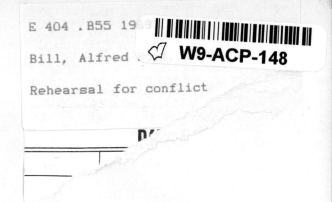

REHEARSAL FOR CONFLICT

REHEARSAL FOR CONFLICT

The War with Mexico

1846—1848

by ALFRED HOYT BILL

NEW YORK
COOPER SQUARE PUBLISHERS, INC.
1969

Originally Published 1947 by Alfred A. Knopf, Inc.
Copyright 1947 by Alfred H. Bill
Published by Cooper Square Publishers, Inc.
59 Fourth Avenue, New York, N. Y. 10003
Standard Book Number 8154-0316-X
Library of Congress Catalog Card No. 79-105298

Printed in the United States of America
by Noble Offset Printers, Inc., New York, N. Y. 10003

TO

CREED FULTON COX

PREFACE

THIS BOOK makes no pretension to profound scholarship. It is intended to acquaint the general reader with a period which, although one of the most picturesque and fateful in our history, has been one of the most misrepresented, misunderstood, and, by all but the special student, neglected. It has long been our national habit to deplore the War with Mexico as an act of unprovoked aggression, to belittle the victorious campaigns of Taylor and Scott, and while enjoying to the full the fruits of conquest, to shed crocodile tears over the means by which they were won. The eloquent polemics of the Whigs and the abolitionists have been accepted as sober history and have branded the war as a conspiracy, a disreputable plot, favored by Tyler and executed by Polk, with the aid of self-seeking and unscrupulous "slave-drivers." And against this presentation of it more recent historians, free from the passions and prejudices engendered by the War of Secession, appear to have labored in vain.

Mexico has been generally understood to have been the harmless and almost pathetically helpless victim of a brutal and grasping assailant. Actually the Mexican nation of a hundred years ago was a backward and illiterate people exploited by a small plutocratic upper class, stultified by a Counter-Reformation Roman Catholicism, and brutalized by an army that was the ready tool of oppression. Save for the brief and infrequent administrations of usually incompetent constitutional presidents, it was ruled by a series of dictators, who ranged from the Emperor Iturbide to Santa Anna, the self-styled Napoleon of the Western Hemisphere. Revolution was endemic in the body politic.

Forgotten are the double-dealing, the provocations, and the outrages for which an international arbitrator awarded to the United States large damages. Unknown are the moderation, the patience, and the restraint of the government at Washington, whose conduct was admitted by not too friendly British dip-

lomats to be eminently "correct." Unappreciated is the fact that
after a war that cost the United States a hundred million dollars and many thousands of lives, Mexico was paid for the territory she surrendered five sixths of the sum that had been offered
her on the eve of hostilities.

In connection with the annexation of Texas, it is seldom
remembered east of the Sabine River that only a twice broken
promise forced the American settlers to fight for independence
through years of smoldering and barbarous warfare. The existence of the weak Texan Republic was a potential threat to the
security of the United States. Great Britain and France were
manifesting an only too benevolent interest in Texas. Combined,
as this interest was, with the presence of the British on the
Great Lakes, in Oregon, and in the West Indies, it suggested
encirclement; and memories of the War of 1812 were only
thirty years old.

There were rumors, moreover, of a British or French protectorate for California, where the sovereignty of Mexico was
hardly more than nominal; and in London and on the Continent
talk of a European monarchy for Mexico seemed to threaten
the validity of the Monroe Doctrine. But since the wise and far-
sighted policy of Tyler, and Polk's energetic execution of that
policy, prevented these things from coming to pass, they have
been generally forgotten, and the period of the war of which
they were contributing causes has been dismissed as a time of
partisan politics at home and of shameless brigandage abroad.

It was, in fact, a period as heavily charged with momentous
consequences as any in our history, a period of change, of new
alignments, and of new issues, or old ones heavy with a new
significance. In Washington the widows of James Madison and
Alexander Hamilton brought a sense of the stately past to
assemblies of a sophistication almost incredible amid the surrounding squalor; the law had only lately compelled quarreling
politicians to go farther than Bladensburg to settle their differences at the point of the dueling pistol; Clay and Webster still
wrought in the spirit of the Founding Fathers. But the old
spirit of compromise that made the Union possible had begun to

die. The flowers of idealism and the weeds of sectional prejudice, whose fruit was to be civil war a little more than a decade later, were sprouting far and wide. Old John Quincy Adams had to fight long and hard to win the mere right of petition for his constituents who were opposed to slavery. Calhoun was striving to solidify the South in defense of its "peculiar institution." Throughout the land the poems of Whittier were awakening a sense of the moral wrong of slavery. James Russell Lowell was writing that he preferred a divided country to Union with slavery. And of the rising men Seward and Chase in the North and Jefferson Davis in the South were typical. By the end of the war with Mexico the sectional cleavage was obvious. The shibboleth of the Wilmot Proviso split the old political parties. The Free-Soil Party appeared, and squatter sovereignty became the standard doctrine of all thoroughgoing Southerners.

Of the war itself — the disease-ridden camps, the heart-breaking waterless marches, the bloody battles — only the conquest of California and the Southwest, the great marches of Stephen Kearny and Doniphan, and the exploits of Frémont have escaped the prevailing neglect or oblivion. It is as if the campaigns had been hardly more than military picnics, the victories won over mere mobs of ill-armed and worse-led foes. Yet it was seldom that the American troops, who were mostly volunteers lately come from civil life, were not faced by two or three times their number of resolute adversaries. Against these odds they stormed tortuous mountain defiles and took strongly fortified cities. Of the battles in the Valley of Mexico Matthew Forney Steele says in his *American Campaigns* that no chapter in the history of American arms is more glorious. To this statement the percentage of losses bears witness. And the same may be truly said of Monterrey and Buena Vista.

For the great conflict that was to come, this war was a singular preparation. Almost all of the officers who became famous in the armies of the Union and the Confederacy learned their grim trade in Mexico and gained there some knowledge of the virtues and shortcomings of the American volunteer soldier, who was to make up the bulk of the armies they were to lead

against each other. Grant and Lee, Jackson and McClellan,
Meade and Beauregard, the two Johnstons, Thomas and Long-
street, are but some of the best-known of their names. And in
the navy were Farragut and Franklin Buchanan, Raphael
Semmes of the *Alabama* and Winslow of the *Kearsarge*, David
Dixon Porter, and Josiah Tattnall.

The hero of the piece, however, turns out to have been none of
these, nor their magnificent commander-in-chief, Winfield Scott,
nor Zachary Taylor, whose fortuitous glory lighted him to the
Presidency. It is the little man in the White House whom the
student of those times finds ever taking the center of the stage
— "Little Jimmy Polk of Duck River," as Scott described him;
"accidental president" and "Jackson's chief cook and bottle-
washer," according to the Whigs.

Essentially a small man, he was guilty of petty spite, abysmal
meannesses, and the basest ingratitude, and was so unconscious
of the real nature of these actions that he left a record of them
in his diary for all the world to read. But he cherished one
great ideal, the preservation of the Union, and one great vision,
the expansion of his country to the Pacific Ocean. And for these
he worked with an inflexible will and a self-forgetful devotion.
He risked war with Great Britain for Oregon, and kept his
country fighting against Mexico until he had made sure of the
acquisition of California, New Mexico, and the Rio Grande
boundary. Keen party man though he was, he told the fiery
Calhoun that they had "a country to save as well as a party to
obey," and he saw his party go down to defeat as a consequence
of the success of his policy of expansion. He offered up his
health and life itself as a willing sacrifice to the performance of
his duties, dying before he was fifty-three and but little more
than a year after his retirement from office.

*   *   *   *   *

For valuable advice and assistance and for invaluable encour-
agement in the writing of this book I am deeply grateful to
Professor William Starr Myers and Professor Walter Phelps
Hall of Princeton University, to Professor Livingston Hall of

the Harvard Law School, to the late General Oliver Spaulding, U. S. Army, retired; to Colonel Arthur Poillon, U. S. Army, retired, who permitted me to consult his excellent military library and collection of military prints; to Mrs. David Arnold Wasson of Kittery Point, Maine; to Miss Elizabeth Braxton Preston of Norfolk, Virginia, for the words of the recruiting song on page 240; and to Dr. Frank P. Graham, President of the University of North Carolina, for his kindness in obtaining for me a photograph of the Sully portrait of President Polk.

Again I have the pleasure of thanking Dr. Julian Parks Boyd, librarian of Princeton University, for his cordial permission to use the university library; Mr. Malcolm Oakman Young, reference librarian, for his expert and indefatigable assistance: and the other members of the library staff for their unfailing courtesy and efficient services.

Formal and grateful acknowledgment is made to the American Missionary Association of New York City for permission to reproduce from *The War with Mexico* by Justin H. Smith the maps of the Valley of Mexico, the Battle of Monterrey, and the Battle of Cerro Gordo.

ALFRED HOYT BILL

Princeton, New Jersey
June 7, 1947

CONTENTS

ILLUSTRATIONS

CHAPTER I

An Explosion and Its Consequences

§1

THE FEBRUARY of 1844 had been cold in Washington. All the way up the Potomac the ice was so thick that the new United States steam sloop-of-war *Princeton* demonstrated the extraordinary power of her novel means of propulsion by smashing her way through it to an anchorage near the city. February 28 was fine but still cold enough for Mr. Secretary of the Navy Gilmer to wear his handsome circular blue Spanish cloak as he stepped on board that morning.

There was a great piping of bosuns' whistles, rolling of marine guard drums, and banging of saluting guns. For he was only one, and not the most important, of the distinguished guests whom Captain Robert Field Stockton had invited to observe the power of the engines of his fine new ship and the range of its great new gun. That weapon — with a mischievous slant at the simmering dispute with Great Britain — he had named the Peacemaker, and to point the moral he called its 225-pounder fellow the Oregon. President Tyler headed the party. Among the assembled notables were Secretary of State Upshur and other members of the Cabinet, several foreign ministers, Senator Thomas Hart Benton of Missouri, Mr. Virgil Maxcy, late chargé d'affaires at The Hague, Captain Beverly Kennon, Chief of Naval Construction, and Colonel David Gardiner of Gardiner's Island, the President's intimate friend.

Colonel Gardiner brought with him his two beautiful young daughters. Old Mrs. James Madison, who in spite of her seventy-seven years never refused a promising invitation, though it might be only to a children's party, was among the two hundred ladies socially or politically important in the capital who came on board. There were some four hundred guests in all.

It was a great day for Captain Stockton. The *Princeton* was the first, and that day the only, screw-propeller-driven warship in the world. Her engine was entirely below the water-line and thereby, compared with the engines of the side-wheel war steamers that had preceded her, practically invulnerable to enemy fire; and the credit for the adoption of this innovation was largely owing to her commander. It was he who had brought John Ericsson to the United States after the British Admiralty had tested and rejected the invention of the clever Swede. The wrought-iron Peacemaker, which could hurl a two-hundred-and-twelve-pound shot a distance of three miles with a charge of thirty-five pounds of powder — as it had proved in repeated tests — owed its existence chiefly to him.

As the *Princeton* steamed down the river in the wintry sun-shine and long clear reaches offered the opportunity to do so, the great gun, with a full charge of powder, demonstrated its range repeatedly to the satisfaction of the gentlemen and the half-playful consternation of the ladies. Fort Washington was passed to larboard, Mount Vernon to starboard, and the party went below to partake of what was described as a "splendid collation," after which they drank a toast to "Ore-gon, the Peacemaker, and Captain Stockton."

Most of the ladies remained about the tables, chatting, while most of the gentlemen strolled up on deck as word came down that at the request of Secretary Gilmer the Peacemaker was to be fired once more. It was about four o'clock in the afternoon; the ship had been turned homeward; and there was a fine clear stretch of water ahead.

For some reason a charge of only twenty-five pounds of powder was used this time, but the huge gun burst. Twenty feet of the bulwark was blown away. Stockton, who had been standing with Gilmer near the breach on the port side, was hurled to the deck, scorched, burned, and blinded. Gilmer was flung against the bulwarks, where he lay in his Spanish cloak, dead, crushed and broken, like a wad of blue cloth. Upshur, who had distrusted the gun from the first and had got an experienced sailor to station him behind the foremast, had his head — that head whose massive structure was thought to excel even the majesty of Daniel Webster's — crushed by a ricocheting fragment of wrought iron, while another struck his watch fob, breaking the crystal and stopping the watch.

Colonel Gardiner and Mr. Maxcy were killed outright by the powder blast. Captain Kennon lived only long enough to raise himself on one elbow. A servant standing next to Senator Benton by the starboard carronade was killed instantly. Benton, after a few moments of unconsciousness, found himself lying on the deck, unhurt as he thought, though old Andrew Jackson out at his Hermitage in Tennessee doubted, it was said, that Benton was ever in his right mind afterwards. The wounded included eleven sailors, of whom two died.

A steamboat from Alexandria met the ill-fated ship and turned back to fetch surgeons. The *Princeton* anchored off Alexandria, and the steamboat *Joseph Johnson* brought the shaken guests back to Washington. But the dreadful news flew before them. From the steamboat wharf a hackman brought it to Gadsby's Hotel, where Mr. Henry Alexander Wise, member of Congress from Virginia, sat chatting with his father-in-law, John Sergeant of Philadelphia. John Sable, the celebrated black waiter, told them that the Peacemaker had "busted" and that it was said that Secretary Upshur had been killed and several others killed or wounded. Confirmation followed swiftly, and Mr. Wise spent the next hour dashing about in a hack to prevent the news from being broken to the bereaved too brusquely.

Old Mrs. Madison reached home to find her drawing-room filled with friends who had come to seek news of her. The gallant old soul, one of the few heroic figures of the dreadful day of Blandensburg in 1814, had gone about the blood-splashed deck of the *Princeton* tending the wounded until professional help arrived. Now she could not trust herself to speak, only to go from one friend to another, bowing, smiling, and pressing their hands.

Ex-President John Quincy Adams, now in his seventy-seventh year and Congressman for Massachusetts, was dining with Mr. Winthrop, Mr. Pakenham, the new British Minister, General Winfield Scott, Mr. Webster, and others when the news reached them and broke up the party. Mr. Philip Hone heard it in New York, where an express arrived with it at two o'clock the following afternoon, and entered it with bitter comment in his diary. He considered that toast coupling the Oregon question with the Peacemaker in execrable taste. The Peacemaker, he wrote, was meant to "hurl defiance at Great Britain or any other nation which might stand between the wind and Colonel Benton's popularity." Stockton he called "the firebrand which was to ignite the whole."

In Washington the adherents of the administration were worrying about another international issue — what Henry Alexander Wise called the Southwestern question, the treaty of annexation with the Republic of Texas. With Hugh Swinton Legaré as Secretary of State *ad interim* it had been in safe hands, but Legaré had died untimely at Boston the previous summer. It had been safe with Upshur, who had told his friends recently that he believed he had at last rounded up the requisite number of votes in the Senate for ratification of the treaty. But now that Upshur was dead, who would be able and willing to carry it through? Only one man, thought Mr. Wise, and that man John Caldwell Calhoun. But would Calhoun consent to become Secretary of State? It seemed doubtful, but Senator McDuffie of South Carolina, who had fought the administration's battles sometimes almost alone in a Senate that had determined to confirm none of John Tyler's appointments, might be able to persuade him to do so.

Before sunrise on the morning after the *Princeton* disaster Mr. Wise, his hawklike features and saffron complexion ghastly in the cold light of dawn, was being jolted in a hack over the abominable macadam that served as a pavement on Pennsylvania Avenue. He found McDuffie in his dressing-gown, not yet sat down to breakfast. Did not the Senator agree with him that Calhoun was the only man to be trusted with Texas annexation? Then would not the Senator write to Calhoun at once, urging him to accept the appointment?

The Senator would, and Wise dashed off to the White House, where the President was awaiting his breakfast in a state of profound sorrow and humility at the thought that he had been spared when so many of his friends and associates had met a dreadful death. All that had kept him from being near the fatal gun had been somebody's calling him back to talk with him as he was about to mount to the deck. He wept when he spoke of it.

Wise stated his errand. The President objected. Texas was important, of course, but he did not think Calhoun the man for the place. They argued it out through breakfast, the President still unconvinced until Wise, in despair, laid his cards on the table. He had, he confessed, committed the President to McDuffie in advance. He had not, to be sure, actually told the Senator that the President had already made the appointment, but he had allowed him to infer as much, and McDuffie was too much of a gentleman to question him on the point, which, between gentlemen, was surely to be inferred. Now was John Tyler going to let down his fellow Virginian, his champion, and his old friend, Henry Wise: force him to go to McDuffie and confess that he had deceived him or, at best, allowed him to deceive himself?

Between annoyance and amusement at the way in which his hand had been forced, the President laughed and gave in, and Mr. Wise went down the river to the *Princeton*. There he viewed the ruined deck and the dead bodies bound up with sailorlike neatness and laid out decently in their clothes, and he talked with poor Stockton, who lay with bandaged eyes in his cabin, the prey of grief and mortification that were sharper than the pain of his burns. But shocked and sorrowful as Wise felt over the fatal accident, he had an inward glow of satisfaction at his morning's work. As he saw it, he had struck a good blow for the future greatness of the United

States, and if it was also a good blow for the strengthening of the Southern states in the Union, so much the better. For there was a growing jealousy of the South in the North, a feeling that the Southern states exercised more than their fair share of influence in the national government.

There was, moreover, the growing antagonism to slavery. Some of Wise's enemies, who were also enemies of the South because they could not separate their ideas of the South from their ideas of slavery, might and did maintain that he had struck his blow for the cause of slavery. And these were not only the avowed abolitionists. A great many other Northerners wished to see slavery abolished by a process of gradual emancipation, and many Southerners shared that wish. Wise himself was far from viewing his accomplishment as they did. When he went as United States Minister to Brazil, as he did not long after, he worked hard to persuade the Emperor Dom Pedro II to join in the effort of other powers to suppress the slave trade. But it was dreadful to him, and to most enlightened slaveholders, to think of what would happen to their kindly, simple, sheltered, and well-cared-for Negroes if they should be suddenly set free by a stroke of the pen as the abolitionists demanded that they should be.

§2

Death, Death in the White House! Ah, never before
Trod his skeleton foot on the President's floor. . . .
From the round at the top he has stepped to the sky —
It is blessed to go, when so ready to die.

Thus had N. P. Willis lamented the passing of William Henry Harrison, whose death in 1841 had brought John Tyler to the presidential chair. Mrs. Tyler had died in the White House in the following year; and now, on March 2, four plain coffins lay in the East Room: those of the two Secretaries and Captain Kennon's covered with the Union flag, Colonel Gardiner's with a black pall. The room was crowded with the President and his family, members of the Cabinet, of the two houses of Congress, the foreign ministers, the mayors of Washington, Georgetown, and Alexandria, and many officers of the army and navy. The Reverend M. Hawley, rector of St. John's, read the burial service, and "the long funeral," according to ex-President Adams, "blackened all the way . . . to the Congressional burial ground, near the eastern branch of the Potomac."

Looking about the handsome East Room, Mr. Adams could recall the White House as it had been when he had entered it as President nineteen years before, and his wife's struggle to make livable what was little better than a dreary monument. Jackson's eight years' tenancy had undone much of her work. But the Van Burens had restored the furnishings and the decencies of service; and although Congress in its bitterness against John Tyler had refused to vote the customary funds for redecoration and maintenance, and even for lights and fuel, the Tylers had seen to it that the house continued to be a beautiful and stately residence befitting the high office of its occupant.

By frequent and lavish entertainment the Van Burens had healed the breach that Jackson's uncouth manner of living had opened between the administration and Washington society. Jackson's receptions had been mere riotous scrambles for the presidential refreshments, with young ladies perched on the mantelpieces to watch the fun. At Van Buren's first reception there had been no suggestion of formality, few uniforms or jewels worn, and even the members of the diplomatic corps in plain clothes. But Van Buren had soon changed all that. Something like protocol was re-established. The Napoleonic chairs, with their imperial crowns changed to American eagles, which Monroe had bought in Paris, were refurbished. The gold spoons, also his purchase, reappeared to excite the wrath of the professional champions of republican simplicity in Congress, though they were only washed gold really.

Tyler mitigated the stiff ceremonial of his predecessor. He lived in the White House, it was said, as if he had been on his Virginia plantation. A caller was likely to be asked to "take something" at the sideboard, where the eggnog bowl stood ready in the winter, and in summer the materials for a julep were at hand. But due ceremony was observed on all occasions. On the evening of the first Fourth of July of his administration Tyler received invited guests in the Oval Room. The Marine Band played in the hall; and while the company sipped iced champagne, the candles in the crystal chandeliers flared in the warm breeze from the open windows and dropped their melted wax until those who stood beneath them acquired, said the local wits, a classical look or, at least, the look of having been in Greece.

President Tyler revived the old custom of having a majordomo announce the guests at these invitation affairs. At first there were some funny blunders in consequence: couples oddly mismated and diplomats assigned to strange countries. But in the long run the amenities profited. On New Year's Day the diplomatic corps were resplendent in their uniforms; and although the public were described as "rushing in," their restraint and decorum on a similar occasion were admired even by Charles Dickens, who found so little to admire in the United States in 1842.

The presence of Mr. and Mrs. Dickens and of Washington Irving, who was about to go abroad as Minister to Spain, drew a tremendous crowd at the last of the public receptions in March. And there were other distinguished foreign visitors that year. The sailor Prince de Joinville, third son of King Louis Philippe, who had brought Napoleon's body back to Paris from St. Helena two years before and was a tall, fine-looking youth, danced a *quadrille d'honneur* with Miss Tyler in the East Room. Lord Morpeth, the future Earl of Carlisle, came to town and stayed for some time — a great disappointment to the ladies, since his red face, light hair, and awkward manner differed so greatly from what the novels of Scott and Bulwer had led them to expect of an English nobleman. He spent most of his time listening to the debates in the halls of Congress and made himself so agreeable to the members that they voted him a seat on the floor.

Lord Ashburton arrived in April, sixty-eight years old, six feet tall, and wearing a look of mildness. A member of the great house of Baring, he had married, in the days when Philadelphia was the capital of the United States, Miss Maria Bingham of that city and seemed well chosen to negotiate the Maine boundary dispute with Great Britain, with which his portfolio was heavy. His three secretaries, five servants, carriage and horses, mountain of luggage, and the rent he was to pay for his house on the President's Square — $10,000 a year and $1,000 more to cover damage caused by his occupancy — quickened the popular interest in his arrival.

It was President Tyler's custom to give two dinners each week during the season: "plain, substantial affairs," people called them. One of them would be for some twenty gentlemen, the other included diplomats, Federal and state dignitaries, and their wives. On other evenings he received informally until ten o'clock; there were occasional informal invitation balls that ended at eleven, and one public levee each month.

Until the death of his wife, who was a confirmed invalid, his daughter-in-law, his son Robert's wife, acted as his hostess. She was Priscilla, daughter of the English Shakespearian actor Thomas Apthorpe Cooper, her mother having been the fascinating Miss Eliza Fairlie of New York, whom Washington Irving had put into his *Salmagundi* as Sophie Sparkle. For a time she had acted in her father's company, and it gave her a Cinderella-like feeling at a ball in her first White House season to find herself in the same ballroom where a few years before she had played Lady Randolph in one of his unsuccessful efforts to retrieve his broken fortunes — "a miserable engagement of a few rainy nights."

At one state dinner she did what she had never in her life done before, fainted, and at the very table. Daniel Webster, who was seated next to her, caught her up in his arms and held her while her distracted father-in-law dashed ice-water

over both of them. On all other occasions she played her part
with distinguished success and great tact, followed old Mrs.
Madison's advice and returned all calls in person instead of
merely sending cards. At one party she wore rose-colored
satin trimmed with blonde lace and flowers, and a little headdress of white bugles, which were "all the rage." As she con-
fided in a letter to her sister, she was considered *"charmante"*
by the French, "lovely" by her own countrymen, and by the
English "really quite nice, you know."

When old Marshal Bertrand, Napoleon's faithful companion at St. Helena, came to Washington in the President's
absence, she acted with courageous initiative and energy, assembled the members of the Cabinet, received the marshal to
the strains of the *Marseillaise,* and extemporized a ball in the
East Room for his young attachés, whom she found notable
for their "full pantaloons and mustachios."

In Washington society Mrs. Madison, with Mrs. Sigourney
and the aged Mrs. Alexander Hamilton as her supporters,
was the uncrowned queen dowager. A gambling, spendthrift
son had made her so poor that Congress had voted her the
franking privilege. But she contrived to keep her residence
on Lafayette Square in a kind of shabby state. There, surrounded by a bevy of pretty grand-nieces, she kept open
house on New Year's and Independence Day, as the John
Quincy Adamses did, and her receptions were as crowded as
theirs or the President's. Dye kept her hair its original brown;
she used a bit of rouge and a touch of the powder-puff, wore
the faded, well-saved brocades and velvets of her great past,
with their gores, short waists, and puffed sleeves, and a tur-
ban; and she went everywhere and was everywhere welcomed,
admired, and liked.

At the Swann house near by, Daniel Webster, with his un-
fathomable eyes, faced his wife's commanding presence across
the table at dinner parties at which Florida shad was followed
by Kentucky beef and prairie chickens from Illinois. Monica,
their colored cook, was famous. Webster's dinner-table talk

was delightful: amusing nonsense or agreeable gossip about the great English country houses where he had been a guest. In January 1842 he gave a great party at which eight rooms were open and lighted and the President, members of the diplomatic corps and other people of importance were present. The Websters gave a ball for Lord Morpeth. Lord Ashburton dined at their house with his secretaries and Mr. Adams among the company. The Bentons, Roosevelts, Poinsett, and Fillmore were among the guests when the Envoy Extraordinary repaid his social obligations.

Conspicuous among the younger matrons in society was Mme de Bodisco, the wife of the Russian Minister. The fairytale alteration of her life surpassed even that of young Mrs. Tyler. She had lately been Harriet Williams of Georgetown, one of the several children of the Chief Clerk of the Adjutant General's office. Baron Alexander de Bodisco had first seen her at one of the children's parties he enjoyed giving at the legation and had married her practically out of Miss English's select schoolroom the year following.

She was only seventeen, but "tall and splendidly developed," it was said at the time. "The American Rose," her admirers called her, though certain ladies described her beauty as "robust," of the "milkmaid type," and the French Minister, the Chevalier de Bacourt, called it the "beauty of youth" and thought her conversation "silly." But de Bacourt, sighing amid the chills and torrid heats of Washington for the snug comforts of his former post at Karlsruhe, denounced everything and everybody in the United States, including his own compatriots.

He considered Bodisco, who was three times the age of his bride, "ridiculous, vulgar and disgusting," with his black-dyed hair, mustache, and whiskers. Mr. Adams was revolted by the "coarseness" with which Henry Clay bantered Bodisco about his marriage and the good-humored complacence with which the Russian assured him that "all was right." On the other hand, Mr. Philip Hone on a visit from New York found Bodisco congenial and enjoyed dining at the Russian lega-

tion by the light of eighty wax candles. "It was like dining in
a gold mine," he wrote, so magnificent was the service. There
was whist afterwards, as there always was at Bodisco's. Webster, Clay, and General Scott were frequent players there.
Stakes were high. But one night, after losing a thousand dollars, the unlucky host addressed his guests as follows:

"Ladies and gentlemans, it is my disagreeable duty to
make the announce that these receptions must have an end,
and to declare them at an end for the present, because why?
The fund for their expend, ladies and gentlemans, is exhaust,
and they must discontinue."

But unlucky at cards, lucky in love. In due time a baby
Nicholas, who was only the first of several progeny of the marriage, was brought downstairs at two o'clock in the morning
to be exhibited to his father's guests at a legation ball.

The wedding had been of the kind that subdebutantes
dream of. Eight of Miss Williams's schoolmates, ranging in
age from seventeen to fourteen, were her bridesmaids, in
gowns of white satin damask, which were the gift of the groom
and were made by Mrs. Abbott, milliner and mantua-maker
from London and the most fashionable of her trade in the city.
The bride's dress, of rich white satin and silver lace, was like
that of a Russian bride, and on her blond hair she wore a coro-
net of red velvet and diamonds, from which fell a veil of silver
lace. Two of the groomsmen were Smith Van Buren, the son
of the President, and Secretary Paulding's son Kemble, both
under twenty. The rest were Bodisco's contemporaries, Senator James Buchanan and Mr. Fox, the British Minister, being of their number.

The marriage took place at the modest home of the bride's
father, but immediately afterward carriages took the wedding
party to the legation, where the wedding dinner was served;
and in spite of the warmth of the April day the groom insisted on his bride's wearing her lovely swansdown cloak and
her attendants the swansdown tippets he had given them. The
festivities ended only the following morning, when bride and
bridesmaids breakfasted together.

Another notable figure in the younger set at Washington in these early forties was Mrs. Philip Kearny, a niece of George Rogers Clark and the wife of Lieutenant Kearny of the cavalry. He was already distinguished. A graduate of the French Royal School of Cavalry at Saumur, he had made a campaign with the famous Chasseurs d'Afrique, "the Lions of the Desert," in Algiers, where their commander had bidden them: "Charge, and when you hear the recall sounded, remember it is not for you." And it was reported to have been Kearny's custom to charge with saber in one hand, pistol in the other, and the reins in his teeth.

Upon his return from abroad his knowledge of the mounted services and experience with them in actual war caused him to be detailed to the headquarters of the army as aide-de-camp to General McComb and later to General Scott. With inherited wealth estimated at a million dollars, he was a soldier for the love of soldiering, and he and his young wife enlivened a rather dull social season by giving a splendid ball.

At the assemblies, which were given by a club of gentlemen at Carusi's, the "sparkling and attractive" Miss Julia Gardiner, so soon to be orphaned, had been much admired. Her beauty, it was said, had made a sensation in London and caused crowds to follow her about Paris. In the winter of 1843–4 Mr. Pakenham had replaced Mr. Fox as British Minister, a change that was all to the good for society; and in that same December Ole Bull gave a concert at which a member of Congress from Alabama got himself thrown out by the police for shouting: "None of your highfalutin, but give us *Hail Columbia* and bear hard on the treble."

The President's New Year's Day reception of 1844 was exceptionally brilliant. The Mexican minister, General Almonte, was splendid in a profusion of gold embroidery; the French Minister "rich and unpretending," it was observed, in blue and gold; the Spanish in light blue and silver; the Brazilian in green and gold; the Austrian and Swedish in white. Bodisco, who usually glittered in a coat of silver tissue on such occasions, was absent in Russia, where he presented his beauteous young wife at the court of his imperial master, the Czar; but an exciting rumor ran around Washington that he had fallen from favor and been exiled to Siberia. General Winfield Scott towered above the throng, his six feet four and a quarter inches of stature magnificent as always in full-dress uniform.

When the public was admitted, democracy became apparent in the men's coats, which ranged from broadcloth to homespun, and the plain stuff dresses of the women among the silks and brocades of their more fortunate sisters. The weather was fine, and Mr. N. P. Willis wrote that Pennsylvania Avenue, with its gay throngs that day, was like a carnival.

§3

The setting of these sophisticated splendors, the discomforts of living, the sordidness and even squalor of their surroundings seem hardly credible in the present day. The Tiber, that little stream whose name excited the derision of foreigners unacquainted with the American sense of humor, still meandered through the city and stagnated with the filth of many of the city sewers beneath the bridge where it was crossed by Pennsylvania Avenue. Other sewers discharged their contents in the marshes not far from the south front of the White House. The broken and rutted macadam on Pennsylvania Avenue, which Frenchmen observed to be half again as wide as the rue de la Paix, was the only pavement in the city. It was never cleaned or sprinkled, always deep in mud or in dust that the summer winds blew in blinding clouds. The other streets were always muddy, dusty, or filled with slush, and in the outskirts it was a common occurrence for a carriage to be mired to the hubs.

Georgetown, wrote a French lady a few years earlier, was a city of houses without streets, Washington a city of streets without houses. To M. de Bacourt the place wore the miserable, desolate look of being neither a city nor a village. About the White House the houses stood only six or seven to the street, invariably two-story red-brick dwellings with green blinds. There were brick sidewalks, but there was open country within five hundred paces.

Hogs, sows, and pigs roamed everywhere unchallenged, their ubiquity defended on the ground that they did a very necessary job of scavenging. But cows also roamed the streets, and women milked them at the wayside, for many of them had no stables. The nights were made hideous by the grunts and mooings of these roving animals and the encounters of a multitude of stray cats and dogs. Oil lamps on wooden posts did little more than make the darkness visible except around the Treasury Building, where gas lamps had been installed experimentally. Fires were frequent. Wild young bloods ranged the dark streets after the manner of the "Mohawks" of eighteenth-century London, transposing signs, tearing off knockers, and breaking windows.

There had been no police force until Van Buren, annoyed by the booing of rowdies in front of the White House, had got an appropriation through Congress for seven thousand dollars for a small force equipped with stars and batons, though his opponents charged that this would prove to be the nucleus of a "pretorian guard." Dickens saw no policemen on duty at an evening reception of President Tyler's and thought that there was less delay and confusion among the crowding carriages than on similar occasions at home under the supervision of the London bobbies.

Housing was a perennial problem. The dwellings available for temporary sojourners were quickly taken up. The less fortunate — diplomats, senators, congressmen, and the like — flocked to boarding-houses and hotels. Baron de Bodisco had a house in Georgetown, but the First Secretary of his legation lived at Mrs. Ulrich's opposite the State Department along with the Argentine Minister and the chargé d'affaires from the Netherlands. A Vice-President might be found at Mrs. Gadsby's on President's Square, a British attaché and an attorney general at Mrs. Latimer's fashionable establishment, a large, brick mansion on Lafayette Square. The National

Hotel was headquarters for the Southern set. Fuller's was little more than a long row of small houses backing on a common yard in which a great triangle clanged continually to summon the leisurely service of Negro waiters and chambermaids. In winter Franklin stoves waged unequal war with the penetrating cold, and one Minister from France lined his walls with buffalo skins against the ague-laden chill.

Hotel guests formed messes and catered for themselves. Generally it was the men who did the marketing, whether they were hotel-dwellers or had houses of their own, and of an early morning Senator Webster himself might be seen in blue coat with bright buttons, cassimere waistcoat, and black trousers, returning from the Marsh Market with a handkerchief filled with vegetables in one hand and a leg of mutton in the other. There was little other buying in Washington. Clagett's dry-goods store and most of the other shops were on Pennsylvania Avenue. Alexandria and Georgetown had always been better business towns than the capital, and people went to Baltimore to make their more important purchases.

But the city ought not to be judged out of its time and country. Hogs roamed the streets of every other American city except Boston. Dickens wrote a choice bit about the porkers and piglets on Broadway. Croton water had only recently replaced well water in New York. The New York police force had lately quit in a body rather than don uniforms, which they considered to be badges of servitude; and bare-legged little ragged girls swept the muddy crossings for the pennies of passers-by.

In the spring Washington turned lovely. The trees that lined Pennsylvania Avenue put forth their bright green leaves, and the shrubs in the grounds of the Capitol and the gardens of the White House, which were well laid out and kept scrupulously, burst into many-colored bloom. From the south portico of the White House, which stood forty-five feet above high water in the Potomac, the view of the two branches of the river was beautiful.

The Marine Band played at the Capitol two afternoons

each week, and there were "music nights" as well. On these occasions people of all sorts streamed up Pennsylvania Avenue on foot, on horseback, or in carriages to wander and gossip and stare at the notables among the shrubberies and about the little lake in the East Garden. Everybody was to be seen there: Mr. Secretary Calhoun; Senator Benton from Missouri in his Spanish cloak, stepping — his admirers thought — "with the air of a tribune"; and the animated countenance of ex-President John Quincy Adams, now for these many years a member of the House from Massachusetts. Short, bald, and stout, he walked briskly, and his glance was piercing in spite of his age.

The variety of conveyances was extraordinary. The foreign ministers turned out in their four-horse coaches: the Frenchman in a beautiful, low-swung Parisian equipage with servants in drab and silver. Blood horses drew the smart carriage of a Congressman from New Jersey, a black coachman and a footman in neat plain clothes on the box. Mr. Henry Alexander Wise's carriage, on the other hand, was "no better than a candle box on wheels," according to his friend John Tyler; to which Mr. Wise retorted by reminding the President that his own carriage still bore on its panels the coat of arms of its former owner, Van Buren's Secretary of State, the late James K. Paulding, at a sale of whose effects Tyler had bought it. Generally the carriages of patrician Virginians were to be recognized by their shrunken and flapping leather curtains, harness mended with rope, and old Negro drivers in torn coats and battered beaver hats.

The equestrian couples and trios that mingled with the vehicles were equally variegated. British attachés appeared clothed and mounted as if for a turn in Rotten Row, whereas provincial dandies were notable for their prominent aristocratic noses, their long spurs, and long stirrups, and military saddles.

With the full coming of summer the streets were so broad, trees so infrequent, and houses so low that there were no shady places that M. de Bacourt could find. Like other people who

cared for exercise, he took his by walking early in the morning and suspected the worst when he met a young society
beauty who was out at the same hour, it might have been supposed, for the same purpose. When Mr. Adams went swim-
ming at sunrise from his favorite rock in the Potomac, he
often had more company than he cared for. Everybody who
could do so went away. But the Tylers remained.

They were the first presidential family that did not remove
at least as far as the heights of Georgetown from the insalu-
brious summer atmosphere of the neighborhood of the White
House. After the Fourth of July the Wednesday band concerts were shifted to the White House garden. Carriages filled
the drive, and people, including many from Georgetown and
Alexandria, the portico; and if it rained, the President invited them to come indoors. They strolled along the shady
paths, listened to the music, and were interested one afternoon in the appearance of two young damsels of the Cherokee
Nation who were escorted by Governor Call of Florida and
Colonel Pendleton, the chargé to Chili. Or of a summer evening the carriages would fringe the plain south of the White
House, crowds would line the terrace, and the President and
Miss Tyler sat in the portico to watch a battery of flying artillery give an exhibition drill.

§4

Except for the periodical race meetings and lectures on
mesmerism and phrenology, the pseudo-scientific fads of the
day, there was a deplorable dearth of public entertainment.
When an occasional musician, singer, or theatrical company
on tour put in an appearance, the interest excited was extravagant. Even old Mr. Adams shared in the unbounded enthusiasm with which the city received Fanny Elssler, the
celebrated Continental danseuse, and she was presented to
the President and members of the Cabinet. When the appa-
ratus of the daguerreotype, "the pencil of Nature," was
brought to town, it was set up in a committee room in the Capitol and people flocked to see it. Professor Morse's electro-

magnetic telegraph made an even greater sensation. The invention had been ridiculed at first as a fit companion for animal magnetism, which had aroused general interest throughout the country, but Morse's champions had finally won for it a congressional appropriation, and it was installed in the basement of the Supreme Court Building.

But there was no lack of the dramatic in real life. In a time when histrionics were a great part of every politician's equipment and dueling had only recently been outlawed in the District of Columbia, the personalities and doings of senators, congressmen, and other public characters were rich with both comedy and tragedy. Rufus Choate, Franklin Pierce, and the bland and courtly Buchanan were in the Senate. In the House, where members slept with their legs on their desks and spat everywhere, it was something to hear the shrill voice of Adams crack in defense of the antislavery people's right of petition. Or one could listen to Daniel Webster's fight against John Sergeant in the Girard will case in a Supreme Court that was presided over by Chief Justice Taney and had Story among its members.

Webster, whom Dickens considered an intolerable poseur, many others thought "a godlike man," though he sometimes appeared both on the floor of the Senate and at White House receptions a good deal the worse for liquor. But then a member of the House need not even apologize for speaking in that condition if he was careful in his use of the name of the Deity: ejaculating "My God!" if he would, but never "By God!" which was swearing. And Henry Clay's intemperance spiced the gossip of these years. There was the scene he made with Choate in the Senate Chamber, for instance, and that row between him and General Scott over the whist table at Boulanger's restaurant.

Dueling was still practiced by gentlemen from the South and the West, though illegal in the District since the notorious and tragic Graves-Gilley affair had jolted the public conscience. Mr. Wise, who had been a second at that meeting, horsewhipped a gentleman who jostled him at the racecourse.

Senator Clay challenged Senator King. Both quarrels were patched up. But it was well known that many members of both House and Senate went onto the floor with deadly weapons concealed beneath their coats. The *Philadelphia Ledger* said that Congress had become a bear garden, and Mr. Philip Hone likened the House of Representatives to the Five Points, the most lawless and dangerous of the New York slums.

There were plenty of issues to arouse bitter passions, and they were debated with a vituperative animosity that passed the bounds of decency. The Whigs, with old General Harrison as their standard-bearer — "Tippecanoe and Tyler too!" — had marched into power to the strains of : "Van, Van, Van is a used-up man." But Harrison had died a month after taking office, and in Tyler, at heart a Democrat of the Calhoun school, whom they had nominated to get the Virginia vote, they had found a sorry substitute for their purposes. As he vetoed their financial bills one after another, the "two dollars a day and roast beef" of their campaign promises dwindled, jeered the Democrats, to "ten cents a day and bean soup." For they lacked the strength to pass their measures over his veto.

Everywhere banks had failed and mobs attacked them. Many a state defaulted on its bonds. The poet Wordsworth wrote to Bishop Doane that his brother's lifetime savings would be wiped out if the bonds of Pennsylvania were repudiated, and that his sister had lost most of her little all by Mississippi's default. Eighty acres of wheat went for three dollars at a constable's sale, and state after state passed exemption laws to save debtors from utter destitution. In 1841 the Treasury had warned that the nation would face a deficit of fourteen million dollars at the beginning of 1843 if something was not done about it. But Tyler had stood by his guns, and the next elections brought widespread Whig defeats and a House of Representatives that supported him during the last two years of his administration.

His perseverance had required an iron endurance. His vetoes had been hissed in the gallery of the Senate. Of the

Cabinet that he had inherited from Harrison, every member but Webster, who was deep in negotiating the Maine boundary dispute with Britain, had resigned in protest, and his enemies had gloated, thinking that he could not form another. The Whigs had repudiated him; Clay had resigned from the Senate in disgust; there had been a time when Henry Alexander Wise had been his only supporter in the House. At a dinner in honor of Lord Ashburton in New York, only the plenipotentiary and members of his staff had risen to their feet at the toast to the President of the United States, whereas all present stood up and cheered "the Queen."

Webster had left the Senate to become Secretary of State, but the patriotism that he had placed before personal considerations and those of party won him small approval. His treaty with Ashburton was bitterly attacked on all sides. By it, said its detractors, Great Britain had received 893 square miles more territory than even the King of the Belgians had awarded her — a tract, moreover, of enormous strategic value; and it had left untouched the question of impressment, the Oregon boundary, and other important matters. At a Whig dinner Webster was compelled to defend himself, his chief, and his chief's accomplishments. Merely because he had stuck to his post Adams wrote him down "a heartless traitor to the cause of human freedom."

For by this time the fiery little septuagenarian ex-President had reached such a degree of fanaticism over Negro slavery in the South that he saw a nigger in every woodpile and a nigger-driver in every Southerner. To him John Tyler — not President but "Vice-President acting as President" — was a "slave monger," Henry Alexander Wise the bearer of a "three-colored standard" in which black stood for the slave overseer, blood red for dueling, and for nullification "a dirty, cadaverous white." He was disgusted by the "dirty trick" of Andrew Johnson, the new member from Tennessee, who was among those who made long speeches only to prevent his petition measure from getting a hearing.

It was less than ten years since the abolitionist lecturer

Thompson had been chased out of Boston by a "mob of gentlemen of property and standing" and William Lloyd Garrison had been dragged half naked through Boston streets at the end of a rope. But times had changed swiftly since then. In 1838 the general assembly of Vermont had asked the Senate of the United States for the abolition of slavery in the District of Columbia and the abolition of the slave trade between the states. Many similar petitions came in, some of them signed by women who "forgot their sex," it was observed, to meddle in such matters. In 1839 Governor Seward of New York dared assert that men could not be held as property. Five years later three New England states had passed personal-liberty laws to hamper the search for runaway slaves, and there were numerous and active centers of abolition in the Western states. When the question of the annexation of Texas came to the fore, as it did when Tyler succeeded to the Presidency, these people could see nothing in it but a plot by the Southerners to increase the territory of the slave states and the power of slavery in the Union.

They were less than fair in this. Many in the South favored annexation, as Andrew Jackson did, as a measure for the military defense of the country. But Henry Clay had opposed even the recognition of Texan independence lest it endanger Whig unity and his own chances for the Presidency. Crittenden of Kentucky agreed with Clay that Texas in Tyler's hands was "a firebrand to be noticed as little as possible." But the situation had so far defined itself during Van Buren's administration that when Texas, on the verge of national bankruptcy, had begged for annexation, Van Buren had turned a deaf ear to her importunities for fear of the sectional feeling that would be aroused if he listened to them. And Harrison and Webster had both opposed annexation, seeing clearly that it was likely to divide their party on sectional lines.

Adams, however, suffered from no such deterrent. He was delighted to present to Congress a memorial from Georgia people who objected to him as chairman of the Foreign Relations Committee as unfit to deal with the Mexicans because of his "monomania" on the subject of people as dark as the Mexicans were. The presentation of a petition from the people of Haverhill in his own state asking for the peaceful dissolution of the Union on account of slavery was only one more move in his unceasing struggle for the reception of petitions against slavery. He gloried in a daily mail that was filled with letters on the subject: letters of praise and poetry from the North and the West; letters of insult, profane obscenity, and filth from the South, he recorded in his diary.

In John Tyler, however, he had an opponent who feared the sectional issue as little as he did. Since Webster could not be relied upon to carry Texan annexation through, Tyler, regardless of Webster's recent loyalty, cold-shouldered him out of the Cabinet; and in choosing his successors — Legaré *ad interim,* Upshur, and finally Calhoun — he made sure of men whom he could rely upon for the purpose. Mexico through the mouth of her Minister at Washington threatened war, but Tyler did not hesitate for that. Calhoun worked rapidly. Within six weeks of Upshur's untimely taking off, the treaty of annexation was signed, and marching and sailing orders were sent to army and navy to provide for the defense of Texas lest Mexico attack her while the treaty awaited ratification. The treaty went to the Senate; and with it, Adams wrote pessimistically in his diary on April 22, went "the freedom of the human race." The whole business Adams considered to be "a conspiracy comparable to that of Lucius Sergius Catalina." Senator Benton saw in it a plot for Calhoun for president, for Texas script, and for the dissolution of the Union.

From his Hermitage out in Tennessee Andrew Jackson wrote that this "golden moment" must not be lost. But Clay, who was again a candidate for the Whig nomination for president this spring, came out against annexation in his famous "Raleigh letter"; and Van Buren, who expected to be the

Democrats' candidate, called it "inexpedient" since Texas and Mexico had never concluded a peace and Mexico had threatened war on the United States if the treaty was ratified.

In New York United States six-per-cent bonds dropped four per cent. It was remembered there how Mexican warships, led by David Porter, late of the United States Navy, had harried Spanish merchantmen in the Mexican struggle for independence, for New York had many a ship upon the sea. On April 25 New York saw a great mass meeting of protest against annexation, and Mr. Hone thought Tyler ought to be impeached for moving troops and ships to support the treaty before it had been ratified.

But it was Calhoun himself who gave the treaty its deathblow. Seizing on a statement by Lord Aberdeen, the British Foreign Secretary, to the effect that Britain wished to see slavery abolished everywhere, Calhoun replied that it was to prevent the abolition of slavery in Texas that President Tyler had decided to annex that country.

§5

A month went by, but the Senate took no action on the treaty. Could it be that they waited for guidance from the great National Conventions that met in Baltimore that May? These were bound to deal with the annexation question somehow, for late in April, "by some treachery," as Mr. Adams saw it, the *New York Evening Post* obtained and published the text of the treaty and the secret and confidential correspondence related to it.

If the Senate was indeed waiting on the action of the conventions, the Whigs gave them no uncertain answer. Assembling early in the month in a welter of "Clay sticks," "Clay hats," live coons, "Ashland coats," and other fantastic campaign emblems, they promptly nominated Henry Clay by acclamation and went on their way rejoicing, though to the disgust of Winfield Scott, who had received sixteen votes for the nomination four years before. It was "ridiculous," Scott had written to Thaddeus Stevens, that Clay should be allowed to lead the Whigs "to the slaughter every fourth year to the end of his life."

There was nothing so cut-and-dried about the Democratic Convention, which met, also at Baltimore, near the end of the month. At Washington May 23 was a "music night" — "a musical sylvan levee," it was called — in the gardens of the Capitol. The conventions had filled the town with political visitors, and the walks and shrubberies buzzed with prognostications of the coming campaign and the probable action of the Democrats at Baltimore. Few, however, can have guessed at what was actually to happen there. As the manuscript bulletins posted on the walls of the rotunda of the Capitol made known the information brought by Professor Morse's electro-magnetic telegraph a full hour and a half before "the cars" arrived with it, the astonishment of the public passed all bounds: Van Buren, the party's standard-bearer, repudiated, betrayed by the adoption of a two-thirds rule, and rejected for James Knox Polk!

"Who is James K. Polk?" asked the Whigs in derision. "Little Jimmie Polk of Duck River," Scott called him in sour satisfaction some months later at the defeat of Clay by an opponent so obscure. To Philip Hone, Polk was Jackson's "chief cook and bottle-washer." And the platform the Democrats had adopted: the annexation of Texas, the occupation of Oregon! Only they called it *re*-annexation and *re*-occupation.

"Polk, Dallas, Texas, and Democracy," had drowned out the slogan of another convention: "Tyler and Texas," which had emanated simultaneously from Calvert Hall, where briefly and vainly, headed by the corporal's guard of Tyler adherents that had excited the mockery of his enemies, a faithful few had flashed their broad gold campaign buttons. But less than a fortnight later the Senate rejected the annexation treaty by a vote of thirty-five to sixteen.

Of those who voted against it, thirteen were from Southern or border states. All but one Whig voted "Nay," and seven of the twenty-two Democrats did likewise. Party, it seemed, was still stronger than sectional feeling on the issue. Wise laid the defeat to the "unreasoning malice of the Whigs." There was wrath in certain parts of the South, to be sure. Numerous local gatherings in South Carolina, Alabama, and Virginia demanded annexation or the dissolution of the Union. It was proposed to hold a convention on the subject at Nashville. Tyler, undiscouraged, appealed to the House. If the thing could not be done by treaty, a joint resolution might accomplish it. Mr. Spencer, the Secretary of the Treasury, a New York man — "a Wall Street man," Wise called him — resigned from the Cabinet in deep disapproval.

But Congress — "the most perverse and worthless Congress that ever disgraced this Confederacy," Adams thought it — adjourned without taking action, and without a protest from its Southern members. There was much opposition to the annexation-or-dissolution feeling where they came from. Nashville did not want the proposed convention, and that project died a natural death. There were matters of more immediate interest to engage the country's attention.

Since 1837 a spirit, new in the land and deplorable, had been manifesting itself in the growth of the Native American movement. All foreigners, and especially the Roman Catholic Church as the emissary and missionary of European absolutism, were the objects of its attack. This May it broke out in Philadelphia in bloody riots. Roman Catholic churches and schools were sacked and burned by armed mobs. The Governor of Pennsylvania was forced to send troops from Harrisburg. A landing party of sailors and marines from the *Princeton* went on guard around the Girard Bank. A grand jury spent the month of June investigating the troubles, which the celebration of Independence Day set off afresh. Churches were searched for arms, a boy was shot by a member of the Hibernia Greens, and the militia fired on the mob, killing and wounding a number of people.

Up in Rhode Island Thomas W. Dorr was sentenced to prison for life for his insurrection against a state government that still functioned under the charter granted by Charles II.

JAMES K. POLK IN 1847

m a portrait by Thomas Sully, now at the University of North
olina

THE EXPLOSION ON THE U.S. STEAM FRIGATE PRINCETON, FEBRUARY 28, 1843

Virginia, New York, and Massachusetts were united in calling the sentence an outrage against republican principles. But what interested Washington most was the sensational event in the President's private life.

Believed to have gone to the Rip-Raps for a few days of sea air and recreation, John Tyler suddenly appeared in New York; and almost before the Stock Exchange could react to rumors that his presence was ominous of war over Texas or Oregon, it became known that he had been married by Bishop Onderdonk at the Church of the Ascension at one in the afternoon of June 26 to Miss Julia Gardiner, the beauteous daughter of his old friend, the lately deceased colonel. The happy couple sailed away on the steamer *Essex* amid the salutes of all the vessels in the harbor, including some of Mexican register. "The old fool," was Mr. Hone's unsympathetic comment: John Tyler was fifty-four that year, his bride just thirty years younger.

In the wedding reception that signalized their return to Washington, the magnificent bride's cake and champagne and the Marine Band playing soft airs in the White House garden, Mr. Adams saw "circumstances of revolting indecency . . . Captain Tyler and his bride the laughing stock of the city." But if he was right about this, one gathers that people were careful not to laugh in the new First Lady's face. She revived a bygone formality at her receptions, at which she sat in a large armchair on a slightly raised platform with the long train of her purple dress swept regally about her feet and three feathers in her hair; and when she drove out in her carriage, her four horses were finer than even those of Bodisco.

It was whispered about that she was much criticized by her new relations-in-law. There was more stateliness than hospitality in her entertaining, people complained. Undoubtedly, familiar as she had been with society in London and Paris, she introduced into the White House an air of European sophistication. She enjoyed a dinner-table flirtation with Calhoun, who was nine years older than her husband; and the East Room saw for the first time what a newspaper described as

the "connubial coupling [for the waltz and the polka] ex-
acted by the ameliorated morals now gaining ground in New
York" — and this in spite of Queen Victoria's condemnation
of the latter dance.

§6

The summer of 1844 was not half gone before the heat of
the Native American riots passed into the presidential campaign. Vigilant Protestants who were above rioting found
cause to ponder certain contentions of the Native Americans.
The new Mrs. Tyler was reported to be a Roman Catholic,
and a young, beautiful, and delicate daughter of General
Scott had been admitted into the Convent of the Visitation at
Georgetown that spring, to her father's great distress.

The Democrats were quick to disclaim all connection with
the movement and to champion the rights of citizens of foreign birth. It seemed as if they could not have enough of them
in New York, which promised to be the key state in the election. The New York courts were busy for many weeks with
the naturalizing of immigrants, and the question of how long
the applicants had been in the country was not gone into too
thoroughly. Twenty-five hundred were thus illegally enfran-
chised in the city, according to the indignant Whigs, and
twenty thousand in the state. Hundreds of Irishmen got jobs
on the canals, with a corresponding increase in the Democratic vote in up-state counties that had been held to be doubtful. In the city, where Whigs and Natives had elected a mayor
in April, the Democrats won by a majority of sixteen hundred. They carried the state by a majority of fifty-one hundred. There were great frauds throughout the country, the
Whigs being only less successful, not less culpable, than their
opponents in the perpetration of them.

On November 9 an Albany newspaper admitted bitterly
that New York had gone for "Polk, Texas, free trade and
slavery." The English papers, headed by the London *Times*,
deplored the outcome as a victory for an "adventurous and
unscrupulous democracy," a victory of the South over the

North, of slavery over freedom, of the repudiating states over the honest ones, and of the worst of the United States over the best.

Mr. Adams was at his home at Quincy when "the train of cars from Albany" brought the news of the vote in the western counties of New York, on which finally the result in state and nation depended, and the sound of the guns of Democratic celebration was a sinister one to him. Back in Washington on November 25 he wrote in his diary: "The partial associations of Native Americans, Irish Catholics, abolition societies, Liberty Party, the Pope of Rome, the Democracy of the sword and the dotage of a ruffian are sealing the fate of this nation, which nothing less than the interposition of Omnipotence can save."

To James Knox Polk at his home at Columbia, Tennessee, the news of his election came by mail via Franklin from Nashville, whence the postmaster had dispatched a mounted messenger to bear it to him. The fact that he had failed by one hundred and thirteen votes to carry his own state made it doubly welcome to him. John Tyler received the glad tidings by the telegraph. Polk's platform being what it was, Tyler could and did consider that by the election the country had endorsed his policies. For the Democrats' triumphal procession on the night of November 29 he had the East Room, the dining-room, the hall, and the circle in front of the White House illuminated; and he turned with renewed confidence to what had been from the beginning of his administration his chosen task.

It mattered not to him that the Historical Society in New York gave a grand dinner on the 20th of November, with old Mr. Gallatin in the chair, John Quincy Adams on his right, and on his left General Almonte, the Minister from Mexico. In his message to Congress, which assembled early in December, he was urgent for the annexation of Texas; and the machinery he had assembled for that purpose went promptly to work. In the Senate McDuffie, Benton, Foster of Tennessee, Heywood of North Carolina, and even Niles of Connecticut

introduced resolutions to that end. In the House the friends
of annexation were equally busy; and it did no harm to the
cause when the President's private secretary, his son Robert,
who was said to look like the poet Shelley, appeared at the bar
with a message telling how Mexico had made a new threat of
cruel and barbarous war.

Through December and January, and into February the
work went on, slowly but with the deliberateness of the inevitable. On December 3 Adams won his fight for the right of
petition on the slavery issue. But that was about all that the
opponents of annexation had to comfort them. To the White
House the political situation, coupled with the presence of its
young, beautiful, and accomplished new mistress, brought
gaiety and brilliance, which were by no means diminished by
the arrival in Washington of the President-elect and his
handsome if somewhat formidable wife in the latter part of
February.

Democracy along the Tennessee and the Ohio had done its
utmost to make their journey a triumphal progress. A small
but brand-new cedar-built steamboat brought them from
Nashville to Wheeling, and when it was blown ashore near
Louisville, that city gave them a warm welcome for the night.
Cincinnati opened its arms to them. From Wheeling to Cumberland, the western terminus of the railroad, they traveled
by carriage over the great National Road, the construction
of which Polk had opposed in Congress and Clay advocated.
At Relay House they were met by Mr. George M. Dallas, the
Vice-President-elect, and welcoming committees from Baltimore, Washington, and other cities; and as their train
clanked into Washington that evening, cannon roared in
salute on Capitol Hill, fireworks blazed, and a torchlight procession celebrated their arrival.

They were in time for the annual Birthnight Ball at the
White House on the 22nd. The heads of all the departments,
the diplomats in court dress, Mrs. Madison, Mrs. Alexander
Hamilton, who was now nearing ninety years of age, and representatives of the beauty and fashion of New York, Phila-

delphia, and Boston graced the occasion. But the "parting invitation ball" that the Tylers gave a few nights later was not less brilliant. For that the invited numbered two thousand, the lamps of their carriages stretching, said one observer, "down the long avenue to President's Square and far away."

The gigantic Scott and the aged and portly one-time commander of *Old Ironsides* were conspicuous among the guests. In the East Room the Marine Band played in a great window recess that was draped in blue with an American flag above it, and the crowd was marshaled so as to leave space for "three large quadrilles." At the magnificent supper wine was like water in its profusion.

Mrs. Tyler, who "looked like Juno," in embroidered satin with loops of lace and a Shepherd's bonnet ornamented with ostrich feathers and diamonds, opened the ball with Mr. Wilkins, the Secretary of War. The young and beauteous Mme de Bodisco joined her in the cotillion — "the godless German cotillion," according to the stricter sect of the pharisees — with the representatives of Prussia, Austria, France, and Russia for partners.

An illness kept Mr. and Mrs Polk from being present. But what she thought of such levity of behavior in the First Lady was to be inferred when she succeeded to that station. She had already silenced a German band that had come on board the steamboat at Cincinnati to gladden the voyage up the Ohio on the Sabbath day.

On March 1 the President gave a grand supper to the members of his Cabinet and their ladies in honor of the President-elect and Mrs. Polk. His attitude in these last days of his administration was that of *nunc dimittis in pace*, and his wife's was the same as his. For that very day he had signed the joint resolution of both houses of Congress by which Texas became a member of the Union.

Two days before, the Senate by a vote of twenty-seven to twenty-five — it was as close as that — had adopted the resolution of the House to that effect. "A signal triumph for the

slave representation," Mr. Adams called it. The thing had
been done, thought Mr. Hone, "by means the most unconstitutional . . . the foundations of the Republic have been
broken up." But John Tyler cared for none of these things.
In the face of every sort of opposition, in spite of enemies, and
at the cost of many friendships and of his political future,
regardless of danger to the integrity of the Union, and fearless of the threat of war, he had removed the military menace
of a weak neighbor on the country's southwestern frontier and
had added to the country's domains it remained to be seen
how many thousands of square miles of territory at least
potentially rich. What if the Mexican Minister should follow a formal protest with a demand for his passports? Polk
could be trusted to see that the good work was carried on.

The Cabinet supper was followed by a reception. It was a
Saturday evening. Monday was spent in packing, with the
President's daughter, Mrs. Semple, and Mrs. Mason, whose
husband had succeeded Gilmer as Secretary of the Navy,
coming in to help in the final flurry. Late in the afternoon a
crowd of friends that included Mrs. Roosevelt and Mrs.
Beeckman saw the President and Mrs. Tyler into the carriage
that took them to Fuller's Hotel. Mrs. Tyler was in a black
dress and bonnet, but they symbolized no mourning mood.
Suspended around her neck she wore "the immortal gold pen"
— as it was called by a chronicler of the time — with which
her husband had signed the annexation bill.

CHAPTER II

Manifest Destiny

§1

TUESDAY MARCH 4, 1845, brought terrible weather for Mr. Polk's inauguration. It was cold and cheerless, and the rain fell in torrents. The members of the diplomatic corps in their ceremonial magnificence were drenched before they reached the Capitol, for there was an order that all carriages must be left a hundred yards away, and profusely beribboned marshals with batons of young hickory enforced it.

Chief Justice Taney, who was to render the Dred Scott decision twelve years later, administered the oath of office. Bishop Johns, the Episcopal assistant bishop of Virginia — the same who took a similar part in the inauguration of Jefferson Davis in front of the Capitol at Richmond in just such a downpour in 1862 — offered the prayer. The new President delivered his inaugural address to a host of dripping umbrellas, and what Mr. Adams, who declined to be present, called "a draggletail procession" escorted him to the White House.

The spirits of good Democrats, however, were nowise dampened. President Tyler rode to the Capitol with Mr. Polk in an open carriage, standing up with him and bowing the whole way to acknowledge the plaudits of the multitude. The Empire Club escorted them with a small cannon, which they managed to unlimber and fire from time to time en route. Mrs. Polk, tall and handsome, in a becoming hat of purple velvet and a long black velvet cloak that was heavily fringed and tasseled, and richly braided, looked young in spite of the dismal daylight.

What was called an "aristocratic committee" sponsored an

inaugural ball at Carusi's that night, with tickets priced at
ten dollars to keep out the common herd. But unfortunately
they forgot to invite the diplomatic corps, who went to the
"Democratic" five-dollar ball at the National Theater, to
which they had been invited. The fashionables followed the
diplomats, and some odd assortments were the consequence.
One Foreign Minister's wife found herself dancing in the
same quadrille with her gardener, and a pickpocket filched
Commodore Elliott's wallet.

The new President and First Lady appeared at both func-
tions, naturally. She wore a ball gown of mazarine blue velvet
and a deeply fringed cape and carried an ivory-handled fan
decorated with the portraits of all eleven of the Presidents.
But evening dress could not save her husband from looking
much as he always did — rather like a Methodist parson, in a
coat to which his spare habit of body gave the appearance of
being two or three sizes too large for him.

He was a Methodist indeed, and became a member of the
Methodist Foundry Church, but as a rule he went with his wife
to the First Presbyterian. She was a firm believer in the doctrine and discipline of that denomination, frowned on cards,
and put a stop to balls and dancing at the White House as
"undignified" and a cause of "unseemly juxtaposition" in
that place. Her sense of propriety had always kept her away
from horse races. She announced that she would attend no
public balls or other public amusements. No refreshments
were served at her weekly receptions, where, like her predecessor, she received her guests seated. An English lady said that
not one of the three queens whom she had seen could compare
with the truly feminine, yet distinguished and regal presence
of Mrs. Polk: a very handsome woman, with very black hair
and dark eyes, in maroon-colored velvet and a pink headdress.
So it was perhaps not unnatural that the conversation on
these occasions was said to be frigid and affected, and "whole
regiments of the raw material of Democracy" in frock coats
lined the walls and stared at the President and the chandeliers.

Her White House dinners were excellent, however. She had

sound ideas on the subject of food and wines and knew how
to be easy and fascinating as a table companion. A "plateau,"
which was a long, narrow mirror, was laid down the center of
the table, its edge covered with vines and flowers and its
length punctuated with three pyramids of fruit; and long
napkins, which the servants rolled up and removed before the
dessert, covered the rest of the board. She and the President
sat opposite each other at the middle of the table: the ends
were "the lowest room."

She knew her Washington and her country as few wives of
presidents have known them. As a girl, Sarah Childress, she
and her sister had ridden on horseback over the mountains
from their home in Tennessee to their school at Salem in North
Carolina in care of an older brother, with a trusty Negro
servant to convey their portmanteaus. During the many years
that her husband had been in Congress she had made the
similar journey to Washington with him in their own carriage, stopping overnight at farmhouses, with their Negro
man and maid in the rumble, and sometimes young Sam Houston, also a Congressman from Tennessee, accompanying them
on horseback. Her husband's lucrative law practice made life
easy for them. They had lodged at Williamson's Hotel, with
Calhoun as a member of their mess, and among her Washington friends of those days were Mrs. Van Ness, Mrs. Benton,
Mrs. Clay of Alabama, Mrs. Edward Livingston, Mrs. Lewis
Cass, Mrs. Hayne and Mrs. Preston of South Carolina, Mrs.
Marcy of New York, and Mrs. Rives of Virginia.

She displayed no overweening sense of her own importance,
declined with thanks a proposal from some citizens of New
York to present her with a carriage and four, and treated the
offer of a saddle horse the same way. During the long, hot
summer, while the long-neglected renovation of the White
House went forward, filling the whole first floor with the
smells of white lead and oilcloths, the rooms upstairs remained
as they had been. What had been good enough for Mrs. Tyler,
said Mrs. Polk, was good enough for her.

She enjoyed politics and liked the society of gentlemen.

She was "always in the parlor," it was observed, when the
President was there; and for him, who shocked a reporter
from the *New York Herald* by saying that he had no time to
read the newspapers, she read them assiduously and marked
the passages she thought it desirable for him to see. Before
long there began to be some who called her "the Presidentess,"
but, all in all, she was admired and well liked.

"Madam," said one gentleman on being presented to her,
"I have long wished to see the lady on whom the Bible pro-
nounces woe," and went on to dissipate her astonishment by
quoting: "Woe unto you when all men speak well of you."

§2

The new President had need of his wife's social ability. He
had but little inclination toward the lighter side of life and
gave even less time to it. But he, too, knew his Washington
thoroughly. The sarcastic query of the Whigs: "Who is
James K. Polk?" had been absurdly rhetorical. He was no
Henry Clay, to be sure — no Van Buren or Lewis Cass, both
of whom had also been his rivals for the nomination. But he
had served fourteen consecutive years in Congress, had been
chairman of the Committee on Ways and Means, and for four
years Speaker of the House, retiring only in 1839 to become
Governor of Tennessee. Now he came to Washington with
Andrew Jackson's special blessing: that fierce old fighter
had cast his last vote for him in the 1844 election.

A thoroughgoing Democrat, he cherished no jealousy of
the more famous members of his party. Buchanan became his
Secretary of State, George Bancroft his Secretary of the
Navy, John Young Mason Attorney General. He made full
use of their abilities, but his policies were his own. For himself, though he lacked some months of being fifty years old,
he had no further political ambitions. In the November of his
first year as President he told Bancroft that he would retire
at the end of his term and would take no part in choosing his
successor.

Upon the great and intricate tasks that confronted him

he threw himself with an industry and a singleness of purpose that disregarded amusement, recreation, and even consideration of his health. During his whole administration he was absent from Washington only thirty-seven days, whereas Tyler had been out of town a total of a hundred and sixty-three. Up at daylight, he breakfasted only after an early morning walk, worked in his study until noon, gave audiences until two, dined early — the usual dinner hour of the time was three o'clock — and went back to work again. Often he would spend half the night over his papers, though they might relate only to some quite insignificant appointment to office.

His wife, who soon became concerned for his health, could seldom persuade him to drive out with her of a fine afternoon. It was an event when he crossed the Potomac in Mason's carriage to watch the fishermen draw their seine, and another when he and Mrs. Polk paid a call on Postmaster General Cave Johnson in March 1846. That, he recorded in his diary, was the first visit of its kind that he had made since the previous summer, when he had called on Mrs. Madison and on Mr. Mason, who was ill; and he had dined out but once: with Secretary Bancroft and the Secretary's handsome, elegant, and somewhat chilly wife. He found his informal receptions on Tuesday and Thursday evenings "pleasant," but this, one gathers, was quite as much because they left his other evenings free for work as for the enjoyment he got out of them.

He found plenty of work cut out for him. There was the reconciliation of his low-tariff pledge with Pennsylvania's demand for a protective tariff. There was the Oregon boundary dispute with Great Britain, which had been darkened by threats of war ever since Van Buren's time. There was Texas, which he was pledged to bring into the Union. And there was California, which he told Bancroft he intended to add to the territory of the United States.

The question of the title to the Pacific Northwest between latitude 42° and 54° 40′ was of long standing. Pending final settlement the treaty of 1827 provided for a joint occupation of the territory: an arrangement, however, from which either party might withdraw on giving one year's notice. Negotiations had continued, had got nowhere while Britain was represented at Washington by the eccentric Henry Stephen Fox, and had been brought to a sudden pause by Secretary Upshur's death, which occurred soon after Fox had been replaced by Mr. Richard Pakenham.

Pakenham came to Washington from a long and successful diplomatic career at Mexico City; he had lately been made a Privy Councilor. Where Fox had been slow in paying his bills, had turned night into day, and had earned the name of "antiquated mummy," Pakenham's look and manner of the "frank John Bull" and his lavish entertaining made him immediately and generally popular. When negotiations were resumed, he proposed to Calhoun to compromise on a boundary that should follow the forty-ninth parallel from the mountains to the northeasternmost branch of the Columbia River and thence, by way of that branch and the Columbia itself, to the Pacific, with free navigation of the Columbia and a large tract of territory at the entrance of the Strait of Juan de Fuca for the United States along with any ports on the mainland or on Vancouver Island south of 49° that the United States might desire. Calhoun held out for the valley of the Columbia and refused Lord Aberdeen's proposal to arbitrate. Tyler, he said, believed that negotiation would succeed eventually.

Thus the matter stood when Polk came to deal with it in his inaugural address, and he sounded no uncertain note. We had a clear title to Oregon, he told the world, and our people would soon establish it by settlement. The only way to deal with John Bull, he wrote in his diary some months later, was to look him straight in the eye; and Lord Aberdeen's statement that, while he hoped for peace, Great Britain would maintain her rights did not cause him to hesitate. In any dispute with Great Britain he knew that he would eventually have the country behind him.

Much had happened since 1827 to strain relations between the two countries. In Britain there were many sore hearts and empty pocketbooks as a result of the defaulted bonds of various states of the American Union. As late as 1846 the news of Iowa's admission to statehood was greeted in England with the gibe that one would rather the States had admitted I O U than I O A. On the other hand, Americans could not forget the episode of the ship *Creole*. A cargo of Negro slaves of American ownership had seized that vessel and carried her into Nassau, where the slaves had been declared free; and the British government had refused Secretary Webster's demand that they be returned to their owners.

There was also the affair of the *Caroline*, which had been engaged in transporting supplies from the United States to Mackenzie's rebels in Canada in 1837. Canadian troops had violated United States territory to seize her, had killed an American citizen in doing so, had captured the rest of her crew and set the vessel on fire and adrift on the Niagara River. One could buy lurid (and lying) colored prints of her plunging over Niagara Falls with her wounded writhing helpless on her deck.

The situation in Oregon itself, moreover, had altered greatly with the passing of the years: and especially of late, owing to the activities of an obscure lieutenant of the army and his charming and determined young wife. The Baron Bodisco's bride had not been the only precocious young lady at her wedding. Among the bridesmaids was Miss Jessie Benton, daughter of the Senator from Missouri. She had been sent as a boarder to Miss English's school because, though only fifteen, she had already received two formal proposals of marriage. At her father's Washington home for brief holidays she might have been supposed to be safe in the pleasant living-room, where the Senator and his wife sat reading on either side of the fireplace and the girls had their books and their needlework around the lamp on a table near by. But Jessie did not need the aids of privacy and moonlight for the exercise of her witchery.

Evening callers were frequent at the Bentons'. Among them was Lieutenant John Charles Frémont of the Topographical

Engineers, who was a special favorite of the Senator's because of his knowledge of the upper waters of the Missouri and the Mississippi and his interest in the Oregon country, all of which formed the Senator's pet hobby. The love that sprang into being between him and Jessie at first sight, however, soon made him, a poor and very junior officer, decidedly less welcome to her father; and Mr. Joel Poinsett, Van Buren's Secretary of War, was quite willing to oblige the influential Senator by shipping him off to survey the lower course of the Des Moines River in what was then the distant territory of Iowa.

But absence had its proverbial effect. Frémont, his mission accomplished, returned to find Jessie's heart, like his own, grown fonder, her determination to marry him as adamantine as it had ever been, and her father set as firmly as ever against the union. They were married secretly. There was a tremendous domestic explosion, but it was followed by a immediate reconciliation. Backed and protected by the powerful influence of his father-in-law, the bridegroom set forth on fresh and wider explorations, and almost at once young Jessie took her place as the tutelary deity of Western Expansion.

While Frémont crossed the South Pass and ranged the Wind River Mountains, with Kit Carson as his guide, examining scientifically the Oregon Trail and fixing the location of future stockaded forts to guard the coming tide of emigration, Jessie waited steadfastly at St. Louis, renewing her childhood memories of the city, which was still French in its atmosphere and still very much of the frontier. In streets shaded by the abounding locust trees one looked down from the long galleries that fronted both stories of every house upon hunters and trappers in fringed buckskin, Indians in paint and blankets, and tough soldiers from Jefferson Barracks, who mingled with French peasant women in white caps, sabots, and full red petticoats, with large blue or yellow kerchiefs crossed over white bodices. Along the levees the air rang with the songs of the Negro stevedores as they loaded and unloaded the steamboats that plied to New Orleans, up the Mississippi to Fort Snelling, and far up the Missouri.

When her husband came back, she helped him write the report of his expedition. They modeled it on Washington Irving's *Adventures of Captain Bonneville* and wrought to such good purpose that it sold thousands of copies as a government document and thousands more when it was republished commercially.

The following year, 1843, at President Tyler's order, Frémont was off again, with forty men, Kit Carson again his guide, and a twelve-pounder howitzer, which he borrowed from Colonel Stephen W. Kearny and which came near to stopping him before he was fairly started. The authorities at Washington thought it made the expedition look too much like a military reconnaissance, whereas its mission was to find a different route to the South Pass from that of the Oregon Trail, to proceed thence to the Columbia, and to check the coastal surveys made by Commander Wilkes. An order for his recall was hurried to St. Louis, but the uncompromising Jessie, who opened all his mail there, suppressed it and sent him cryptic word at Kaw Landing (later Kansas City), where he had paused, that he had best be off without delay.

He stood not on the order of his going, and it was August of the following year before either she or St. Louis saw him again. He had not found a new route to the South Pass, but from Fort Vancouver he had struck southward that winter. January 1844 had found him on the Carson River in what is now Nevada. In spite of perishing cold he arrived at Sutter's Fort on the Sacramento early in March and came home over the "old Spanish trail" to Santa Fe and on by Utah Lake and Pueblo and down the Arkansas River. His return to Washington, with Jessie at his side, caused a sensation. Her father doughtily defended her suppression of the recall order, and Senator Buchanan moved the printing of ten thousand copies of his report. For the Oregon fever had reached its height by that time.

When, in 1817, young William Cullen Bryant had written of

> *the continuous woods*
> *Where flows the Oregon and hears no sound*
> *But its own dashing,*

it seems to have been the first time that the name had been mentioned in print since Jonathan Carver in the previous century had told what he had heard of the great river that was soon to be called the Columbia.

In spite of the joint-occupation treaty the Oregon country had remained the special preserve of the Hudson's Bay Company, and the company had naturally discouraged settlement as detrimental to its trapping and fur-trading activities. But in 1824–5 a liberal-minded factor had made Fort Vancouver, on the north bank of the Columbia, a port of entry for ocean-going vessels. In 1829 Oregon City had been founded. Christian missions had been established in the Willamette Valley in 1834 and at Walla Walla and eastward as far as what is now Idaho soon after. In 1843 American settlers, who found the Hudson's Bay Company's laws inadequate for their growing numbers, organized a provisional government of their own ; and that year came the Great Immigration : nearly nine hundred men, women, and children made the long journey overland from Independence, Missouri.

For the American people had no such feeling against expansion westward as manifested itself against the annexation of Texas. Ever since the acquisition of Florida in 1819, American diplomacy had been directed toward establishing the security of a United States that should be continental in its extent. The idea of the peaceful displacement of Spain, and even of Great Britain, in North America was popular. Manifest Destiny, it was called, and it was increasingly in the air.

John Tyler felt a warm sympathy for the movement. As president, in the spring of 1842, he appointed Dr. Elijah White to be Indian agent in Oregon and bade him set off from Independence as soon as possible, taking with him as many emigrants as he could assemble. Tyler was all for building the forts that he sent Frémont to locate along the trail. But Congress in one of its periodical spasms of penny-wise economy proceeded to deprive of their horses the dragoons whose duty it was to guard the travelers from roving bands of mounted Indians, and the Senate rejected a resolution to request the President to give notice for the ending of joint occupation.

There were many on the eastern seaboard, to be sure, who maintained that Oregon, except for a hundred-mile-wide strip along the coast, was not worth having and, if obtained, could not be defended against the British Asiatic squadron, the Hudson's Bay Company's servants, and the heavily armed steamboats the London *Times* was advocating for the defense of the Columbia Valley. Many Eastern newspapers called the migration a mania and wrote of the dry, hot summers and rainy winters of the Oregon littoral, of timberless inland regions covered with prickly pear, and of deserts still farther east.

To New Englanders with a snug competence and satisfied that theirs would be the best of all possible worlds as soon as they had made over the rest of the country in the image of New England, any desire for a change of environment was naturally incomprehensible. Young Francis Parkman, just out of Harvard in the summer of 1846, speculated on the "insane hope of a better condition in life" and the "desire of shaking off the restraints of law and society" that must animate the emigrants whom he saw as he set out from Fort Leavenworth on the journey he afterwards described in his *Oregon Trail*.

But the spring of 1843 saw pro-Oregon meetings at Pittsburgh, St. Louis, and Cincinnati. A convention of citizens from six Mississippi Valley states demanded that the right to the whole of Oregon up to 54° 40' should be maintained by troops and a fleet in the Pacific Ocean, that emigration should be encouraged and forts built from the Missouri to the Pacific to protect it. In the past ten years the British, it was charged, had dotted the valley of the Frazier River with forts and fringed the Columbia with forts, fisheries, sawmills, and settlements while denying to Americans the right to settle there. American blood ought to boil, said one leading newspaper, at reading in Farnham's *Travels in the Great Western Prairies* of the treatment given Americans by the Hudson's Bay Company employees, who were merely the cat's-paws of England.

Meanwhile the great ox-drawn wagons, with "Oregon" painted on their swelling canvas tilts, had been creaking out of Illinois, Kentucky, Tennessee, Arkansas, the Iowa country, and Missouri itself to gather at Elm Grove near Independence that spring. The next year men, women, and children to the number of fourteen hundred followed them, and three thousand in 1845.

§3

That spring of 1845 Washington had a glimpse of another of the leading literary lights of the time: Mr. James Fenimore Cooper brought his daughters to see the sights of the national capital. In June the death of Andrew Jackson caused the Capitol and the doors of the departments to be hung with black. Mr. Louis McLane went to the Court of St. James's to replace Mr. Edward Everett, who came home in disgust at the administration's Texas policy. The Polks took a picnic party to Mount Vernon. As the season advanced, picnics over at Arlington, Mr. George Washington Parke Custis's place, became the rage. And the Oregon negotiations came to what looked dangerously like a dead end.

Thoroughly convinced of the justice of the American claims to the whole of that territory, Polk nevertheless felt himself bound to continue the negotiations begun by his predecessor in office, especially as he thought that a war for the comparatively worthless country north of 49° could hardly be justified by civilized standards. He directed Buchanan to offer to compromise at that parallel. But now Pakenham refused, refused flatly, was angered by the offer, and declined even to refer it to his government. Polk promptly withdrew it. Let Lord Aberdeen make an offer now if he would; or let war come if it must.

Buchanan demurred, believing that the country would not support a war for the territory north of 49°. But Bancroft, accompanying the President on one of his rare horseback rides, commended Polk's firmness. This was late in August, and two months later a dispatch from McLane justified Polk's action. Lord Aberdeen deplored Pakenham's rude rejection of the offer and asked if the President would be willing to negotiate further. But the international atmosphere had become so tense that the Barings' agent came down from Boston to try to find out from the President himself whether it was to be war or peace.

Polk thought that at any rate the twelve months' notice for terminating the joint occupancy ought to be given, that the laws and jurisdiction of the United States should be extended to American citizens in the disputed territory, and that, in addition to the proposed forts along the trail, two or three regiments of mounted rifles should be raised for the protection of the emigrants: all of which could be done without violating the terms of the convention.

Buchanan still held that a majority in Congress favored compromise. Polk thought not, and a good many congressmen called to express their approval of his forthright message in December. Even Mr. Adams, though he said that he would refuse an invitation to dine with the President when Buchanan sounded him on the subject at Polk's request, added that he would support the administration's Oregon policy. Pakenham made a second offer of arbitration, and on the 27th of December Polk made up his mind to refuse it.

New Year's Day came in so cold that the hackmen who clustered about the north portico of the White House during the President's reception pulled their muskrat caps over their ears and thrust the hands that carried their whips deep in the pockets of their rusty greatcoats. Indoors two little Negro slaves guarded the piled-up wraps of the guests and collected twenty-five-cent tips for their services, while a policeman, who sported a large A on his otherwise plain clothes, shepherded the crowd, intoning: "Gentlemen who have been presented, please walk forward into the East Room. Don't stop up the passage."

Dr. and Mrs. Elijah White, who were about to return to Oregon by way of Mexico — which was the quickest way to get there — were the lions of the occasion. Mrs. Madison promenaded the rooms on the President's arm, it was observed, "with almost youthful agility," while a "few horny faced strangers" chewed tobacco and stared. Polk was in fine form at these affairs. A master of the ordeal by handshaking, he possessed a gentle voice and a manner both unassuming and cordial.

He hated, however, to be dragged down from his study for no better reason than to watch a certain Herr Alexander perform sleight-of-hand tricks before some forty or fifty ladies and gentlemen. An amusement "innocent in itself," he called it, but "time unprofitably spent." Other distractions were bad enough: the receiving of the Pottawatomie chiefs, for instance, who came in ceremonial splendor of paint and feathers and delighted in their reflections in the great pier glasses in the East Room. And then there were the sittings for his portrait to Mr. Healy, the American artist whom King Louis Philippe had sent over from Paris to paint the portraits of Andrew Jackson, Henry Clay, and John Quincy Adams. At a state dinner in February the earnest, hard-working little man enjoyed the conversation of eighty-seven-year-old Mrs. Alexander Hamilton, but in his diary he added rather unkindly that, "dressed in the style of fifty years ago," she looked "comical enough."

He had good reason to feel harassed. Since the beginning of January congressmen from the Northwestern states had been pressing for giving the notice to terminate joint occupancy. But certain Democratic defections in Congress, headed by Calhoun, made him feel that he lacked reliable support there and made him fear for his policies and the success of his administration. These recreants were even saying significantly that the only way to deal with an unruly Negro was to give him "a d— good drubbing at the start."

Calhoun wished him to compromise at 49°. Polk refused. He would never, he repeated, agree to the free navigation of the Columbia. The Whigs rejoiced at his dilemma: one faction of his party ready to curse him if he compromised, the other to curse him if he did not. "Was ever gentleman in such a fix?" Crittenden, the Whig leader, asked with sardonic satisfaction. In his diary Polk unburdened himself with one of his few witticisms. The Senate, he wrote, had been more interested in '48 [the next presidential election] than in 49° or 54° 40′.

That entry was made in April. Nothing had yet been accomplished in the Oregon negotiations, and Webster, Calhoun, and others were weakening the administration's position in them by making speeches in favor of a large part of the British claims, although such information of Britain's warlike preparations had reached the Cabinet that the Secretaries of War and of the Navy had asked the Military Affairs and Navy Committees of both houses for additional appropriations for national defense.

But by this time the contagious alliteration of "Fifty-four forty or fight" had begun to ring so clearly from all parts of the country that even politicians with ears pressed so close to the ground that they could hear almost nothing could hear that. The cautious Buchanan, lately animated by presidential aspirations, had, as Polk noted, turned "warlike." Calhoun began to flounder out of his opposition to giving the notice on joint occupancy; and although he and his faction voted with the Whigs to defeat one of the President's appointments, both houses on April 23 voted by large majorities that the notice should be given.

Polk had long been convinced that Great Britain had been counting on internal dissensions in the United States and would not settle the Oregon question until Congress had taken such action. Now, with what he considered to be his "first great measure" sustained, he could turn with a less divided mind to the problem of Texas, which had become more and more pressing as the months went by.

§4

Texas had been an interesting subject to the people of the United States ever since Stephen Fuller Austin had established his colony of American settlers at San Felipe de Austin on the Brazos River, with the consent and approval of the Spanish Viceroy, in 1821. It had been a sore spot in international affairs and a sore that rankled among the American people ever since Santa Anna had done away with the Mexican Constitution in 1835, made himself dictator, and proceeded against the Texans as if they were rebels against his government.

Whatever opinion Americans might hold regarding annexation, they could not forget that the Texans were their own flesh and blood, and their fortunes were followed with keen interest. This was especially true in the Southern states bordering on the Mississippi, for from these had gone the largest number of Austin's settlers and of the thousands that had followed them. When Santa Anna treated the Texan request for statehood in the Mexican union as treason and the Texans took up arms in their own defense, the news of their first small victories had hardly reached the United States before a company of volunteers, the New Orleans Grays, landed at Brazoria from a schooner loaded with military stores contributed by the people of New Orleans for the cause of Texan liberty.

In April of the following year, when Austin, as one of the Texan commissioners to the United States, spoke at Louisville, people crowded to hear him. They did the like in New York, where Wharton, another member of the commission, spoke at the Academy of Music. For all over the country of late years adventurous young men had been writing G. T. T. (Gone to Texas) in place of P. P. C. on their visiting cards and had departed to seek their fortunes beyond the Sabine River.

Henry Smith, the head of the Texan provisional government, John W. Robinson, the Lieutenant Governor, W. H. Wharton, Branch T. Archer, Ashbel Smith had all been citizens of the United States before they became Texans. So, too, had been Bowie, Travis, Crockett, and the rest who were massacred at the Alamo while the Mexican band played the Assassin's Song and the black flag flew from Santa Anna's observation post. Volunteers from Nashville and a whole company from Kentucky had been among the helpless victims butchered at Goliad by Santa Anna's orders. Many in the United States had sons and daughters, brothers, sisters, and grandchildren in that terrible mass exodus when the news of the Alamo's fall sent all Texans flying for refuge beyond the Brazos. The whole country could take pride in Houston's magnanimity when he saved Santa Anna from a well-deserved hanging after the knock-down-and-drag-out fight with bowie knife and clubbed rifle at San Jacinto.

Within three or four months after San Jacinto twenty-five hundred volunteers from the United States had joined the army of Texas. From Mississippi came five hundred fully equipped, followed soon after by a thousand more. Several companies were raised in Kentucky. Some volunteers came from Ohio. Albert Sidney Johnston, thirty-three years old and sorrowing over the death of a beloved wife, resigned a lieutenancy in the United States Army and enlisted as a private in that of Texas. Very soon he rose to the command of it — after taking a dangerous wound in the thigh in a duel with the Texan general whom he superseded and who considered himself slighted by Johnston's appointment.

When Santa Anna on his way to repatriation was taken to Washington, there were those who thought it remarkable that somebody did not kill him, so high ran the feeling against him in the United States. At the urgency of Congress President Jackson recognized the independence of the Republic of Texas on March 1, 1837, just three days before the expiration of his term of office. It was only eleven months after the battle of San Jacinto. But he had the additional motive of anxiety lest Great Britain forestall the United States in doing so and thus gain special privileges for herself from the infant nation in return.

Jackson would dearly have loved to take Texas into the Union as the Texans themselves desired, but not for the sake of slavery, the motive that the antislavery people imputed to him. There is no more evidence that he and his young friend Sam Houston plotted the Texan revolution for what the enemies of annexation called the slavocracy than there is for their other accusation: that the settlers of Texas were chiefly animated by a desire to extend and strengthen slavery in the United States. Many of the settlers had slaves and took them with them just as they took what they could of their other property. That was all.

Jackson saw in the existence of a young and necessarily weak nation on the southwestern border of the United States a military menace. Let Great Britain — "England" to him — acquire bases in Texas and, operating from these and from her posts on the Great Lakes, she might crush the United States in a gigantic pincers movement. But this same year 1837 saw the publication of the Reverend William Ellery Channing's *Thoughts on the Evils of a Spirit of Conquest, and on Slavery; A Letter on the Annexation of Texas to the United States.* More and more people of standing were joining the antislavery ranks. Adams, who the next year began his long fight against the "gag rules" in Congress, was already damning annexation as a slaveholders' conspiracy. The gentle Whittier reminded the country that Freedom's soil had no place "for traitors false and base."

For the contention of others that annexation was merely a scheme of speculators in Texas lands and Texas scrip, there was this to be said: the state of the finances of the new republic was deplorable. Some of its other aspects were hardly prepossessing. The quarrel of the Texans among themselves over the location of their capital, a fracas that included the discharge of a cannon by one hotheaded woman, was the reverse of edifying. The French consular agent at Galveston, who

came up to Washington in 1841, told M. de Bacourt that the
Texan Republic was a regular nest of bandits, its government
composed of brigands; and when he added that it had been
settled by fugitives from justice in the United States, he had
thus much of truth on his side: many a Southern planter who
had been ruined by the panic of 1837 escaped the sheriff by a
moonlight flitting to Texas and took his slaves with him.

But events in Texas continued to make an appeal to the
sympathies of many Americans. On the day after San Jacinto
Santa Anna, a captured fugitive with a speedy and painful
death at his shoulder, had been glib in his promises. He would
order an immediate armistice and follow it by a peace treaty
that should recognize Texan independence and the Rio
Grande as the boundary between the two countries, exactly as
the Texans claimed that it should be. But Santa Anna's failure had compelled him to retire from politics for a time; the
war had gone on smoldering; and when he returned to power
a few years later, he sent two of his armies into Texas. Both
penetrated as far as San Antonio before the Texans could
gather to repel them, and the second carried off in its retreat
the judge and lawyers assembled there for the 1842 fall term
of the district court.

A Texan force engaged in besieging the town of Mier on the
Rio Grande was captured. Of its survivors, a hundred and
sixty in number, seventeen were executed as punishment for a
mass attempt to escape, and the rest were marched to Mexico
City, where the dungeons already held prisoners taken in an
episode characterized by still greater barbarities. Again volunteers poured in from the United States though the Texan
government lacked the means to arm and equip them. Two
years later the publication of the *Narrative of the Texan
Santa Fe Expedition,* by George Wilkins Kendall of the *New
Orleans Picayune,* revived American memories of the wrongs
done to United States citizens by the government of Mexico.

Most of the facts concerning that ill-conceived and worse-
executed enterprise were, of course, already well known. It
had set out in 1841: fifty merchants, a few other civilians, and

an escort of two hundred and fifty dragoons to protect them from the Indians, with the ostensible purpose of persuading the inhabitants of Santa Fe to divert to some port on the Texan coast the flourishing trade by wagon trains that they had been carrying on with St. Louis. Two commissioners of the Texan government went with it, however. For it was understood in Texas that the inhabitants of Santa Fe had revolted against the Mexican government, and this seemed to President Lamar like a favorable opportunity to extend to the Santa Fe country the authority that Texas claimed the right to exercise over it.

Mismanagement and miscalculation reduced the expedition to a state of starvation and demoralization many days before it reached the end of its long and terribly difficult journey. Instead of being welcomed as allies and deliverers, as its members had been led to expect, they were met with a general and bitter hostility, disarmed, robbed, stripped, and started on a death march of two thousand miles over waterless deserts and icy mountain plateaus to Mexico City. There the survivors were sent to the filthy dungeons of Perote or incarcerated in the city prisons, whence daily they were driven forth in chains to sweep the streets.

Kendall's book recounted once more the harrowing details: the hunger and thirst on the march, the beating of the laggards, shooting in the back of those who could not keep up, and the ears of the killed cut off and strung on a rawhide thong so that the guards could present a proper count of their charges. Kendall, who had long since made himself a kind of press agent of the Texan Republic and his paper an organ of Texan publicity, had accompanied the expedition and wrote with the authority and vividness of an eyewitness. For though he was an American citizen and bore evidence of the fact in a passport issued to him by the Mexican consul at New Orleans, he and some other American nationals were treated like the rest. Their prison was the one in which lepers were confined, and it was several months before the American Minister succeeded in accomplishing his liberation.

His book was widely read both in the United States and abroad. It was not in human nature to note the many instances of Mexican kindness to the prisoners that it told of, the fact that charges were preferred against the Mexican officer responsible for the worst of the cruelties, and that they were denounced by a leading newspaper in the Mexican capital. What caused his long imprisonment was a letter, published in an American newspaper, which stated that he was actually one of the commissioners of the Texan government. But what people remembered was that a British subject captured in the same circumstances had been released promptly when the British Minister brought his case to the attention of the Mexican authorities. The appearance of the book in that last year of Tyler's administration was timely for the cause of annexation, as its author undoubtedly intended it to be.

§5

But with regard to annexation the administration at Washington had to consider matters more important than outrages against its nationals, although for these an international court of arbitration had assessed a sum of over two million dollars against Mexico. Repulsed by Jackson and Van Buren, Texas had turned to Great Britain and France and had been met with a cordial reception by the governments of both those countries. They received Dr. Ashbel Smith as Minister from the new republic. Captain Charles Elliot of Her Britannic Majesty's Navy and lately engaged in negotiations in China established himself as British diplomatic agent at the Texan capital. The Count de Soligny was sent over by King Louis Philippe to represent France. Daunted by the bottomless mud of Austin's Congress Avenue, its bleak rows of shacks and cabins, President Lamar's two-story frame residence, and the dirty wooden one-story Hall of Congress, the Count removed to the luxuries of New Orleans, but continued at long range to watch over his country's interests on the far side of the Sabine.

The stake was well worth great effort. Texas had a hun-

dred thousand inhabitants now. In spite of the business depression, Texas exports from the port of New Orleans had
taken third place in the last quarter of 1838, although New
Orleans was the great outlet of the whole Mississippi system
and by 1844 its levee bristled with the tall smokestacks of a
fleet of four hundred and fifty steamboats, while seagoing
vessels lay moored three deep in the great crescent of its river.

In an attempt to make the best of both worlds Britain, with
the co-operation of France, strove for the acknowledgment
of Texan independence by Mexico and against the aggran-
dizement of the United States that annexation would bring
about. While British merchants established a direct trade in
Texas cotton between Galveston and Liverpool, British abolitionists interested themselves in slavery in Texas. It was
believed at Washington for a while in 1843 that the British
government would assist in an abolitionist scheme for buying
and setting free all the slaves in Texas by means of a loan to
be paid by grants of Texas public lands.

With Britain on the Columbia as well as on the Great Lakes,
at Bermuda, in Jamaica, and on the Mosquito Coast, many in
the United States saw British machinations in Texas as part
of a policy of encirclement in which the seizure of California
would be the next step. There was in the diplomatic air, moreover, a project to establish a monarchy in Mexico, with a
Spanish prince to sit upon its throne. The London *Times*
frankly advocated this, giving good grounds for President
Polk's belief that in his policy of expansion he was, as he said,
"re-asserting Mr. Monroe's doctrine." He sent Frémont on
a third expedition that summer, with sixty men, the explora-
tion of the Great Basin and the Pacific coast as his ostensible
mission, and secret orders to assist the United States naval
force in California waters in the event of war. To Commodore
Sloat, the commander of that force, he sent orders to keep his
squadron cruising within striking-distance of Monterey and
to seize that port at the first news that war with Mexico had
been declared.

At New Orleans the Count de Soligny enjoyed the society

of cultivated people who spoke his native tongue, the performances at the St. Charles Theater, which was at that time the
fourth largest in the world, and other ameliorations of the
life of a homesick Frenchman. But he left them at once and
hastened to join Elliot at his post of duty on hearing that the
American Congress by joint resolution had offered annexation to Texas. Anson Jones, who had lately become President there, preferred independence to annexation and went
to work with the two foreign representatives to such good
purpose that by the time Colonel Andrew Jackson Donelson
arrived from Washington with official notification of the congressional action Elliot was on his way to Mexico on the British frigate *Eurydice* with the draft of a proposed treaty by
which Mexico was to acknowledge Texan independence,
Texas was to bind herself never to become annexed to any
other country, and the disputed boundary between the two
was to be fixed by a final treaty or adjusted by arbitration.

Elliot returned with the Mexican government's agreement
to this arrangement. But meanwhile an enthusiastic popular
celebration at Donelson's arrival had clearly indicated the
wishes of the people of Texas, whatever those of their President might be. When Jones called his Senate together in mid-
June, it refused to ratify the treaty with Mexico. Ashbel
Smith, his Secretary of State, who was blamed for the treaty,
was twice burned in effigy and took a hasty departure for Europe; and on July 4 a convention of the people, assembled to
pass on annexation, voted for it unanimously.

Lest the seven thousand Mexican troops that lay along the
lower Rio Grande should invade the country while this action
was pending, General Zachary Taylor, who commanded the
United States "army of observation" that President Tyler
had stationed at Fort Jesup just over the Louisiana border
the previous year, had received orders to place his troops at
some suitable United States port where they could be embarked for a point on or near the Rio Grande as soon as the
offer of annexation was accepted. Stockton, now a commodore,
was sent with the *Princeton*, the sloop-of-war *St. Mary's*, and

two or three smaller vessels to the mouth of the Sabine; and one still night in July the streets of New Orleans rang with the music of army bands as the 3rd Infantry marched down to the steamboat *Alabama* on the first leg of the journey that was to end at the city of Mexico. The rest of the little force, which included as its only artillery Captain Braxton Bragg's battery of four brass Napoleons, followed in sailing vessels.

With it, in the 4th Infantry, went Ulysses Simpson Grant, twenty-three years old, two years out of West Point and lately promoted from brevet rank to a full second-lieutenancy. When he wrote his *Memoirs,* an old man, dying, and under the spell of the Civil War, he called the war in which he had been about to engage in 1845 "the most unjust" in the history of his country and this military movement of which he had been a part a mere provocation to hostilities that all else had failed to precipitate.

There were many who held this view at the time the movement was made. It seems not to have occurred to them that, having offered Texes annexation and the offer having been accepted, the government of the United States was in honor bound both to do all in its power to protect its new citizens and to support their territorial claims until these should be brought to a final settlement. They ignored the fact that in moving troops into the disputed area their government was doing no more than the Mexicans had already done. They could hardly have been persuaded that President Polk did not wish for war, had no intention of fighting unless he should be forced to do so, and was convinced that he could get everything he aimed at by negotiation and purchase.

Yet the size and condition of the American army and navy and the little that was done for the next ten months to improve them should have borne witness to Polk's peaceful intentions. It might have done so in a nation less traditionally unmilitary than the United States, even when full allowance was made for the penny-pinching shiftlessness, the high-hearted insouciance, and the valorous ignorance with which, until 1917, the American people always went to war. In 1845 the army had an authorized strength of 8,613, including its generals and staff officers. There were two regiments of dragoons — no other cavalry — eight ten-company regiments of infantry, and four of artillery, of which one company in each regiment was mounted as a light or horse battery — the "flying artillery" of newspaper writers who dreamed not of airplanes armed with cannon that were to come just a century later. There was also a corps of forty-five officers of engineers, whose efficiency is to be judged by such names on its roster as Robert E. Lee, George B. McClellan, and George G. Meade. All these in the summer of 1845 added up to an actual strength of about seven thousand two hundred.

Scattered in small detachments throughout the country, overworked against the Indians on the frontier and sunk in a lethargic monotony elsewhere, even this modest establishment was under continual attack by congressmen who wished to make an easy reputation as watchdogs of the people's money. When Tyler's administration proposed to increase both army and navy, Adams made a move for retrenchment, and Calhoun supported him. The Navy managed to build two fine side-wheel war steamers, the *Missouri* and the *Mississippi*, of 3,000 tons each. The *Missouri* was destroyed by fire at Gibraltar, and nothing was done about replacing her.

On the other hand, Senator Benton maintained that between 1841 and 1842 the navy had increased as much as in the previous twenty years. It had 937 guns afloat in '42, he complained, and 11,000 or 12,000 men on its rolls. The navy's bill for the next year was nine millions. The African squadron alone, which was charged with the suppression of the slave trade, cost $600,000. Adams and Hale of New Hampshire attacked the Home squadron, which was composed of sixteen ships, as a useless expense. Let midshipmen be sent to the merchant marine for training as naval officers.

With his senses somewhat sharpened by his anxiety for Oregon, Senator Benton felt a certain uneasiness about the new fast steamships that could cross the Atlantic in twelve or fourteen days. They could land an invading force from Europe on the American coast before troops could be assembled to resist it. But Professor Morse's invention disposed of that fear, in the Senator's judgment. Summoned by telegraph and transported by railroad, the embattled farmers, whose Lexington reputation was not to be lived down until more than seventy years later, could doubtless be got together in plenty of time to hurl the hirelings of European despotism back into the sea whence they came.

As for the regular army, were not its ranks filled with foreigners and the worst sort of men, whose desertions between the years 1830 and 1836 had averaged a thousand a year? And why? Because, forsooth, promotion was closed to the enlisted man; nobody could be an officer who had not been through the Military Academy at West Point. The remedy? Abolish the Academy, of course. What could be simpler? And on one occasion Congress came within one vote of doing it.

During the war that was soon to follow, the sight of the cadets drilling at West Point gave Ralph Waldo Emerson a slight feeling of mental nausea, though he liked their looks very well twenty years later, when they were being trained to fight slave-drivers in the Civil War. After Monterrey and Buena Vista even such a level-headed observer as Philip Hone wrote with a certain naïve astonishment that the West Pointers had demonstrated the value of their alma mater. The army was the reverse of popular among the people at large. When in his young delight, Lieutenant U. S. Grant rode out in his home town in his first army uniform, a small boy jeered him with: "Soldier! Will you work? No, sir-ee; I'll sell my shirt first."

When Taylor's little army landed in Corpus Christi in August 1845, it numbered only 1,500, and to bring it to that figure Texas had been drawn upon for a party of rangers, and Louisiana for two companies of volunteers whose enlistments expired in November. To augment it further, troops had been taken from little garrisons in the North and East, and when, in that same month, these were assembled at New York, they had to wait until the storeship *Lexington* could be converted into a transport.

But it was the moral effect of this force that Polk relied upon. In this he believed implicitly, and he had confidence in its commander. Taylor's record in the War of 1812 and in the Black Hawk and Seminole wars had earned him the name of Old Rough and Ready. To be sure, he was a Whig. But unfortunately there were no generals who were professing Democrats, and when Polk was President-elect, Andrew Jackson had told him that, if the Oregon question brought war with England, Taylor was the man to command the American army.

Polk sent Taylor orders to regard any Mexican crossing of the Rio Grande in force as an act of war and added that in that event he need not wait to be attacked, but should drive the enemy back across the river and take the towns of Matamoros and Santiago, only refraining from any deep advance into the interior. With such expectations of a force of less than two thousand, which would be opposed by some seven thousand enemy troops, it is not surprising, perhaps, that Polk thought its presence in the debatable land and the naval squadron off Vera Cruz would prevent the Mexicans from declaring war or taking any other hostile action.

He remained confident of this, although President Herrera in July had recommended to the Mexican Congress that they declare war if United States troops entered what he considered to be Mexican territory. In August, after Pakenham had spurned the American offer to compromise on the Oregon boundary and Polk had determined to reject any British offer to compromise at less than 49°, Buchanan had suggested to him that it might be best to temporize until one could see what would follow the Mexican threat. But Polk had replied that he saw "no necessary connection" between the two.

He felt certain that by negotiation and the payment of money Mexico could be not only placated but induced to recognize the utmost of the Texan boundary claims and to part with all the territory lying to the westward of that boundary and northward to Oregon, including California. His friend

Sam Houston had dreamed of a Texas such as that, and had added Oregon while he was about it. Polk deemed the acquisition of those territories essential to the security and future greatness of the United States.

§6

The acquisition of territory by negotiation and purchase was, of course, nothing new in American policy. Thomas Jefferson, fighting down his qualms as to its constitutionality, had begun it with the purchase of Louisiana. Florida had been acquired in the same way while John Quincy Adams himself was Secretary of State. In 1825, when Adams became President, he strove to "rectify" the Texas boundary, instructing Joel Poinsett, the American Minister to Mexico, to offer a million dollars for a boundary along the courses of the Rio Grande and the Pecos or half a million for one that should follow the Colorado of the Gulf of Mexico, or at least the Brazos, the line to run north from the source of any of these rivers to the boundary of 1819.

At the Mexican capital Poinsett sensed so much opposition to any such proposal that he refrained from making it formally. A few years later, when Andrew Jackson authorized his Minister, Anthony Butler, to offer a reasonable price for a boundary following the Rio Grande to the thirty-seventh parallel and thence west to the Pacific, a tract that included San Francisco Bay but not the busy and desirable port of Monterey, Mexico refused to part with even Texas, though Butler approached Santa Anna and the conservative leader Alamán with the idea that they should receive ten per cent of the purchase money and planned to spend $600,000 "purchasing men." With the birth of the Texan Republic the boundary question had become, at least theoretically, a matter for Texas to settle, and it remained so until annexation tossed it back into the lap of the United States to exacerbate the whole annexation issue.

On March 6, two days after Polk's inauguration, General Almonte had lodged a protest against the annexation resolution with the State Department. He called it "the most unjust aggression in the annals of modern history," "the spoliation of a friendly power." Four days later he demanded his passports, and diplomatic relations were closed on March 28th by the Mexican Minister of Foreign Affairs, who at the same time addressed a protest against the American action to the ministers of Great Britain, France , and Spain at Mexico City.

Polk sent a confidential agent to Mexico, Dr. W. S. Parrott, from whom he heard in mid-September of the probability of still another revolution there. It seemed that General Paredes, who represented the Church and the aristocracy, had refused to lead an army into Texas, and Dr. Parrott believed that, in spite of all that had passed, President Herrera would now receive a minister from the United States. Writing two days after Parrott wrote, the American consuls at Mexico City and Vera Cruz expressed the same opinion.

Polk and his Cabinet acted on this information promptly. For their emissary they chose John Slidell, who sixteen years later, as Confederate commissioner to France, was to share with James M. Mason the notoriety of the affair of the *Trent*. The selection seemed a wise one, though the Whigs scoffed that Slidell owed his appointment to the election frauds he had perpetrated in Polk's behalf in Louisiana in the recent election. Born in New York, a graduate of Columbia College, he had settled in New Orleans, where he had been making ten thousand dollars a year by his law practice. He had married into the distinguished Creole family of Deslonde, had represented Louisiana in Congress from 1843 to 1845, and was thoroughly at home in both the French and the Spanish language.

It was arranged that a naval vessel should convey him from Pensacola to Vera Cruz secretly lest, forewarned of his coming, the British and French representatives at Mexico City should be able to thwart his mission ; and as a gesture of amity the American squadron off Vera Cruz was removed by orders to Commodore Conner, its commander, to take it elsewhere. The very day after Slidell's appointment, however, newspapers from New Orleans reached Washington with news from Mexico that looked decidedly warlike, and his departure was postponed pending the expected arrival of a warship from Vera Cruz with further information. In the meanwhile Polk had a confidential talk with a Lieutenant Gillespie, who was going out to join the Pacific squadron. He gave the officer certain secret instructions, which remain something of a mystery to this day, and a letter to Mr. Larken, the American consul at Monterey, which he was to carry to California by way of Mexico.

November had come before Secretary Buchanan entered the President's study late one evening with dispatches from Commodore Conner stating that the Mexican government would indeed receive a minister from the United States. On the 9th Dr. Parrott arrived with the information that Mexico really wished to settle its differences with the United States, and at ten o'clock the following evening the President signed Slidell's commission as Minister and Envoy Extraordinary.

Slidell was empowered to offer the following terms: (1) twenty-five millions for a boundary following the Rio Grande and thence due west to the Pacific; (2) five millions for New Mexico (that is, the Rio Grande watershed above El Paso), or, as a minimum, the release of the two million dollars of claims of United States nationals in exchange for the Rio Grande boundary that Texas had contended for. This last was about what Mexico had been willing to agree to as a result of the Anglo-French mediation just before annexation had been ratified.

Slidell set out at once, but when he arrived at Vera Cruz he learned that his presence was the reverse of welcome. He was met on the road to the Mexican capital with a number of reasons why he could not be received: the United States Congress had not consented to his mission; the Senate had not confirmed his appointment; the Mexican government had agreed to accept a "commissioner" — to receive a minister would be to condone annexation, and that it would never do.

The fact was that Herrera, who was honest, earnest, and married to an American wife, knew that it would cost him his place to receive Slidell. His refusal to do so saved him for only a few more weeks. In January 1846 a revolution overthrew him, and Paredes at the head of a provisional government ruled in his stead.

Slidell, who meanwhile had entered the city and presented his credentials willy-nilly, retired to Jalapa, whence he wrote, on instructions from Washington, to inform the new government through the American consul that if he was not received by March 15, he would ask for his passports and leave the country. He had good hopes of this ultimatum. Buchanan heard from him to that effect near the end of March. Money, he reported, was the essential thing, money to be paid down at the time of signing the treaty: a half-million dollars, of which Paredes stood in desperate need to pay the Mexican army. Buchanan thought that Congress would appropriate it, considering the precedents of 1803 and 1806. But Calhoun, on being consulted, doubted the wisdom of even asking Congress for it. And nine days later Slidell's dispatches brought word that he was coming home.

Actually the situation was even more discouraging than that news implied. The Mexican government had intimated to him that if the United States persisted in its present course, Mexico would call on all its citizens to defend the country. Paredes looked for help from the European powers, Slidell suspected; and the American consul at Mexico City wrote that Paredes was making secret visits to the British Minister. Polk was of the opinion that he ought to tell Congress that the time had come for the United States to take the redress of its wrongs into its own hands. When Calhoun objected, hoping that the Oregon question might be settled first, Polk replied that he saw "no alternative but strong measures," and coupled the two issues by adding that he believed it was British influence that had prevented Slidell's reception. To himself he could say that if he had failed in his efforts for negotiation, the failure had strengthened his position for war. Through-

out the country Slidell's rejection was taken as a clear indi-
cation that there remained now no alternative if the Mexican
question was to be settled at all.

As a matter of fact, war might well have come before this
from the situation that Polk had created on the border,
though his purpose in doing so had been a perfectly proper
one in the circumstances. To show President Paredes that the
United States meant business he had directed Secretary
Marcy in mid-January to order General Taylor to advance
and occupy positions "on or near" the Rio Grande as soon as
the season and the weather made it convenient for him to do
so. It was not Polk's fault that heavy rains and the Texas mud
delayed the movement until the second week of March.

CHAPTER III

Church Bells and Bugles

§1

Travelers from the United States who entered Mexico at
Vera Cruz were struck by the contrast between the cheerful
bustle and untrammeled enterprise they had left behind them
and the air of lethargy, of age and stagnation, that brooded
over their new surroundings. Their ship steamed past the
formidable stone ramparts of the sixteenth-century castle of
San Juan de Ulloa and landed them at a ruinous mole. They
entered the city through a gateway that, after three centuries, was still unfinished. The city, of 6,500 inhabitants, was
substantially built, its flat roofs bright with gay-colored
awnings. The pebble-paved streets were scrupulously clean
— kept so by chain gangs of galley slaves and the other official scavengers, the buzzards that strutted the pavements,
arrogant in the protection of the law, and blackened the roofs
and towers of the churches to the highest cross. The people
promenading in the evening cool were silent and seemed sad.
There was a fine new custom house, but it was built of stone
from Quincy, Massachusetts, though stone equally suitable
was to be had for the quarrying only ten miles away. In the
cities of the States the nights were noisy with business and
roistering. Here after dark there reigned a stillness that was
shattered hour by hour by the watchman's cry of *"Ave María
Purísima,"* while, in between, the numerous church clocks
boomed the quarters and from time to time the streets echoed
with the drums and bugles of the changing of the guard.

At New York, Philadelphia, or Baltimore, where the traveler had taken ship, he had perhaps lately descended from the
"steam cars," on which the fare was a little over three cents

a mile, and which were capable of a speed of twenty-five miles an hour under favorable conditions. For the journey to Mexico City from the country's principal seaport the available means of transportation was the *litera*, a sort of hammock borne by men or mules, or, if one would save time and money, one of the excellent stagecoaches built at Troy, New York, driven by American drivers, and operated by an American concern.

In one of these vehicles, at eleven o'clock at night, the traveler rolled out upon a road by no means of the smoothest. Over the fine stone National Bridge and up through the mountains the coach toiled on to arrive at Jalapa, a distance of seventy miles, at three the next afternoon. Wretched habitations of upright canes, roofed with palm leaves, punctuated the route at long intervals. The villages one saw were composed of filthy hovels of unburnt brick and surrounded by little patches of chili and Indian corn. In the States the farmers were adopting mechanical reapers, but these wretched cultivators were toiling with wooden plows and hoes that were no more than poles pointed with iron spikes such as they had used in the time of Cortes. For all the land in Mexico was owned by a few great proprietors who grazed cattle by the scores of thousands on estates a hundred leagues square and saw to it that their Indian laborers were always in their debt.

Jalapa was an attractive place, clean and bright, and notable for the beauty of its women. It had an excellent hotel, where one paid four dollars for a dinner, a bedroom, and breakfast, although the same could be had at the best hotel in New York for half that sum. But Perote, the next stop, was a dismal place of 2,500 inhabitants, situated in a barren waste and cringing beneath the walls of its fortress prison, where more than one deposed dictator and many of the victims of the Santa Fe and Mier episodes had languished.

Highway robbery was rife in the land, though two or three bandits were publicly garroted each week in Mexico City under the stricter administrations. The prudent traveler armed himself before leaving Vera Cruz; and now he looked to his rifle, shotgun, or Colt's revolving pistols, for the road ahead was lined with crosses that marked the graves of murdered wayfarers, and the escort of three mounted guards in long yellow coats looked none too reliable.

A band of jackals was all that was usually encountered otherwise. But as one approached the city of Puebla — Puebla of the Angels — broad fields of wheat and Indian corn and barley began to appear. The city itself boasted tall handsome houses, a multitude of churches, of which the bells were seldom silent, and a great square where the population circulated under the surrounding arcades as the traveled visitor had seen the people do at Bologna. There were great cotton manufactories here, which were protected from foreign competition by a tariff so high that it encouraged smuggling. Mr. Waddy Thompson, the American Minister, called Puebla the Lowell of Mexico, and thought the land about it the richest and best-cultivated that he saw anywhere in the country.

After leaving Puebla the coach climbed over the backbone of the continent, it crossed a stream that flowed into the Pacific Ocean, and presently one saw below, surrounded by snowy peaks, the valley of Mexico, with its flashing lakes and its capital city as a long line of turrets, domes, and spires in the distance. Within its gates it was as if one had left the nineteenth century on the steamer at Vera Cruz and by a few days' journey had entered a somewhat backward stronghold of the seventeenth.

The walls of Cortes still contained the city, though it was so crowded that often thirty or forty families were to be found living in a single one of the flat-faced houses whose iron balconies looked down upon the stony street. On the ground floors heavily barred windows and the massive gates of portes-cocheres bore witness to the inadequacy of the police. There were no good hotels, for travelers were few, and those of quality stayed with friends or relatives. But at the new French Gran Sociedad two Frenchified meals a day, a room, and a multitude of fleas in one's bed could be had for seventy dollars a week. Churches, monasteries, and convents were everywhere, some of them occupying an entire square; and late each evening their bells rang out to the satisfaction of the pious, for it was well known that while they pealed, the souls in purgatory had respite from their torments.

In the streets, except for the lumbering coach of some aristocrat or dignitary of Church or state, scarcely a wheeled vehicle was interspersed in the traffic. Men and pack mules, even for lumber, were the sole means of transport. The rich folk's ice came the forty miles from the snowy heights of Popocatepetl on the backs of half-naked Indians. The arches of two splendid aqueducts bestrode the surrounding plain to furnish the city with water. But it was not piped into the houses, and all day long the streets rang with the cries of the water-vendors. *Evangelistas,* professional letter-writers, squatting in shady corners, offered their services to a generally illiterate public with displays of stationery of various colors and ornamentation like that of valentines in the States.

Of the men on the streets, which seemed always to be crowded, eight out of ten were priests, friars, and monks in the habits of their profession, soldiers and officers in showy regimentals, or *léperos,* who were not lepers, but inhabitants of the squalid suburbs, so debased and wretched as well to deserve the name. The rest of the men wore, summer and winter, long black cloaks. Women of the lower classes swarmed everywhere, bare-legged, in satin slippers and the *rebozo,* the long shawl, which was worn over the head and held close about the chin, but had a way of slipping frequently to expose the full bosom under the white chemise beneath. To the fine new market came the Indians from Chalco and Texcoco across the lake in canoes laden with vegetables, fruits, and flowers, and Brantz Mayer, the secretary of the American legation, thought the scene worthy of the brush of a Canaletto.

But the quintessence of the city and, indeed, of the whole country was the great central square; the Plaza de la Constitución, when a constitution was in force, and at all times the Plaza Major. On three sides of it arched *portales* shaded the fronts of smart shops and cafés and the Casa Municipal, which housed the fine Merchants' Exchange, while gambling-houses flourished in the stories above. The fourth side was filled by the National Palace, where the President had his residence, and the huge mass of the Cathedral, which was built of undressed stone, the head and center of a rigid Counter-Reformation Roman Catholicism that had grown moribund and corrupt through three centuries of complete and rarely challenged predominance.

Brantz Mayer, who had been educated by the Sulpicians at St. Mary's College in Baltimore, noted the contrast between the luxurious lives of the high prelates and the splendor of shrines and sacred images decked with precious stones and pearls, and the gaping, half-clad wretches who knelt in adoration before them. Even that devout Catholic of Maryland and Alabama, Raphael Semmes, who visited Mexico in both peace and war, deplored the public pomp of the religious ceremonies and the wearing of ecclesiastical and monastic habits on the streets and deprecated the lax morality of the lesser clergy. Others Americans, reared in a bigoted and militant Protestantism, were horrified by the street names such as "Jesus" and "Holy Ghost."

At almost every hour the Host would be carried forth to bless some passing soul. A priest bore it in a carriage to the ringing of little bells, and singing boys or a dozen friars with lighted candles followed. The guard at the Presidential Palace turned out and presented arms. The cry: "*¡Dios viene! ¡Dios viene!*" ran before it, and woe to the ignorant or thoughtless Protestant who did not fall on his knees like everybody else and remain kneeling till it had passed. In 1824 an American shopkeeper had been murdered because he had knelt only on his threshold instead of coming out into the street to do so. It took soldiers with loaded muskets to ensure him even a decent burial, and his body was dug up and stripped by *léperos* who had been told that the heretic had wine and clothing buried with him "for his journey."

When the church bells stopped, the drums began to roll. The President drove out in state and never without a strong guard of cavalry: fifty hussars in front and fifty behind his coach, which was decked with crimson and gold. A Yankee coachman drove its four white American horses, and six aides-de-camp galloped alongside. If he happened to be Santa Anna, he wore the uniform of a general of division, with a medal set with diamonds among the numerous other decorations on his breast, and a gold-hilted sword. His hands were clasped on the gold head of a cane, and he bowed gracefully in acknowledgment of the *vivas* of the crowd.

To balance or curb the executive power in the government there was only the Congress of Deputies, which was distinguished for an orderly and dignified procedure very different from the behavior to be seen in the halls of the Congress at Washington. But Mr. Waddy Thompson thought that it was backed by too little of general intelligence, public virtue, and the spirit of liberty to be able to accomplish much. Armed revolutions were the accepted means of dealing with political ailments. But they were never truly popular movements — merely the uprising of one rich and powerful faction against another. Still visible on the buildings of the city were marks of the bombardment by the guns of Chapultepec and of the fighting through the streets that had brought Santa Anna in again in 1841.

But for the commonalty and the poor a perfect climate in which the severities of heat and cold were unknown, a soil whose fertility richly rewarded the most superficial cultivation, the pageantry of Church and army, numerous fiestas, cockfighting, and the cheap entertainment of frequent bullfights made life easy and pleasant, poverty and wretchedness endurable.

On Corpus Christi Day ten thousand cavalry, with the Host at their head, escorted through the streets *Nuestra Señora de los Remedios*, who, underneath her three petticoats of pearls, diamonds, and emeralds, was a little broken-nosed alabaster doll, with one eye gone. She dated from the *Noche Triste* of Cortes's expedition and was venerated as the agent of its ultimate success. In Holy Week there were endless religious ceremonies and processions, and on Easter Even, for the vulgar herd, firecrackers, fireworks, the hanging of Judases and heretics in effigy on ropes stretched across the streets, and a wild racket generally.

Every day there was the Alameda, the forty acres of sweet public garden where the principal fountain dripped beneath a gilded figure of Liberty, and the notes of doves, wrens, and mockingbirds lulled the stillness of groves that were "almost druidical," Mayer wrote. And every evening there was the free show of the Paseo, the mile of broad road bordered by fine trees and ending at the aqueduct, with the Castle of Chapultepec at one end of the view and snow-crowned Popocatepetl at the other. Here all who made any pretension to importance assembled on horseback or in enormous and splendid carriages that were drawn by two small mules with a postilion on one of them. There were hundreds of these equipages, thousands of cavaliers in roundabout jackets embroidered with gold and silver, who rode the fiery little horses of the country on gorgeous saddles that cost anything from a thousand to five thousand dollars.

This was the occasion, too, for Mexican ladies of quality to show themselves in public. Since ten in the morning they had been at their windows, watching and gossiping about those who passed in the street below. They were not, Mr. Thompson thought, well educated, excepting General Almonte's wife; it was the porter at the gate, and the institution of the duenna, that kept their idleness from turning to mischief, and they had the diversion of dressing extravagantly. At a ball Mr. Thompson was told that the headdress of one of them was worth twenty-five thousand dollars and that those of several others cost a thousand.

At the Paseo they turned out in all their splendor, languorously attractive and expressing by intricate movements of their fans their interest in the feats of horsemanship that were performed for their attention. After the Paseo came the theater — the new theater on Bergera Street, which was said to be finer than any other in the world, except the San

Carlo at Naples, and was named after Santa Anna when he was in power and after somebody else at other times. The performances were indifferent: the actors merely recited their lines. But that hardly mattered. The members of the audience were more interested in one another than in the play.

On other evenings persons of quality were at home to such callers as could pass the rigid examination as to their identity that was carried on through the grilled peephole in the barred doors of the porte-cochere. Once admitted, the visitor was conducted across the patio, past stabled horses, carriages, and servants' quarters, and up the great staircase to the princely apartments above or, on warm nights, to the flat roof, the *azotea*, where he was entertained with stately conversation or a rubber or two of whist.

Once a year gentle and simple alike partook of the pleasures of the Feast of San Augustín, when the entire population of the capital flocked to the neighboring village of that name and spent whole days together at cockfighting and gambling. Tables of monte received stakes of gold, silver, and coppers graduated to every purse, and the highest ladies of the land vied with the President and the members of the Cabinet in their interest in the performance of the birds.

§2

Even the revolution that had freed Mexico from the mother country had been a conservative movement motivated by apprehension of the excesses of the liberals who seized the power in Spain in 1820. The Mexican prelates feared for the Church's wealth, the rich for their own. Within a year the new government became an empire under Augustín Iturbide, who had fought on both sides in the sporadic struggle for independence that had been going on since 1810. The next year saw his abdication and exile, and when he sought to return to power in 1824, he was defeated and placed before a firing squad by the oligarchical republic that had replaced him.

The change from Spanish viceroys to native presidents brought little alteration in the life of the people. The government of the viceroys had been arbitrary and corrupt. The presidents frequently became dictators and exercised unquestioned authority over the public revenues and expenditures. Of the law courts it was said that even a bad compromise was better than a good case. Throughout the nation of 3,000,000 people there were only 300,000 producers. The relatively few who were politically conscious were divided into two great parties: the Centralists, who stood for the Church, the army, and privilege generally; and the Federalists, who were liberals, at least by profession, and favored local government. There was no regular middle class. So the path to dictatorship was easy.

For a quarter of a century president followed president into exile, one high-sounding pronunciamento succeeded another, and frequently to the sound of cannon and the rattle of civil musketry. Constitutions, liberal and anti-liberal, were successively adopted and abolished, and there had been one period of complete anarchy when in 1838 a French fleet had taken vengeance for outrages against French nationals by battering the walls of San Juan de Ulloa and occupying Vera Cruz.

Through all this confusion one figure came and went, now helping another to power, now seizing power himself, now passing into more or less brief eclipse, but only to reappear with greater strength and brilliancy enhanced. This was Antonio López de Santa Anna, "the Napoleon of the New World." An officer in the colonial army, born at Jalapa in 1795, he had helped Iturbide to his throne and at the head of a single regiment had led the revolution that dethroned him. He had earned the title of "Hero of Tampico" by defeating the Spanish in their attempt to reconquer the country in 1829. Five years later he had ruled as dictator until his abject failure in Texas forced his retirement. But the loss of a leg in fighting the French at Vera Cruz had restored him to popular favor, and in 1841 he returned to the Presidency, succeeding the liberal Bustamente, whose laws he abolished.

The principal streets of the City of Mexico were covered with awnings, the balconies gay with tapestries. The military and high functionaries of the state attended in glittering procession, and that leg, enclosed in a crystal vase, was solemnly interred in the Cemetery of Santa Paula beneath a monument erected by the commissary of the army. Soon after, a protest against receiving it, supposedly written by the neighboring dead, was found on a near-by tomb. But the limb remained there until in the next upheaval some thorough-going insurgents found time to dig it up and throw it to the buzzards.

Meanwhile its owner had again retired on finding the make-up of his Congress too Federalist to suit him and in 1844 had again made himself dictator. This time he ruled only by violence. But an attempt to raise a forced loan for means with which to pay the claims the United States was pressing in behalf of its nationals caused a mutiny at the end of the year. Amid popular outcries of "Death to the lame man!" he was overthrown, sent as a prisoner to the castle of Perote and thence into exile, and General José Joaquín Herrera succeeded to the Presidency.

Such had been the state of affairs since Joel Poinsett had become the first Minister of the United States to the Republic of Mexico in 1825. It was further complicated, moreover, by the intrigues of the representatives of France and, especially, those of Great Britain. Neither he nor any of his successors received more than a grudging reception. Accused of an improper sympathy with the Federalists, he had the Church, the aristocracy, and the influence of what was virtually a British protectorate against him. He was constantly insulted "unofficially," and both he and Anthony Butler, who followed him, were recalled at the request of the Mexican government as *personæ non gratæ*.

To Powhatan Ellis, who was chargé d'affaires in 1836

and Minister from 1839 to 1842, fell the difficult task of dealing with relations still further strained by the rebellion of Texas. The Mexican government complained bitterly of the pro-Texas meetings that were held all over the South-western United States, of the thinly disguised recruiting of volunteers to fight for Texan independence, and of the numerous shipments of munitions and supplies to the insurgents. To all this the reply of the United States was that whereas Jackson's administration had refused armed help to the Texans and even recognition of their belligerency, the laws of the United States did not forbid its citizens to expatriate themselves and enlist in the service of a foreign state or to export contraband of war. For fitting out expeditions to help the Texans the Federal government had brought some individuals into court, but the juries had refused to convict them, just as they had refused in like circumstances when the South American countries were in revolt against Spain. When, a few years later, Mexico threatened war for these causes, Secretary Webster snubbed her sharply, pointing out that American citizens were no longer aiding rebels, since Texan independence had been recognized by Britain, France, and the Netherlands as well as the United States; and even the British Minister told Santa Anna that the American attitude was entirely correct.

On the other hand, to rasp American feelings, there was the long list of outrages committed against Americans by officials of the Mexican government. Among these were the shooting at Tampico without trial of twenty-two Americans bound for Texas, the arrest and maltreatment of Americans in California, the case of those captured with the Santa Fe expedition, and many others. Even United States naval and coast guard officers landing at Mexican ports in performance of their official duties had not escaped insult. And the list grew longer day by day. The Mexican government evaded and delayed the payment of the two-million-dollar claim that the international commission headed by the King of Prussia had assessed against it. By 1842, relations between the two countries had become such that in October of that year Commodore T. Ap Catesby Jones, commanding the American Pacific squadron, actually seized the port of Monterey and held it for a few days in the belief that they had gone to war.

Mr. Waddy Thompson, who succeeded Ellis at Mexico City, was happier than his predecessors in his relations with both the government and the people. The sort of man apparently who sees most clearly the best side of everybody, he wrote of his stay in Mexico that he was never treated with the slightest discourtesy there, although he was known to have favored Texan independence and to desire annexation. He was able to enjoy and admire, for different reasons, both the stately Archbishop in a violet cassock, who said that the Puseyites were good enough Catholics for him, and the saintly old Bishop of California, who had given all that he had to the poor and had retired from office to live on the charity of others.

President Herrera he found to be a good character though remarkable for nothing in particular; Paredes lacking in information and experience, but brave and patriotic. He thought highly of Bocanegra, the Minister of Foreign Affairs, and held Bravo to be courageous, virtuous, and humane, though he had to threaten Bravo with a declaration of war to prevent the wholesale slaughter of the Mier prisoners. He got on well with Santa Anna, considering his rule to be patriotic and wise: the Mexican press, for instance, to be at least as free at the contemporary press of France under the Citizen King Louis Philippe; and he condoned the dictator's vices as being only those of his country and education.

In a book that he published some years later he described Santa Anna as a man of olive complexion and fine proportions, five feet ten inches in height, who was well aware that his mutilation was the best item in his political stock in trade and, far from trying to conceal it, stumped about on an old-fashioned wooden leg. His face, Thompson thought, showed

Sonoma ✳ Sutter's Fort

San Fransisco
(Yerba Buena)

Monterey

Santa
Barbara

• Los Angeles

• San Diego

Gila River

Tucson•

Fronteras •

SLOAT 1846

N
W   E
S

MILES

0   50 100   200   300

THE UNITED STATES AND MEXICO

f cities and operations of the War, 1846–8

talent and firmness and the capacity for both the greatest benevolence and the greatest ferocity.

Thompson spoke Spanish fluently and, a born South Carolinian, shared so fully Santa Anna's keen interest in cockfighting that when he returned to the States, Santa Anna sent him as a present one of his finest birds. But perhaps it was because he could listen with a straight face while Santa Anna lied smoothly out of his responsibility for the massacre at Goliad that Thompson was able to persuade him to release two hundred of the Santa Fe prisoners. In Thompson's time in Mexico all the installments so far due on the award for damages against American citizens were paid: fifteen per cent of the principal sum and nineteen per cent of the interest; and by demanding his passports he forced the Mexican government to rescind an order expelling all United States citizens from California — an order, by the way, that had never been executed; but Thompson did not know that.

These were creditable accomplishments for an American Minister to Mexico, but any British representative could have taken them in his stride. Kendall and his American companions had lain for months in a filthy jail in spite of Powhatan Ellis's protests, whereas British subjects who had accompanied the Santa Fe expedition had been released within a few days. In the city streets at night Americans who were accosted by the police were taken to the lockup unless they falsely declared themselves to be British. If they did that, they were allowed to proceed about their business.

The United States had been the first of the nations to recognize Mexican independence, only fifteen months after the defeat of the Spanish Viceroy in 1821. But it was Great Britain that put a stop to the plan by which the nations of the Holy Alliance were to have helped Spain to recover her American colonies, and the moral support Mexico had received from the promulgation of the Monroe Doctrine was forgotten by the Mexicans in their resentment of the various American schemes for the acquisition of Texas. The Mexicans, it was Thompson's belief, feared that not only Texas but their whole country was coveted by the *Americanos del Norte;* and they undoubtedly looked to Britain for help if it came to war.

There was a considerable colony of English merchants in Mexico City. The genial Pakenham had been dean of the diplomatic corps there for many years. After his departure for Washington the British representative was for a time General William Miller, who had been a subaltern in the British Army in the War of 1812, participating in the battles of Blandensburg, Baltimore, and New Orleans. Later he had served as an aide-de-camp under Bolívar and owed his title to having commanded a division at Ayacucho in the final battle of the Peruvian struggle for independence. Thompson found the general an accomplished gentleman, the English merchants enlightened, hospitable, and generous. But he was not less well aware than his predecessors had been of the machinations by which Great Britain and France were still striving to curtail the growing power of the United States.

It was his opinion that if war should break out between the United States and Mexico, a blockade of the Mexican coast by the American navy would bring Britain into it on the Mexican side, for the stoppage of shipments of Mexican specie was bound to derange the British monetary system. But he felt that, even so, it would be worth a war — twenty years of war — to keep Britain out of California, on which he, like many of his compatriots, believed that she had fixed a longing eye. California might be too far away to be joined to the Union, but she might become the center of a sister republic with the same language, institutions, and laws. There was not, as Thompson saw it, more than five or six hundred miles between the heads of navigation on the Arkansas and Red rivers and the navigable waters of streams flowing into the Gulf of California. Let a railroad connect the two, and the commerce of China and India would pour into New Orleans, which would become the greatest city in the world.

Neither Thompson nor most other citizens of the United States at that time could believe that Great Britain under

the government of Sir Robert Peel was not bent on aggran-
dizement in North America.

§3

The greatest barrier to prosperity and progress in Mexico was the army. At least that was Mr. Thompson's opinion, and it would seem to have been a sound one. There had
been a time when it numbered 44,000, of whom 24,000 were
officers. By 1844 this absurdity had been corrected. There
still remained two hundred generals, but only such as commanded regiments were rated as *generales efectivos*. Its
peacetime strength on paper, including the 9,000 militia
that were always kept under arms, amounted to about 30,000.
Actually it was far less. The troops were distributed throughout the country to preserve order and, especially in the
larger cities, to check the endemic tendency to revolution.
But they themselves constituted a fertile soil for the prop-
agation of dictators.

Of the officers as a corps the British Minister to Mexico in
1846 said that they were perhaps the worst to be found in
any part of the world: "ignorant, incapable, and insubordinate." Thompson doubted that there was one of them who
was able to handle a force of five thousand in a tactical maneuver. The ranks were filled chiefly by Indians and poor laborers who were marched in, handcuffed or roped in pairs, by
press gangs, and who deserted at every opportunity, for
their life was bitterly hard. They were scantily and poorly
clothed, and for food were at the mercy of their regimental
commanders, who were their own commissaries and generally
made a personal profit out of the rations. In emergencies
their numbers were increased by the liberation for military
service of prisoners convicted of minor offenses. They were
not lacking in courage, however, as they were to prove repeatedly in the war that was about to come, and they were
untiring on the march.

There were twelve battalions of regular infantry, most of
them armed with muskets that had seen service in the Brit-

ish army. Of cavalry, nearly all of them lancers, there were
twelve regiments. They were mounted on the horses of the
country, which were active and enduring animals, but so
small as to have little chance in shock action against the
more heavily mounted cavalry of the United States. The
three brigades of artillery were probably the weakest arm.
Their gun was of French design and far from efficient by the
standards of the day, and they were lacking in technical
training. There were, however, some troops of excellent appearance. Brantz Mayer noted that in the 11th Infantry,
which he saw passing in review in June 1842, the white uniforms were clean and good and the muskets shining. The
regimental bands were excellent, generally the best parts of
their organizations.

But of the ability of these troops to defeat any army that
the United States could send against them, people in Mexico,
and people elsewhere who ought to have known better, were
confident. A colonel of Mexican cavalry expatiated on the
ability of his troopers to break squares of hostile infantry
with their lassos. The members of the British merchant colony were sure that Mexico would win the war. In an outburst
of Latin enthusiasm the Spanish Minister at Washington
said that there were no finer troops in the world than the Mexican. The London *Times* correspondent wrote that they were
superior to those of the United States. Captain Elliott told
the Mexicans that the United States was incapable of fighting a successful war.

General Almonte, who seems to have taken too literally the
remarks of his Whig friends during his stay in the United
States, shared that delusion. He foresaw a brilliant invasion
of Texas, made easy by the disaffection of the Northeastern
states of the Union and a servile insurrection in the South,
and then the armed intervention of Great Britain on the side
of Mexico. Lord Aberdeen seems to have hinted at something
of that sort to a Mexican diplomatic agent, or so the Mexican
understood him; and the Oregon boundary question was still
unsettled.

Abroad the frequently disgraceful behavior of American troops in the War of 1812 was still remembered: it was hardly more than thirty years since the signing of the Treaty of Ghent. Reports from Corpus Christi told of disease, hardship, mismanagement, and incapacity in Taylor's army. When word came that Taylor was advancing toward the Rio Grande, the European press concurred with that of Mexico in expecting disaster for the little force now far from its base and at the end of an unprotected line of communications. The London *Morning Herald* prophesied that United States commerce would suffer from swift Mexican slave ships that would turn to privateering. The London *Times* mocked openly: "The invasion and conquest of a vast region by a state which is without an army and without credit is a novelty in the history of nations."

On April 23 General Paredes declared war. His appeal to all loyal Mexicans to rally to the defense of their country was received with enthusiasm.

§4

Mexican reports of conditions prevailing in the American army since it went into camp on the beach at Corpus Christi in the previous August only exaggerated the unhappy truth. Nostalgia, diarrhea, and dysentery prevailed among the troops. There was a lack of firewood. The drinking-water was frequently brackish, the camp sanitation deplorable even by the rudimentary standards of the time. The commissary was inadequate at first. The Quartermaster Department was slow in providing everything necessary for the comfort of the troops. The first tents that were issued were like sieves in the heavy rains, worthless against the blasts of the northers that became more and more frequent as the season advanced. Rattlesnakes infested the camp. Lightning killed two Negro servants. The boilers of the old contract transport *Dayton* blew up, wounding seventeen and killing eight. The schooner *Swallow* was wrecked in a storm. All in all, it was well that there were seldom any volunteers in the camp, and that those were few. The regulars, then as always, were accustomed to being required to make bricks without straw.

During the fall and winter, while Herrera was playing fast and loose with Slidell, reports and rumors of all sorts poured in to distract and discourage the impressionable. Taylor himself believed that there would be no war. Arista, the Mexican commander, was said to hold that opinion also. Commodore Conner was authority for the statement that Herrera had said that Mexico was too weak internally to expel the Americans from the Rio Grande country. Again and again, on the other hand, came stories of warlike preparations in Mexico. According to these, the garrison of Matamoros varied from day to day between five hundred and two thousand; Herrera had issued a war message; General Ampudia was advancing from Victoria with ten thousand men. And not one man in the army knew enough Spanish to sift these reports for the small particle of truth they might contain. The camp was fortified after a fashion, but it was evident to everybody who had any military knowledge that the army lay for weeks at the mercy of an active and energetic enemy.

Corpus Christi was a Mexican hamlet of between twenty and thirty houses and about a hundred inhabitants when the Americans landed. Kenney's Ranch was its other name, and a Colonel Kenney had ruled supreme there, flouting the Indians and the Mexican customs guards alike and trading American goods, Negro slaves, and tobacco with the Mexicans of the interior for cattle, horses, saddles, the beautiful Mexican blankets, and bars of pure silver. The native traders poured in when it became known that the United States Army would pay $36 a dozen for wild horses and from $8 to $11 apiece for mules. There was an American influx, too; generally a less desirable one. By November a town of a thousand inhabitants and buildings that mostly housed gambling-dens and drinking-places had sprung up at the edge of the camp. There was a theater, for which some of the army officers painted the scenery and which was occupied by a company of strolling players. By February the place had a weekly newspaper.

General Taylor was criticized for keeping slack discipline, for tolerating too much gambling and drinking. Lieutenant Colonel Ethan Allen Hitchcock, who commanded the 3rd Infantry, held that neither the general nor most of the other high-ranking officers could form the army in line of battle, except in a sort of militia fashion. Lieutenant George Gordon Meade, untroubled by premonitions of Gettysburg, found Taylor "a plain, substantial gentleman." Lieutenant W. S. Henry had observed him in August on St. Joseph's Island, the expedition's first landing-place, and noted that he was pushing forward his troops and supplies "with his usual energy."

By mid-October his army numbered 3,900, without counting the 150 dragoons in the interior. It had strained the resources of the regular military establishment to assemble so many. Five companies of the 5th Infantry had come all the way from Detroit, down the Ohio and Mississippi and across the Gulf, a distance of 2,500 miles in twenty-one days. Eight companies were "red-legged infantry," artillerymen without their cannon, armed and drilled as infantry. There were four batteries of horse artillery and, for a time, two companies of volunteer artillery that had been rushed from New Orleans on the news that Taylor's force was in danger of an immediate attack.

Small as this force appears by modern standards, it was large enough by the standards of the time to be divided into three brigades. Something of the same sort is to be seen in the organization of the British army in the Crimea ten years later. And the dragoons were kept separate under the immediate command of Colonel David E. Twiggs, who had led them overland to Corpus Christi by way of San Antonio. Brevet Brigadier General William J. Worth commanded the 1st Brigade, and between him and Twiggs there soon broke out an unseemly professional quarrel that complicated the life of the whole army.

According to persistent camp gossip Taylor, who, in spite of his hale and hearty appearance, was sixty-two years old, intended to retire, and both Worth and Twiggs laid claim to the right to succeed him in command. Worth, who had been in the regular army since 1813 and had rendered distinguished service at the Battle of Chippawa and against the Seminoles, based his pretensions on his brevet rank. Twiggs, who was also a veteran of 1812 and of the Florida war, held that his lineal seniority in rank gave him the right to the position. The other officers promptly took sides. The dispute was referred to Washington, where General Scott pronounced in favor of Worth. Thereupon Colonel Hitchcock prepared a memorial condemning Scott's decision as contrary to regulations, and sent it off to the President of the Senate over the signatures of 130 out of the 251 officers in the camp.

But in spite of sickness, dissipation, and dissension the work of training and organization went steadily forward. There were continual drills and parades and much target-practice. Taylor had a young and highly professional adjutant general in his future son-in-law, Captain W. W. S. Bliss — "Perfect Bliss" to his West Point classmates. The white-haired and white-bearded Twiggs, bull-necked and heavy-shouldered and six feet tall, was like a snow-clad volcano on the drillground. Worth, of middle height, strongly built, trim, and soldierly, was a thorough master of his work. The Rangers, a visiting Texas colonel wrote to Albert Sidney Johnston, were teaching the American troopers what riding really meant. Lieutenant Meade and the other "Topogs," the army's name for the Topographical Engineers, explored the thirty miles of the Nueces River up to San Patricio, and the Laguna Madre, the great, sheltered coastal waterway that ran a hundred and twenty miles to Point Isabel and made a perfect route for the transport of supplies to an advance base at the mouth of the Rio Grande. And all day long the corrals were lively with the roping, branding, and breaking of horses and mules to harness and the saddle.

Tents were fortified against the blasts of the northers with linings, embankments, and the planting of hedges of the dark green chaparral until the camp looked as if it had been pitched among orange groves. Nevertheless the men suffered severely from the cold. But one of these ill winds blew on shore quantities of green turtle and large fish rendered torpid by the icy blast, and at all times the army rations could be varied with game that abounded and fish that were to be had for the catching.

If some of the officers shared too freely in the gambling and drinking that beguiled the brief leisure hours of the enlisted men, most of them were well educated and of high character. Hitchcock, Bliss, and others read Spinoza, Swedenborg, Schiller, Kant, and Hobbes in their spare time. Most of the younger officers bought good saddle horses, which could be had for twenty or thirty dollars, and horse races became week-end fixtures. Hunting leaves were granted freely. Parties rode into the interior and returned with geese, deer, and panther.

On New Year's Day the general and the brigade commanders entertained the other officers at eggnog parties. The rest of the day was given to horse racing, a performance at the theater, and even a ball, though one doctor's wife was the only lady in the camp and there were few women in the town. On February 4 Taylor got his orders for the Rio Grande, and early in March the troops, who were thoroughly sick of their camp, the sandy shore, the cold, and the everlasting drills, hailed with delight the order to advance.

The weather was fine, the ground, after the first few stages, dry enough to make marching easy, and the country was beautifully interspersed with handsome groves of chaparral and bright with the scarlet Texan plume, the Mexican poppy, and the indigo. A mirage of great blue mountains, lakes, and farms brought memories of the Old Dominion to one observer. Wild hogs were shot along the road. A herd of antelope dashed away to halt and gaze at the column from a distance, and an immense drove of mustangs galloped close enough to satisfy their curiosity.

Twiggs led the march with the 2nd Dragoons and Ringgold's battery. Worth followed next day at the head of the 1st Brigade. The other two came on, each at a day's interval after the one before it, and a supply train of three hundred ox-drawn wagons creaked along with the 3rd, which brought up the rear. Presently the grass grew thin, the country waterless, the dust blinding. Faces turned red and peeled in wind and sun, though there was frost at night. But again the country changed. The chaparral reappeared in dense groves, and the soil turned from sand to stiff black clay.

So the army plodded peacefully onward for more than a week. On the 16th a Mexican patrol, which might have been the advance party of an army but turned out not to be, was encountered by a patrol of Twiggs's dragoons. Its leader forbade the Americans to advance farther but only rode away when the American lieutenant proposed to refer the matter to his commander. On the 20th, at the arroyo of the Colorado, Mexican bugles sounding for some distance up and down the wooded farther bank seemed to indicate that the crossing was to be resisted in force. A party of Mexicans showed themselves and threatened to open fire if the Americans attempted to advance. But again there was no fighting.

Taylor, who had been riding with the 1st Brigade, replied that he would open with his artillery if his passage was interfered with. At the first contact with the Mexicans he had sent back orders for the other brigades to join him by forced marches, leaving their trains behind them, and the 2nd had already done so. The field guns were unlimbered and trained on the opposite bank, with portfires burning. The steep nearer bank was cut down to facilitate the assault. Four companies of the "red-legged infantry" dashed through the breast-deep water, with Worth and his staff riding at their head, and the Mexicans vanished.

The army rested two days at the Colorado while the 3rd

Brigade and the supply train caught up with them. Taylor had intelligence that two thousand Mexicans now held Matamoros and had occupied Point Isabel, where he had expected to meet his supply ships. It was reported to him that General Ampudia had succeeded to the Mexican command and was about to arrive at Matamoros with a reinforcement of five thousand men. But the spirits of his troops were high. They cut down the steep banks of the river still further for the passage of the supply train and snaked guns and caissons, wagons and unwilling animals across the stream at the ends of ropes. And on the 23rd the advance was resumed across a prairie country fragrant with flowering acacia and so open that the army could march with Twiggs and the dragoons on the right and the brigades in columns abreast at deploying distance from each other.

The next day, on word that the Mexican guard at Point Isabel had burned the little town and retired, Taylor set out thither, with the now empty supply wagons and the dragoons for escort. The army, under the command of Worth, continued its march, and at eleven o'clock on the morning of March 28 the troops stood on the banks of the Rio Grande and gazed across its rolling waters at the town of Matamoros.

They were spoiling for a fight. The place looked inviting and exciting. A cathedral and substantial houses of stone and brick showed through the trees. Every roof and window was crowded with spectators to watch their arrival. The Mexican flag flew from General Mejia's headquarters, from the Plaza de Artillería and the barracks of the sappers and miners. The dust of marching columns of cavalry and infantry rose here and there among the fortifications, and the notes of bugles were wafted across the stream.

On their side the Americans planted a flagstaff. The Stars and Stripes went up to the strains of *The Star-Spangled Banner;* the field music followed, with *Yankee Doodle* on their fifes and drums; and the pet rooster of one of the regimental commanders flapped its wings and crowed defiance. Across the river the British, French, and Spanish colors were hoisted above their respective consulates, but not the American. Its absence struck some of the Americans as sinister. Did their consul not dare raise his flag? Was he not permitted to do so?

Not war, however, but only negotiation was the immediate sequel. Following implicitly his instructions from Washington, Taylor had given Worth his orders accordingly, and the latter, as soon as he could obtain a boat, crossed the river to explain to the Mexican commander that the purpose of the expedition was only to take peaceful possession of what was rightfully United States territory. When Taylor rode in from Point Isabel, as he soon did, with his wagons loaded with supplies and four 18-pounders that he had got from his ships, he reiterated this statement, but in vain. General Mejia persisted in regarding the American movement as an invasion. Taylor planted the 18-pounders in a battery that commanded the town, the center of which was only half a mile distant. The Mexicans placed a heavy gun on the opposite bank and protected it with sandbags.

The troops amused themselves by strolling along their side of the river, imagining the delights that Matamoros would afford. They watched a priest blessing a new Mexican fortification by sprinkling it with consecrated oil. At a narrow stretch they tried their Spanish on the handsome, scantily clad girls who were washing clothes in the stream in the age-old manner of all Latin countries, and were answered with laughter. On the northern bank there were only wretched one-room hovels in which a goat and a gamecock, tied by the legs, shared the brick floor with the human inmates. But eggs and fowls were to be bought at them, and "chicken fixin's" were a welcome change after the many days on salt provisions.

Some soldiers deserted — forty-three of the "Northern barbarians," according to the *Matamoros Gazette*. A few of these, in attempting to swim the river, were shot and killed by the American sentinels. Most of the others returned as soon as they could do so on discovering that they must either enlist in the Mexican army or work in the salt mines. On April 2 an order arrived from Secretary Marcy, reversing Scott's decision on the question of brevet rank, and Worth took leave, tendered his resignation from the army, and departed for Point Isabel and the States, though a man less angry or possessed of less moral courage might have been deterred from quitting his post by the atmosphere of tension that grew denser from day to day. For if it was not war on the Rio Grande, it certainly was not peace.

On the 12th General Ampudia sent warning that the Americans must retire to the Nueces or there would be war. He added that he, for his part, would wage it according to the usages of the most civilized nations — which was reassuring, since he had made himself notorious by boiling the head of one of his political opponents in oil. Two dragoons who had been taken prisoner were well treated, but Colonel Cross, the commissary general, had ridden out on horseback one morning and had not been seen or heard of since. One of the patrols that went to search for him was caught, first by the heavy rain that wet their priming, then by a party of Mexicans, who routed them and murdered their leader, Lieutenant Theodore Porter, son of the famous commodore, who had fallen wounded in the fight. Colonel Cross's body, stripped and with a crushed skull, was found a few days later. These outrages were charged to the bandit gang of a certain Romano Falcón, but it was believed in the American camp that they were looked on complacently by the Mexican authorities.

To Ampudia's warning Taylor replied quietly that he had been sent to the Rio Grande by his government and intended to remain there, and he set all hands to work at building an impressive fortification, which he named significantly Fort Texas. Ampudia retorted by expelling all American residents from Matamoros. Then Taylor requested Commodore Conner to blockade the mouth of the river.

Since Matamoros imported its flour from New Orleans and Conner promptly turned back two shiploads of it that were about to come in, this was serious for Ampudia. He protested to Taylor that under the circumstances the blockade was unauthorized by the law of nations and that if it were not raised it would have grave consequences. Taylor replied that he had already been three times informed that his advance into the country would be regarded as a declaration of war and once that his presence opposite Matamoros was considered to be an act of war, and since Ampudia himself had ordered him to retire to the Nueces within twenty-four hours, the blockade of the river was the least offensive act of war he could think of in return. He offered an armistice until the boundary should be settled or war declared formally. If that offer were accepted, he continued, he would raise the blockade, but not otherwise, unless his government, which had been informed of it, should order him to do so.

He entrenched his camp, with Fort Texas at the apex of a triangle of which the base and the sides, where they could be approached from the ferries above and below the town, were strengthened by parapets and ditches, and the troops manned the defenses each morning before daybreak. On the 25th a grand review on the other side of the river celebrated the assumption of command there by General Arista, an event of which he informed Taylor in a courteous note. In the afternoon word came that the Mexicans had crossed the Rio Grande in great force both below and above the camp, and in the evening Taylor sent Captain Thornton with Captain William J. Hardee and a detachment of dragoons to verify the report as to the upper crossing.

Next morning Chapita, the Mexican guide who had accompanied Thornton, rode in to report that the dragoons had been surrounded and either cut to pieces or made prisoners. At eleven a country cart brought in a wounded dragoon who had been sent by General Torrejón, the commander of the force that had engaged Thornton's patrol, with his assurances that the prisoners would be well treated. According to the dragoon, Thornton and one of his lieutenants were dead, and Hardee, who was to distinguish himself sixteen years later as a Confederate general at Shiloh, was among the prisoners. Actually Thornton was a prisoner also, but the killed included a lieutenant, two sergeants and eight privates.

§5

Taylor's situation was now a perilous one. This was war. A post that he had established halfway between his fort and Point Isabel had been attacked with a loss to its little garrison of five killed and four wounded, and he had a report that Point Isabel itself was being assailed. With his force of 2,700 he had to deal with an enemy numbering between 6,000 and 8,000. He was absolutely dependent on his communications with Point Isabel to maintain himself where he was, and the Mexican superiority in cavalry — 2,000 to his 200 — gave them an advantage in mobility that might easily make contact with his base impossible.

He acted promptly, with decision and rare insight into the power, capabilities, and mentality of his opponents. Leaving the 7th Infantry, Bragg's battery, and a company of artillerymen to man the four 18-pounders — about 500 in all — to hold Fort Texas, under the command of Colonel Jacob Brown, he set out with the rest for Point Isabel at four o'clock in the morning of May 1. The troops under his command marched until midnight, slept on the open prairie without fires, and reached their destination at noon the next day without incident, to find that the report of an attack there had been a false one.

For five days he remained there, resting his men, loading his great wagon train, which he had brought with him empty, and strengthening Fort Polk, the fortification that guarded his beach-head, though all that while he could hear across the intervening twenty-seven miles of prairie and chaparral the thunder of the guns at Fort Texas. But he had been able to leave the garrison there provisions to last them for a month, and Captain Walker of the Rangers, one of the old Mier prisoners, whom he sent back for news of the siege on the 3rd,

returned two days later with word that the superior skill of
the American cannoneers had silenced every one of the Mexican heavy guns in the first thirty minutes, and that though
the Mexicans continued to shell the fort with a mortar, they
were doing little damage.

It was three in the afternoon of the 7th before Taylor was
ready for his return march. His anxiety for his base was diminished that day by the arrival of a reinforcement of two
hundred and fifty men for its garrison. He still had, to be
sure, only his 2,200 for his field force. He would be encumbered by his enormous train. His scouts brought the intelligence that the enemy were encamped across his road in large
numbers with the evident intention of giving battle. But
"The General has every confidence in his officers and men,"
he said in his Order No. 58. ". . . He has no doubt of the result, let the enemy meet him in what numbers they may. He
wishes to enjoin upon the battalions of infantry that their
main dependence must be in the bayonet." And the hearts
of his troops were as high as his.

What with his laden wagons and his late start, his army
made but five miles that afternoon. At dawn next day the
scouts brought word that the Mexicans had broken camp and
retired. But when, some hours later, his advance guard
rounded the point of a thicket near the ponds at Palo Alto,
they discovered the enemy less than a mile distant, drawn
up across the road in a line of battle a mile and a half in
length. Ranchero cavalry (irregulars) formed their right;
infantry, with guns interspersed between the battalions,
the center; and the lancers of the regular cavalry, the left.
There were six thousand of them in all, and Arista was in
command.

Taylor halted, made a park of his three hundred wagons
under guard of the 3rd Infantry and one of his squadrons of
dragoons, and when his men had filled their canteens, for the
day was hot and they had already marched twelve miles, he
formed the rest for attack and, sword in hand, led them forward. It was the first time that American troops had gone

into action against the army of a civilized nation since the Battle of New Orleans in 1815.

The enemy guns opened fire at 700 yards. The American column deployed, with Ringgold's battery on the right, Duncan's on the left, and two 18-pounders, which had been picked up at Point Isabel, in the center. But the Mexican powder was poor. Their cannon balls — they had no shell — struck the ground far short of the target and rolled and bounded forward so slowly that often the American infantry, most of whom had been ordered to lie down, had only to open their ranks to avoid them. A body of lancers about a thousand strong swung to their own left under cover of the chaparral and, with a couple of guns, made to outflank the American line and seize the wagons. But the shell fire of two of Ringgold's guns caught them in column; the 5th Infantry changed front to the right and, along with the 3rd, formed such bristling squares of bayonets that the Mexican horsemen retired without pressing home their attack.

Burning gun wads set the dry prairie grass on fire. Dense clouds of smoke drifted across the front, hiding the combatants from each other. When the smoke blew away, Arista, finding that his left was being badly cut up by the American artillery, drew it back and advanced his right, where his own artillery had been more effective than elsewhere. Taylor changed front accordingly. Two of Duncan's guns galloped forward and enfiladed the new Mexican position from its right, his shell and shrapnel making such havoc in the enemy's dense formations and spreading such confusion among them that many of the American officers believed that a charge would have routed them. But Taylor had his train to consider. His mission was to re-establish his position at Fort Texas. On that depended the success of his whole campaign, and he was not to be diverted from it by the chance of an easy victory. The guns thundered on till sunset, when the Mexicans withdrew. The Americans bivouacked on the battlefield.

They were elated, and not without good reason. Hampered

by the necessity of guarding their train, they had neverthe-less defeated an enemy that outnumbered them almost three to one and was enormously superior in cavalry, the arm by which, in the circumstances, a victory might most easily have been won. As regulars they were especially pleased at achieving a success before the arrival of the volunteers, who were expected and to whom the newspapers would have given the whole credit for it. The Mexican dead and wounded lay in heaps and were estimated to number at least five hundred.

The American loss was only nine killed, forty-four wounded, and two missing. But if it was small in numbers, it was great in quality. The gallant Ringgold, both of whose legs were mangled by a cannon ball, lived only long enough to be carried to Point Isabel. A captain whose jaw had been shot away died before morning. Most of the other wounds were severe. The surgeon's saw kept going all night long, and the groans and screams from the improvised field hospital, where tobacco and brandy were the only palliatives, made sleeping difficult.

The Mexicans were expected to renew the battle next day, for they had retired only a short distance. At daybreak some of them showed themselves amid the dense chaparral and mesquite that covered the country ahead, but the dragoons and Walker's scouts, who were sent forward to feel out their strength, soon reported them to be in full retreat. The Amer-icans spent the early hours of the morning in policing the battlefield, burying the dead and searching the thickets for any wounded who might have been overlooked in the brief Southern twilight.

Taylor rode back to the supply train to send off to Wash-ington a report of his success. He caused the wounded to be collected there for transport to Point Isabel, ordered the parked wagons to be fortified with a hasty entrenchment, and left five hundred men to guard them. Then, with a hun-dred and twenty picked infantrymen ahead of him to probe the dense jungle that walled in the road, he led the rest for-ward until, about three miles from his destination, the Mex-

ican army was found to be strongly posted behind a series
of ponds where the road crossed the concavity of a horse-
shoe curve in what had once been the channel of the Rio
Grande.

Dense lines of skirmishers held the thickets on the nearer
bank. Artillery, some of it entrenched, was in position to
sweep the road and the few other avenues of approach. Any
attack would be exposed to flanking fire, and the whole front
was masked by thorny undergrowth so dense as to limit
greatly the employment of the American artillery, which had
proved itself to be Taylor's greatest strength on the day
before, and to make co-ordinated movements by his infantry
impossible for any unit larger than a platoon or, at most, a
company.

The Mexican guns opened fire with grapeshot and canister. With a dash and intrepidity worthy of its late commander, Ringgold's battery, now under Lieutenant Ridgely,
went into action on the road, which ran well over to the right
end of the front. On its left, deployed in successive lines of
skirmishers, the American infantry pushed their way forward through the jungle of undergrowth, and the enemy in
large numbers advanced to meet them. The battle quickly
degenerated into numerous isolated combats in which a squad
or two, a platoon or, rarely, a whole company fought it out
with bayonet and clubbed musket against groups of Mexicans who contended for every glade and thicket with stubborn courage.

A party of lancers caught Ridgely's battery as he was
moving his guns forward. He had only one unlimbered. But
a sergeant rammed home a load of canister on top of a shell,
and it accounted for all but four of them. These Ridgely
charged singlehanded and drove off. But his six light pieces
could do no more than hold their own against the artillery
opposed to them. The Mexican cannon continued to sweep
the road and the adjacent thickets. The American infantry
could make but slow, if any progress.

Taylor, calmly sitting his faithful charger, Old Whitey,

amid the flying shot, ordered Captain May of the dragoons to charge and take the enemy battery, and when May rode back to report that the Mexican artillery had slightly changed its position, Taylor exclaimed: "Charge, captain, *nolens volens!*" Ridgely, overhearing him, shouted to May: "Hold on, Charlie, till I draw their fire"; which he proceeded to do.

Then down the road, which was so narrow that his men must ride in column of fours, May, with his long black hair and beard flying, led his squadron at a gallop. In spite of Ridgely's precaution some of the Mexican guns had remained loaded and now opened fire. A lieutenant fell, several other saddles were emptied. On went the rest, down into the shallow watercourse and up and over the guns, making a prisoner of the Mexican General de la Vega, who scorned to follow the gunners in their flight to the near-by undergrowth. But the horses of the dragoons were running away now. Their formation was broken. They dribbled back by twos and threes, targets for the Mexican infantry, who shot at them from the brush; and the plucky Mexican gunners ran out of hiding, back to their pieces, and opened fire afresh.

Taylor turned in disgust to the commander of the 8th Infantry, which he had been holding in reserve. "Take those guns," he ordered, "and, by God, keep them!" So down that road in column went the gallant 8th and, with the help of some of the 3rd, who had worked around through the jungle onto the Mexican left flank, did as they were bidden. A crack battalion, the Veterans of Tampico, fought them sword to sword, bayonet to bayonet. Arista, who almost up to this moment had remained in his tent, writing a report of the action of the previous day and insisting that the present affair was only a skirmish, now put himself at the head of his lancers and led them to the attack. But he was too late. His charges were beaten back with bitter loss. Duncan's battery galloped up to support the American infantry. Taken in flank, the Mexican center resisted stoutly for a while, then broke, spreading panic down the rest of the line. The entire army dissolved into a terror-stricken mob that fled along the road to Matamoros and by every bypath leading to the river.

Yelling like mad, the Americans, with their artillery galloping ahead, unlimbering and hastening the Mexican flight with charges of canister, surged after them past the enemy camp, where the packs stood in order on the ground, campfires were burning, and carcasses of beeves hung ready for cooking a few hundred yards from the battlefield. There was no real pursuit, however. There could not be one. Taylor had put every man he had into the battle. They had been on their feet since daylight, marching and fighting; the dragoons were spent, horses and men alike. But as the demoralized rabble that had been a Mexican army streamed down to the lower ferry, the guns of Fort Texas opened upon them, killing many as they crowded onto ferry boat and scow, and many more were drowned in attempting to swim the river. So ended the Battle of Resaca de la Palma.

From headquarters on the battlefield two days later Taylor congratulated his troops on their "coolness and readiness" at Palo Alto and the "brilliant impetuosity" with which they had carried the enemy's position on the following day. They well deserved his praise. Seventeen hundred in number, they had defeated and routed an army estimated at 6,000, inflicting a loss estimated by Mexican officers at 1,200 killed and wounded and 300 drowned in the river. They had captured eight guns, 2,000 stand of arms, 200 pack mules, 150,000 rounds of ammunition, the standard of the Veterans' Battalion, and General Arista's personal baggage and private papers. Among their prisoners were a general, two colonels, and several captains and lieutenants. Their losses at Resaca de la Palma were 39 killed and 71 wounded. Meanwhile Fort Texas had easily withstood its seige. Only two of its garrison were killed. But one of them was its commander, Colonel Brown, and in his honor it was promptly renamed.

After some days spent vainly in striving to reorganize his beaten troops Arista asked for an armistice. Taylor replied that the Mexicans must evacuate Matamoros, leaving all government stores behind them, or he would demolish the place with his guns. He had no other means of attacking it, for his repeated requests for a pontoon train had been ignored at Washington, and to have brought up lumber and built boats before hostilities began, as the armchair strategists criticized him for not having done, would have nullified his protestations of purely peaceful intentions. During the week after the battles, however, he had not been idle. Parties of daring American swimmers had been collecting boats from the farther bank. On the 18th his army crossed. The Mexicans retired. As the Americans advanced, they fled, and the two hundred American dragoons chased the four thousand of them for nearly sixty miles.

CHAPTER IV

"Mexico or Death!"

§1

Palo Alto, Resaca de la Palma, Fort Brown, Matamoros! The *New Orleans Picayune* had word of the two victories in the field within a week of their occurrence, and they made a splendid story. From the office in Camp Street a courier spurred with the news to the dock on Lake Pontchartrain. A swift steamboat carried it to Mobile. Certain Northern and Eastern newspapers, anxious to get early intelligence from the front and disgusted with the slowness and uncertainty of the government mails, had established a service of mounted messengers from Mobile to Montgomery and thence northward across the other intervals where the railroads did not serve their purpose. With this news one of their riders, a boy of fifteen, is said to have covered a hundred and eighty-six miles in thirteen hours. Philip Hone in New York heard a strong and, as it turned out, remarkably accurate rumor of the battles on the 19th, just ten days after Resaca. President Polk received accounts of them by the Southern mail on the 23rd, and Taylor's official report reached him on the 25th.

Rejoicing was general throughout the country, for anxiety for the safety of the army on the Rio Grande had been keen. It was believed to have been cut off from its base, and so alarming had been the reports of the Mexican preparations for attacking it that Conner, who was in the best position to appraise them, had made sail from before Vera Cruz and landed five hundred sailors and marines at Point Isabel on the very day of Palo Alto.

Dispatches from Taylor, dated April 16th and telling of the position he had taken up opposite Matamoros, had reached Washington on Wednesday, May 6th. The Cabinet discussed them at its meeting on the following Saturday and, with the exception of Bancroft, agreed with the President that early in the coming week a message should be sent to Congress recommending a declaration of war if the Mexicans should commit any hostile act against Taylor's troops. Bancroft thought that the message should wait until a hostile act had been committed. But he also favored war if it were committed.

At six o'clock that same evening General Jones, the Adjutant General, hurried over from the War Department with fresh dispatches from Taylor bearing the fateful news of the attack on Thornton's patrol: Taylor added that he had called on the Governors of Texas and Louisiana, each of them, for four regiments of volunteers, a total of eight thousand men. A hasty summons brought the Cabinet together again at half past seven. Here was American blood shed on American soil, and all were agreed that a message asking for a formal declaration of war should be sent to Congress on Monday.

The Secretaries of War and State and other members of the Cabinet lent their clerks to copy the correspondence between Slidell and the Mexican government and that of the War Department with General Taylor to be sent with the message. Almost all day Sunday, with time out only for church and dinner, the President and Secretary Bancroft worked on the message, while Secretary Buchanan read and approved their effort and two confidential clerks slaved with the President's private secretary making copies, one for the Senate and one for the House. The Military Affairs Committee of the House met that morning and agreed to support a war bill that would provide ten million dollars and authorize the creation of an army of fifty thousand men.

The war spirit — that ebullition of evanescent bellicosity that flared up so readily in all countries in the nineteenth century — swept the Southwestern states. New Orleans echoed with cries of vengeance for the blood of Thornton's dragoons. The city hummed with the recruiting of the Washington Regiment, the Jackson Regiment, the Montezuma Regiment, and the Louisiana Volunteers. In all they numbered forty-five hundred in ten days. The legislature voted $100,000 for their equipment. When enlistments fell off, the Governor offered a bounty of ten dollars and a month's pay and talked of a state-wide draft. At Mobile the citizens planned to charter a steamboat to start for Point Isabel the next day with as many volunteers as could get ready to go. It is small wonder that Taylor, on hearing of such ill-considered enthusiasm, feared that he would soon have only too much of such raw material on his hands.

All over the country, in city after city, great war meetings were held. Park Benjamin, Irishman by birth and New Englander only by adoption, though he had been a Harvard classmate of Oliver Wendell Holmes, sounded a clarion call:

> *Arm, arm! Your country bids you arm!*
> *Fling out your banners free —*
> *Let drum and trumpet sound alarm,*
> *O'er mountain, plain and sea.*

Many people everywhere felt that the Mexican government's refusal to receive Slidell indicated that further forbearance was useless and drastic action necessary. A strong suspicion that England was at the bottom of most of the trouble did nothing to dilute the war spirit. At Indianapolis nineteen-year-old Lewis Wallace left his law studies and *The Fair God* unfinished, hired a fifer and a drummer and, parading down Washington Street with a transparency that read: "For Mexico, Fall In," raised a company, of which he became second lieutenant. Indiana had an adjutant general though no organized militia, and it could soon offer fourteen regiments for the four that the Federal government asked of it. Tennessee had 30,000 volunteers for 3,000 places. In Kentucky volunteering had to be stopped by Governor's proclamation. North Carolina offered three times its quota. Even

Ohio, where popular feeling had been against Texan annexation, raised 3,000.

In New England opposition to annexation generally grew into opposition to the war. In Boston young Mr. Lowell's Hosea Biglow encountered a recruiting officer of a different sort from Lew Wallace. This one "hed as much as 20 Rooster's tails stuck onto his hat" and "enough brass . . . figureed onto his coat and trousis . . . to make a 6 pounder out on." Hosea called war murder and touched on "the overreachin' o' them nigger drivin States," and his editor prefaced his remarks with a fable in which Farmer North proposed that, if his neighbor South did not agree with him, they "instantly divide." But even in Massachusetts ex-Governor Lincoln's son George and Daniel Webster's Edward were far from being the only fine young men who put patriotism before sectional prejudice. Both of them died in the war — George Lincoln at Buena Vista, and Edward Webster of disease near Mexico City.

In the central Atlantic states the anti-annexation argument had ceased to be valid with regard to the war. At meetings in New York, in Baltimore, at Easton and Harrisburg it was held that not annexation but the "aggravated and multiplied wrongs" perpetrated against the United States were the cause of it. The New York newspapers were against it at first, especially against the President's statement in his message that "a state of war" existed. But on the publication of the correspondence between Secretary Buchanan and Slidell during the latter's mission in Mexico the *Herald* led them in a change of tone.

Times were bad, had been bad for years now, and young men, seeing little likelihood of early success in civil life, were strongly attracted by the prospect of adventure and possibly fortune in a land of exotic beauty, romance, and fabulous wealth. "Mexico or Death" and "Ho, for the Halls of the Montezumas" were the headings of the recruiting posters. It was not for nothing that Prescott's *Conquest of Mexico* had been widely read in the past three years. Various corps made special appeals:

> *Come all ye gallant volunteers*
> *Who fear not life to lose,*
> *The martial drum invites ye come*
> *And join the Hickory Blues:*
> *The gallant Hickory Blues,*
> *The daring Hickory Blues —*
> *To Mexico they proudly go,*
> *The gallant Hickory Blues.*

In comparison with the country at large, however, Congress was lukewarm. At least the Senate was. The message that Polk and Bancroft and their secretaries worked so hard to have ready by Monday morning, May. 11, requested, to begin with, that Congress recognize that a state of war existed. The House promptly did so by a vote of 174 to 14 and passed all the rest of the President's recommendations. But the Senate balked. The Whigs were not alone in their opposition. News of Paredes's declaration of war had not yet been received, and Calhoun and other Democrats denied that there was any proof of the existence of a state of war: Mexico might disavow the attack on Thornton. Houston and Cass retorted by asking what further proof they wanted, considering Mexico's repeated threats that if Texas were annexed, war would follow.

Benton, who was of the opinion that Calhoun had engineered the war and left it on Polk's hands, called at the White House that afternoon and voiced his disapproval of an aggressive war. He seemed to hold that the Nueces was the legitimate boundary and wanted to know how many men and how much money would be required to *defend* the country. He sounded as if he might join the Whigs and defeat the measure. Only fear of the people, Polk was convinced, kept some of the other Democratic senators in line.

At seven o'clock the following evening, however, he received the good news that, after a thrilling debate, the Senate had passed, by a vote of 40 to 2, the House bill, which appropriated $10,000,000 for the prosecution of the war and authorized him to call for 50,000 volunteers for twelve months or its duration. Calhoun had spoken against it, saying that the whole affair ought to be investigated, but he had contented himself with joining Berien of Georgia and Evans of Maine in not voting. The two who voted nay were Davis of Massachusetts and Clayton of Delaware, who charged that Taylor had been the aggressor. Webster was absent.

"The gates of Janus are open," wrote Alexander Hamilton Stephens, future Vice President of the Confederate States of America. He had gone against his party on the annexation issue, but was now the leader of the Whig opposition to the war in the House.

The President had his Cabinet behind him, all but the chameleonic Buchanan, who annoyed him by inserting in dispatches to McLane and other American ministers abroad a pledge that the United States would take no territory from Mexico. Polk struck it out. We had not gone to war for conquest, he said, but if we could get California and other Mexican territory at the peace table, we would do so. Buchanan objected that Great Britain and France might join Mexico to keep us out of California. Polk retorted that he would have war with Great Britain and France before he would give such a pledge as Buchanan proposed. The meeting lasted until eleven o'clock that night, and the spunky little Polk went to bed exhausted. Doubtless he would have slept more soundly had he known that about that time Paredes offered Lord Aberdeen California for British intervention and Lord Aberdeen refused it.

§2

So Mr. Polk had his war — if war, as his opponents charged, was what he wanted. But it was his belief — a belief shared by many — that the passage of the war bill would bring peace, and he lost no time in beginning to work for that end. Counting on the disappointment, confusion, and dismay that the disasters on the Rio Grande must have produced in Mexico, he had Buchanan write to Paredes proposing negotiations. The letter was sent to Conner, who forwarded it through the Governor of Vera Cruz under a flag of truce. He resorted to other means as well.

Among his callers back in February had been a certain Colonel Alexander Atocha. A Mexican by race, the colonel had a somewhat legalistic claim to American citizenship, but he had been deeply engaged in the political and military affairs of Mexico. As an adherent of Santa Anna he had been arrested along with his leader at the dictator's fall from power in the previous December and had left him in his exile near Havana only a month before presenting himself at the White House.

Santa Anna's eclipse, Atocha assured the President, was only temporary. Hundreds of letters came to him from Mexico by every ship, and it might not be long before he was again in power there. If the United States would pay thirty millions for a boundary along the Rio Grande and the Colorado of the West and thence through San Francisco Bay, Santa Anna — according to the colonel — would favor a treaty on those terms. But the United States must keep an imposing force impending by both land and sea in order to bring the Mexican government to negotiation.

The colonel did not inspire the President's confidence. Polk thought him unreliable though evidently a man of education and talents. But he did believe that the words he spoke had been put into his mouth by Santa Anna, and when Atocha called again a few days later, Polk listened for an hour while the colonel elaborated his theme.

Any Mexican government was bound to fall, Atocha assured him, if it attempted to make a boundary agreement with the United States, unless it appeared to be yielding to a force so overwhelming that the Archbishop and the people would understand that the country could be saved in no other way. Let the American army advance to the Rio Grande, the

navy return to Vera Cruz; then let the United States demand
the payment of its claims. Mexico had neither the money nor
the ability to raise it, and so must agree on the boundary instead. Paredes, Almonte, and Santa Anna were all for this
course, but naturally they did not dare say so openly. The
Archbishop would favor it as soon as he understood that it
would result in the repayment to him of the half-million dollars he had loaned to the Mexican government.

All this had been in February. Now, to be sure, the American army had advanced to the Rio Grande, the fleet had long
since returned to Vera Cruz, and not peace but open war had
been the result. But both Slidell and the United States consuls at Mexico City and Vera Cruz had confirmed Atocha's
report on Santa Anna's peaceful inclinations, adding for
good measure that he was opposed to the European scheme
for a Spanish monarchy in Mexico. Santa Anna was still at
Havana, still desired by many in Mexico, and still apparently in a receptive state of mind. On May 18 Bancroft sent
orders to Conner to the effect that if Santa Anna attempted
to pass through the blockade at Vera Cruz, he should be permitted to do so. A little less than a month later a special
emissary sailed from Norfolk on the United States brig
Truxton with a personal message to Santa Anna from the
President of the United States.

The bearer was Commander Alexander Slidell Mackenzie.
A brother of John Slidell, he had adopted the surname of
Mackenzie and had the unique distinction of having hanged
at the yardarm for mutiny on the high seas a son of a Secretary of the Treasury of the United States. The message
stated that the President believed that Santa Anna did not
wish the war to go on, that he would be glad to see him return
to power, and that if he should do so and would agree to negotiate, the President would suspend hostilities by land,
would make no claims for indemnity, and would pay liberally
for any territory that the United States might take.

Santa Anna thanked Mackenzie for the permission to pass
the blockade. If the Americans would advance to Saltillo, de-

feat the Mexicans, and go on to San Luis Potosí, he said, his country would have to recall him. Then he would negotiate such a peace as the President desired. He added, however, that the capture of Tampico and Vera Cruz and an attack on San Juan de Ulloa by the Americans would help him toward that end. But when Mackenzie had taken his departure, Santa Anna exclaimed to his secretary: "Why has the President sent me that fool?" It appears that Mackenzie had decked himself out for his visit in his naval full-dress uniform and driven to Santa Anna's plantation through the principal streets of Havana at high noon in an open *volante*. It was not the Latin idea of conduct befitting a confidential agent. The Mexican did not know that a few days before Mackenzie's departure it had been chronicled in the *Philadelphia Ledger* with the statement that he was said to be charged with a mission to the exiled former dictator.

§3

But Polk did not allow these overtures to interfere with his preparations for carrying on the war. He called at once on Texas, Mississippi, Alabama, Georgia, Arkansas, Tennessee, Kentucky, Missouri, Illinois, Indiana, and Ohio for 17,000 volunteers. He could count on the other states where the war fever was high to bring the number up to 25,000 and he soon had 23,000 under arms. It was planned to organize these into infantry and cavalry regiments for immediate service in a ratio of three of the former to one of the latter. The other half of the authorized 50,000 was allotted to the Northeastern states, where infantry regiments only were to be formed and held in reserve. The regular army was increased to some 15,000 by raising the strength of the companies from sixty-four to one hundred, organizing a company of sappers and miners and a company of pontoniers and, at last, one of those regiments of mounted rifles so long desired by the Oregon expansionists.

Two field armies were created in addition to Taylor's "Army of Occupation," which was to be strongly reinforced.

One of these was to gather at San Antonio and march to the invasion of Chihuahua. The other, assembling at Fort Leavenworth under the command of Colonel Stephen W. Kearny, who was made a brevet major general, was to invade New Mexico, capture Santa Fe, and march thence to California, where it might expect to find Frémont and Commodores Sloat and Stockton with the Pacific squadron already busy in the good cause.

All this, of course, involved the President in many difficult and irritating matters such as the choice of commanders, promotions, and the granting of commissions in the volunteers and the new rifle regiment. But there were others of still greater importance — Oregon, for one — and, do what he would, the inevitable distractions.

The British reply to the notice for the termination of the joint occupancy of the Oregon country had been an offer to settle the boundary along parallel 49° to the middle of the channel between Vancouver Island and the mainland and thence along the middle of that channel and of the Strait of Juan de Fuca to the sea, leaving the navigation of the Columbia south of 49° free to British subjects. Polk, who did not want to have two wars on his hands at once, favored such a settlement. But now Buchanan, who for months had been harping on the danger of war with Britain over the Oregon boundary, declined to commit himself by helping Polk draft a message to Congress in favor of the offer, and there was another disagreeable scene between the two. Polk wrote the message without the assistance of his Secretary of State, and on June 12 the Senate voted, 38 to 12, to accept the British proposal.

Some six weeks later, July 28 and 29, the administration's tariff measure, the Walker bill, was passed, though persons whom Polk regarded as "capitalists and monopolists" had been working hard against it for weeks in the lobbies of both houses and one member reported that a thinly disguised effort had been made to buy his vote. But another matter, and one of high importance to the Mexican situation, was less fortunate. To settle with Mexico, except by carrying the war to a complete and costly victory, money was essential. The President asked Congress for $2,000,000 "to facilitate negotiations." He could cite two precedents for such action from Jefferson's administration. It had the approval of Benton, Cass, McDuffie, and Archer. But in the House the Wilmot Proviso, by which slavery was to be prohibited in any territory that might be acquired from Mexico, was inserted in the bill. When it was taken up in the Senate, on August 8 and only twenty minutes from the hour set for adjournment, the Proviso was attacked, and Davis of Massachusetts spoke against the bill itself until word came that the House had adjourned. The Senate thereupon adjourned without voting on it — amid great disorder, according to the President, who had gone up to the Capitol to sign the final measures. "A most disgraceful scene"; both Webster and Barrow "quite drunk," and the latter "noisy and troublesome," he wrote in his diary of what was told him.

To the harried little man in the White House, rising early and working late into the night, it seemed that Washington had never been so crowded as it was this summer. In May the great Manufacturers Fair was held there, bringing many visitors. The building alone, erected for this occasion only and to be demolished immediately afterwards, had cost six thousand dollars. It was hung with cambric of various colors and lighted at night by gas. Mrs. Polk broke her rule against attending public gatherings and accompanied her husband when he took time to make a visit to it. Later months were diversified by the arrival of delegations of Comanche and Cherokee Indians. The former came to town wearing little more than breechclouts, and at the Marine Band concert in the White House garden, inured to self-torture though they were, could hardly be restrained, especially the women, from tearing off the habiliments of the palefaces, in which their guides and guardians had clad them for their visit to the Great White Father.

But the worst of the minor nuisances were the seekers

after commissions in the newly raised forces. That Sunday afternoon when Polk was working over his war message, two members of the Military Affairs Committee of the House, who called with good news of the Committee's support, remained to propose their own names for high rank in the volunteers. Within a few weeks it seemed as if every congressman and several senators were smelling the battle from afar and snorting "Ha, ha!" louder than Job's war horse. There was, moreover, the question of promotions in the regular army, which was deplorably short of officers in the higher grades, even of colonels, whose age did not unfit them for service in the field. At Palo Alto and Resaca de la Palma Taylor had been the only field officer exercising the command appropriate to his rank; one regiment had been commanded by a captain.

Few applicants got much satisfaction out of Polk, however. His method was to refer them to the Adjutant General or to General Scott. But he had his own ideas on the subject, ideas that sprang from a determination to allow the Whigs to get as little glory out of the war as might be consistent with the winning of it and to see to it that what was popularly known as the "West Point aristocracy" should not profit by it in any way. He held, not unreasonably, that the new mounted rifles ought to be officered by Western men, who knew something of the plains and the mountains. But many of the hard-worked regular officers had served on the Western frontier and, when they were passed over, felt that "any hope of justice or chance of promotion" was ended for them, "no matter how glorious their deeds." Frémont was slated for promotion, but that was on account of his explorations.

Appointments to the higher commands were still more troublesome. In common decency Polk could not do less than make Taylor a brevet major general and approve the prompt action of Congress in giving him that rank in regular line of commission. But he was less impressed by Taylor's victories than by the shortcomings he had displayed as an army commander, and soon Thurlow Weed, who was powerful among the Whigs, came out strongly for the victor of Palo Alto and Resaca as that party's candidate for president in 1848, while at Trenton a non-partisan meeting of citizens named him as their choice.

Of the other generals, Gaines was sixty-nine years old and had recently replied to a well-earned reprimand by a communication for which madness could be the only excuse. Brigadier General John Ellis Wool was a Whig and two years older than Scott, who was sixty. As for Scott, there were Whigs in Pennsylvania who had never given up the hope of making him president, and after the election of 1844 the *New York Herald* had proposed a coalition of Native Americans and Whigs to elect him in 1848, if he "keeps his mouth shut for four years, (which is a pretty hard job)."

Polk gave him command of the army to be sent against Mexico, however, because he thought Scott's position as Commander-in-Chief entitled him to it, though he did not consider him "in all ways suited" for the task. But to make sure that some Democrats should be in a position to gather laurels in the war, he got a bill before Congress authorizing the appointment of two new major generals and four brigadiers. Immediately he found himself at loggerheads with his Adjutant General, with Wool, and with Scott, all three of whom set to work to bring about the defeat of the measure, or so Polk believed.

Between the personalities of Polk and Scott there yawned a gulf. Reserved, repressed, Polk was not a man who enjoyed asserting himself. He wrote in his diary an account of how he had allowed two American diplomats, home on leave, to ignore him when they called to pay their respects, talking over his head of European society and of Powers's statue *The Greek Slave*, which had caused a sensation in Paris that year. Afterwards he had vindicated the dignity of his office by telling Buchanan that one of them had had his head turned by living abroad and had better remain at home in future. Scott in like circumstances would probably have administered a stately rebuke on the spot and proceeded to forget the incident for all practical purposes.

But in purely official contacts Polk showed no lack of force. As Speaker of the House he had presided with dignity and strength. Back in March of this year it had been he who had reversed Scott's decision in the squabble over seniority between Worth and Twiggs. Scott had written such an endorsement on the papers that Benton recommended that he be sent to rusticate in some remote Northern post for the duration of the war by way of punishment. But Polk had been content to treat him like the spoiled and unruly but highly useful subordinate that he was.

Winfield Scott, professional soldier and Virginia gentleman to his immaculate fingertips, experienced and successful in actual war, a thorough student of the military art, and distinguished as a pacificator at Charleston in Nullification times, at Niagara in the Canadian insurrection troubles, and in Maine during the boundary dispute with Great Britain, was forthcoming, genial, and impulsive. He could be charming in conversation, a paragon in any social assembly, when his egotism did not betray him into a hardly endurable pomposity. He was afflicted by an overweening sense of what was due his position and possessed of the pen of an all too ready writer when he felt the necessity of defending it, which was all too often. Perhaps, moreover, he had some difficulty in remembering that he was dealing with the President of the United States and not with "little Jimmy Polk of Duck River," whose ignorance of all things military was abysmal.

A similar imperfection of sympathies existed between Scott and the Secretary of War. William Learned Marcy, a former Governor of New York, had, it was observed by the ladies of Washington, "few of the social graces." His massive head and the shaggy eyebrows through which he peered at you, his voice hoarse from snuff and his everlasting red handkerchief, his professional politician's geniality, and the noiseless laughter that made him shake like Kriss Kringle were not traits likely to appeal to the urbane and polished Scott. Like his chief, he was far more interested in winning the war before the November elections than in the means necessary to that end, and of those he knew as little as Polk knew.

Both men were greatly dissatisfied when Scott, three weeks after his appointment, lingered in Washington instead of rushing to the Rio Grande. The expansion of the War Department to handle the business of an army suddenly increased from 7,000 to 50,000; the necessity of furnishing it with arms, equipment, munitions, and supplies, and with boats and wagons; the collection of information about the country to be invaded, of which very little was known in Washington; and arrangements for the transportation of the troops to the seat of war did not strike them as requiring Scott's superintendence.

Polk had already noted that Scott was "rather scientific and visionary in his views." Now he told Marcy that Scott's delay would not be tolerated, that Scott must either proceed to his post very soon or Polk would supersede him in command. About the same time Scott heard of Polk's bill to create the new generals. He saw in it a "double trick": first to supersede him and then, at the end of the war, to get rid of every general who did not "place Democracy above God's Country." With nerves frayed by working fourteen hours a day, he sat down and tore off a sizzling letter to Marcy, recapitulating what had to be provided before the invasion could begin, his labors in that task, and now the necessity of pausing to guard himself "against, perhaps, utter condemnation" in "high quarters." If he could not feel secure against this, he wrote, let some other command the army against Mexico; he did not wish to place himself where he would receive a fire upon his rear from Washington as well as in front from the Mexicans.

To his amazement, he was taken at his word: told that he was to remain in Washington and devote himself to arrangements and preparations for the prosecution of the war.

He was hurt. He had had no idea of giving offense and, undeterred by the consequences of his previous letter, contented himself with no more than "a hasty plate of soup," as he wrote to Marcy, before sending the Secretary a letter of explanation and apology. He pointed out that he had written of fears of condemnation not in "the highest quarter" but in "high quarters," by which he had meant friends of the President in both houses of Congress who were his enemies. One of these, though he did not say so, had lately called him "too much of an old granny" for the command of the army of invasion. Whether the President sent him to the Rio Grande, which he would prefer, he concluded, or kept him in Washington, he was equally ready to do his duty to the utmost of his ability.

He was, indeed, too good a soldier to do otherwise, and when Polk saw nothing in this letter to cause him to change his decision against sending him to the front, he labored on faithfully and efficiently through the summer's heat, though the newspapers got hold of his letters and published them and the widespread merriment over that "hasty plate of soup" must have galled his sensitive spirit. His reputation as both a gourmet and a gourmand was fresher in the public mind than were his military exploits. A witty diplomat called him "Marshal Tureen," and somebody else suggested "Farrier General" because of his highly proper concern for the hoofs of the cavalry horses. But when, in mid-July, Colonel Payne, wounded in the Rio Grande fighting, arrived in town on crutches, with a sheaf of captured Mexican battle flags, Scott went at the head of a group of other officers and a crowd of ladies and civilians to present the bullet-torn trophies to the President. A lesser man might have stayed sulkily in his office.

§4

June passed. July drew to a close. The army, gathering slowly between Matamoros and the sea, was about ready to advance at last, and Polk's hopes of winning a peace without using the army gradually dwindled. To the proposal to negotiate that he had sent to Paredes after the American victories in May he had received no reply. Santa Anna, however, still looked like a possibility. August brought the news that Mexican discontent at the defeats on the Rio Grande, Parades's reputation for heavy drinking, his demonstrated incapacity, and his well-known monarchical leanings had at length brought about his overthrow. Bravo, the Vice President, succeeded him. At Vera Cruz, early in August, there was a pronunciamento for Santa Anna, and Salas came to power with the slogan: "Federation, Santa Anna, and Texas!"

A few days later the British steamer *Arab*, bound for Vera Cruz from Havana, attracted the notice of the American blockading squadron, and the tired eyes of the naval officer who boarded her were gladdened by the blue glance and golden hair of the "Flower of Mexico," Santa Anna's young wife by a recent marriage, who was accompanying her husband home from his Cuban exile.

Allowed to pass according to the orders from Washington, the couple landed amid the thunder of the saluting battery on San Juan de Ulloa. The 11th Infantry lined the route to the Governor's Palace, and between their ranks, smartly dressed in his major general's uniform, stumped "the Illustrious General, *Benemérito de la Patria*, the Most Excellent Señor Don Antonio López de Santa Anna, Champion of Independence, Hero of Tampico, Immortal Commander." He had grown portly, but he still looked tough, suave, and commanding, and nearer forty than his actual age of fifty-one. But there was an ominous dearth of *vivas* from the multitude that packed the streets behind the files of gleaming bayonets, and one observer saw his tawny face darken at the silence and noted the signs of duplicity, treachery, avarice, and sensuality that marked it.

He issued an allocution against monarchy and the domination of the Church, advised the country to return to the Constitution of 1824 and the complete control of the executive by the Congress, and proclaimed himself to be devoted to the death to liberty and the independence of the Republic. Thereupon, complaining that the stump of his crippled leg was hurting him, he retired to his country house, El Encero, which was near Jalapa, to await events.

There followed a few days of desperate uncertainty. The rich and influential city of Puebla was against him. He was not looked upon with favor by the English colony in the capital, or in England. "That very sorry hero but most determined cockfighter," the London *Atlas* called him. He could not entirely count even upon the army. For if he proved true to his avowed Federalist principles, he would have to replace it with a national guard. And the firing squad was the customary way of dealing with exiled dictators who have made an unsuccessful return.

Within a week the Constitution of 1824 was exhumed and once more adopted, but he was still cautious. Posing as a simple patriot soldier, he called for a levy of 30,000 men but would take no part in the government. The Church accepted him, though the clergy, like the merchants, were reluctant to subscribe to the new government loan. He reached an understanding with both the radicals and the moderates and soothed the army with promises. Almost a month went by before he entered the capital, but when he did so, it was to the sound of artillery in salvos and the chanting of *Te Deums*, and the Cathedral bells rang backwards. Three days later he was appointed Commander-in-Chief of an "Army of Liberation" and soon was off by coach, with mule teams in relays along the three hundred and eighty miles to San Luis Potosí, there to direct the defense of the northern frontier.

Réjón, Secretary of Foreign Affairs under this new dispensation, sent off a negligent answer to Polk's proposal for negotiations that had been written nearly four months before. It would be referred, he wrote, to the Mexican Congress, which was to convene in December. So much for the promises given so readily in Havana in June. Bankhead, now the British Minister to Mexico, believed that only the doubtfulness of Santa Anna's popularity prevented him from keeping them. He may have been right in this belief, but, if so, it was of no help to Mr. Polk as head of the Democratic Party in winning the elections that were by this time only two months away. On the other hand, the American army had only just begun to apply the pressure that Santa Anna had specified as essential to the performance of those promises.

§5

Down at Matamoros, sweltering amid the tropic heat and alternate mud and dust of the Rio Grande summer, General Zachary Taylor was too busy making an army out of the unleavened thousands of volunteers that the Administration was thrusting upon him to have time for more than a half-amused annoyance at the efforts to make a presidential candidate out of him. He was honestly sorry to hear of Scott's trouble, would gladly have served under him. To a friend who wrote to him of Thurlow Weed's proposal he replied that such an idea had never entered his head any more than it was likely to enter the head of any other sane person. The thanks of Congress, the swords and medals that were voted him, he received graciously but with a keen realization of the evanescence of the popularity of which they were the evidence.

A delegation from Louisiana arrived with the thanks of the legislature and, as earnest of a golden sword that was not yet ready, the sash that General Braddock had bequeathed to Washington. There was a ceremony of presentation, a collation of dainties from New Orleans, champagne, and speeches. But the general courteously declined to receive their gift until, as he said, the campaign was finished as far as he was concerned in it.

Other visitors poured in: Governor Henderson with five hundred of his mounted Texans, Dr. Ashbel Smith, and a young nephew of the famous Marshall Blücher, who had made Berlin too hot for him by editing a liberal paper there and wanted to see some fighting. Kendall arrived at the head of a trio of *Picayune* correspondents. There were other newspapermen aplenty, and two French artists went about, taking officers' likenesses for a great painting of the Resaca de la Palma battle.

One and all, they found the general living in a tent on the river bank without so much as a single sentinel to protect him from interruption: "a hearty-looking gentleman," rather like a farmer in appearance, but with keen, flashing eyes. He detested the martial pomp and circumstance that were so dear to Scott, never wore sash and sword, and seldom a uniform, if he could help it. Through his army the story ran joyfully of how, when Conner on one occasion came ashore to confer with him, Taylor, knowing the Commodore to be a stickler for form, arrayed himself in full regalia of cocked hat, frock coat, braided pantaloons, and sword, whereas Conner, aware of Taylor's love of informality, dressed himself with scrupulous negligence. It was difficult, according to spectators of the meeting, to say which of the two men was the more embarrassed.

In general, visitors found him dressed in a pair of Attakapas pantaloons and a linen roundabout and seated at a desk that was formed by a couple of blue-painted chests and strewn with a confusion of official documents. There were camp stools for the callers. "Ben!" he would shout, and his servant would appear with a tin tray bearing two black bottles, shining tumblers, and an earthen pitcher of the tawny water of the Rio Grande. "Help yourselves," would be his hospitable invitation, while behind him, around him, and across the river, town and camp hummed with the work of organization, supply, and training.

Matamoros had a population of 8,000, but when Taylor's troops entered it in mid-May it presented a sad contrast to their romantic expectations. Dismal and dilapidated, it stank from the improvised hospitals that the retreating Mexicans had left crammed with their wounded. Aside from the distribution among the troops of large quantities of tobacco

found among the government stores that the Mexicans had
hidden in houses and down wells or dumped in the river, it
offered nothing of interest to officers or soldiers. The more
genteel of the inhabitants had fled. Ticks, red bugs, and
mosquitoes even larger than those of New Orleans murdered
sleep, and by day the heat was terrific. A rainstorm, the
first of many, flooded the camps, blew down the tents. The
mail rider from Point Isabel lost the mail sack containing
a large quantity of private letters and many important official dispatches from Washington. When the little steamboat *Neva* tied up at the bank, she was hailed as the solitary
sign of civilization.

But in a single month, wrote Kendall, Matamoros had
become an American city. General Taylor might lack steamboats to bring his troops from the mouth of the river, but
what was called "American go-ahead-ativeness" saw to it
that civilians had the chance to make any money that might
be made out of the war. The city was soon thick with grog
shops and gambling-houses. Sutlers followed the regiments,
and merchants swarmed in with stocks of Lowell calicos,
which they found they could not sell, since the Mexican
taste had been cultivated by the products of French looms.
An American newspaper was started, was suppressed by
General Twiggs, the military governor, for printing sub-
versive matter in Spanish on its press, and was replaced by
The Republic of the Rio Grande and the People's Friend,
which was edited by Hugh McLeod, former West Pointer
and leader of the Santa Fe expedition.

Ice was shipped in, and juleps became obtainable — "a
long step toward civilization," Kendall wrote. An American
theatrical company, at this day remarkable only for the presence of young Joseph Jefferson among its members, came to
town and played in the old Spanish theater to what he remembered in his old age as "a most motley audience" of soldiers, sutlers, gamblers, and the rest of the rag, tag, and bob-
tail that used to follow an army in the old, easy-going days.
Gradually the people of substance ventured back to their

homes in the city. Officers discovered that in the cool of the
evening ladies of great beauty sat at the barred windows and
were not disdainful of a little pleasant bilingual flirtation.
Some houses appear to have opened their doors to the more
prepossessing of the invaders. Or one could stroll up to Fort
Paredes in the early twilight and watch Mexican female
beauty bathing in the river, unadorned and unperturbed by
the presence of spectators.

The people grew to like the steady, well-disciplined regulars, the *trupas de ligna,* as they called them. But they hated
and feared the *volonterios,* and with good cause. The regulars regarded the volunteers, of whom about two thousand
had reached Matamoros by the end of May, with impatience
and contempt. Every guardhouse was filled nightly with their
drunken men and officers. The rich gentlemen rankers from
Louisiana balked at hewing their own wood and drawing their
own water. When they moved, they loaded their wagons with
comforts and luxuries and left essential supplies and baggage behind, expecting the regulars to look after it for them.
They rioted and fought among themselves. The Baltimore
Battalion was better behaved than most, but only a few cool-
headed officers prevented its members and those of an Ohio
regiment from going at each other with ball cartridges in a
row that began over the ownership of a catfish and proceeded
from the Ohio colonel's using the edge of his sword on the
Baltimore claimant.

They robbed the Mexicans of their cattle and corn, stole
their fences for firewood, got drunk, and killed several in-
offensive inhabitants of the town in the streets. They were
continually letting off their muskets in spite of Taylor's
strict orders to the contrary. Those encamped north of the
river came down to the bank in crowds and fired across the
stream so frequently that Lieutenant Meade felt that a day in
his tent at headquarters, which were on the opposite side, was
equivalent to passing through a well-contested action. Their
officers had little control over them and often were obviously
afraid of them; Taylor appeared to have given up in de-

spair any attempt to keep them in order. They grew mutinous at not being led at once against the foe. To Lieutenant George Gordon Meade, who little guessed that the valor of similar troops would make him one of the saviors of the Union, they were anathema.

Some of the other regular officers viewed them more sympathetically. And they were deserving of sympathy, these patriotic boys whom a negligent Secretary of War and a moribund War Department had dumped in unseasoned thousands on the inhospitable coast of an alien land with their heads full of nonsense about hoards of Mexican treasure, passionate señoritas, and caballeros who were to become the easy victims of Anglo-Saxon prowess.

The bar at the mouth of the Rio Grande would permit the passage of vessels of only the lightest draft, and while these were being collected, regiments from Missouri, Tennessee, Alabama, Mississippi, Louisiana, Kentucky, Ohio, and Maryland were put ashore through the surf near Point Isabel on Brazos Island, where the wrecks of a number of transport sloops and schooners bore witness to the fierce and sudden storms that had caught them on a lee shore.

The men landed, dizzy from seasickness and poisoned by the liquor that all the vigilance of their officers could not prevent the civilian personnel of the transports from selling them. They were quarrelsome from the gambling with which they had whiled away the tedium of the voyage, and devoured by nostalgia. They found themselves on what was no more than a barren sandbank destitute of even a blade of grass, without shelter from the scorching sun and the torrential rainstorms. Utterly ignorant of what was before them, they were unprovided with the many small comforts and necessities without which no experienced soldier ever willingly takes the field. The water was bad, brackish at best; and they were as yet unaccustomed to the army ration of bean soup, unleavened flapjacks, and bacon. Many organizations arrived already riddled by dysentery and diarrhea, from mobilization camps where the doctors had no other medicine than opium.

Some regiments were so fortunate as to be commanded by graduates of West Point who had left the army for civil life. But the company officers, and sometimes the field officers, were elected by their men according to the militia laws of the various states. Daniel Webster said it would be degrading for free-born Americans to be required to serve under any officers but those of their own choosing. So there were few who felt a sense of responsibility for the welfare of their men, and fewer still with the slightest notion of how to care for them. Green young captains were bewildered to find themselves like inexperienced parents in charge of groups of grown-up men who behaved like spoiled and mentally retarded children after the immemorial manner of volunteers.

Each evening saw a burial at the foot of the dunes, when the band wailed the Dead March, the steady roar of the surf drowned out the reading of the burial service by some conscientious officer, and the triple volley crashed its farewell over the mound of sand that by morning the unresting wind had swept away.

From Brazos Island they were marched to Boca del Rio at the mouth of the river. There the lucky ones were taken upstream by steamboat. Most of them marched, their faces swollen and peeling from sunburn, to exchange the seashore sand for soil that was a deep, fine dust in fair weather and turned to bottomless mud in the frequent rains. They camped in tents of muslin amid jungles infested by scorpions, centipedes, tarantulas, and rattlesnakes. The reason why the campaign was not begun — a lack of steamboats for the advance up the river — was hard for them to accept. Why, after more than a month, were there no steamboats for the army, when there seemed to be no lack of them for civilian traffic?

From the deck of one of the latter the ladies of the theatrical company saw and pitied the wretchedness of the Baltimore Battalion, sang to cheer them, and tossed them bottles of wine. The river rose suddenly, flooding their camps; and when, in August, the Baltimoreans resumed their march to Matamoros, it was by roads, they gibed, "impassable except

for American volunteers." Once their route led for three miles
through water that rose almost to their armpits. They were
toughening now, however. They made eighteen miles that
same day.

But in the camps that by this time lined both banks of the
river from Matamoros to its mouth, there were many who had
had more than their fill of soldiering. When orders came from
Washington that all who had enlisted for six months or less
would be sent home unless they re-enlisted for a year, there
were many among those who had rushed to arms in Louisiana
and Alabama, at St. Louis and Louisville, who sought their
discharge from the service. Soon steamboats that should have
been hastening the advance up river to Camargo had to be
employed in carrying the infirm of purpose down to Point
Isabel, bound for home. Thus departed eight thousand of
them after consuming 240,000 of the government's rations
to no purpose, Meade grumbled, adding that a regular army
large enough to have won the war by this time, or prevented
it altogether, would have cost far less through the years than
the equipment and maintenance of such troops.

§6

For the lack of steamboats and other means of transportation Taylor was being criticized at home as well as in his
own command. It was charged that he had been dilatory in
his efforts to obtain them. His critics overlooked the fact that
such boats as could cross the bar at the river's mouth had to be
collected from the inland waters of the Southern and Southwestern states and were dependent on fine weather to make
the six-hundred-mile crossing of the Gulf. A half-dozen of
the more venturesome of them lay, mere hulks, on surf-beaten
Barra del Bravo. Wagons had to be built in Ohio and even
Massachusetts and shipped to the Rio Grande. Draft animals
and pack mules had to be purchased and collected to serve an
army that grew in a few weeks from 5,000 to 30,000 men.

The calmness with which Taylor dealt with his problems
was mistaken for lethargy by some of his officers. He did not

know how to make use of his staff, especially of the Topographical Engineers, according to one of the latter. But even
that efficient young man had to admit that what the general
left undone generally turned out to have been unnecessary.
Gradually his two or three steamboats were increased to five,
to ten in early July, and finally to twenty. They bore such
names as *Troy, I. E. Roberts, Big Hatchee,* and *Hatchee
Eagle* — enough to make any volunteer homesick at the sight
of them.

Though they drew from six to eight feet of water, the river
was deep enough for them, and, to the delight of their officers,
proved to be free from the snags that were the terror of Western river navigation at home. There were, however, sand bars
that shifted from day to day. And the current was so swift,
and the mesquite and chaparral wood was such poor fuel, that
often the little vessels had to tie up to the bank to get up
enough steam to go on with.

Monterrey, the capital of the state of Nuevo León and the
key to all northern Mexico, was the objective of the expedition. It lay some one hundred and seventy miles west by south
from Matamoros. But a reconnoitering expedition demonstrated that the direct route was rendered impossible for the
army by lack of water and forage. So Taylor decided to establish an advance base at Camargo, about eighty miles up
the river, whence he could march by a fairly practicable road
to his destination.

Early in June he placed a small force of infantry with two
field guns and a company of Rangers about halfway between Matamoros and Camargo at the little town of Reynosa,
where, on a limestone promontory overlooking the river, the
stump of an unfinished church tower dominated a few streets
of half-built stone houses and clustering hovels. The inhabitants received the Americans gladly. They had, indeed, sent a
deputation to Taylor to ask his protection. For not only were
the Comanches raiding in their neighborhood but the Mexican General Canales and his Ranchero cavalry were living
on them at free quarters to their intense discomfort.

The advance to Camargo began early in the following month. The sharp rise in the river made steamboating easy. But the boats were so small that each one could carry only half a regiment at a time, even of the little regiments in that army, of which it took four of volunteers to add up to two thousand officers and men, and eight of regulars made a total of only twenty-five hundred. The consequence was that many had to go by land, where the marching conditions were terrible and the air-line distance of eighty miles stretched out to a hundred and twenty-seven. The high water had flooded the riverside road, making long detours necessary. Guides proved untrustworthy or downright treacherous: one detachment of regulars came close to being led to the Mexican headquarters at Linares. Coveys of plover rose before them, and a herd of wild horses dashed away through the floods. There were some handsome girls who sold them tortillas at the wretched jacals and at the rare ranchos where hides and jerked meat hung drying in the yards, and they bought melons at exorbitant prices from a native who was hauling a cartload of them to the Matamoros market. But though they marched eighteen miles that day, it took the steady playing of *The Girl I Left behind Me* by the fifes and drums to bring them through the glutinous mud in which they sank ankle-deep at every step.

Next day there was no water. A merciless sun made the ground so hot it burned the feet, and at that night's bivouac they found only a hog-wallow in which to quench their thirst. Reynosa, with its two discordant church bells, its depressing air of dilapidation, and only the rain to cleanse its streets, marked the end of the third day's march. From there the road began to climb past ranchos where the number of children rivaled that of the goats. They looked off over the wide valley of the Rio Grande, with the smoke of isolated habitations rising where cornfields interspersed the chaparral, and could trace the roads by the long trains of their covered wagons and the glint of sunlight on the bayonets of advancing columns of their comrades.

Now the weather grew so hot that they gave up marching by day. Reveille sounded at midnight, and the moonlit hills echoed to the tramp of the infantry and the dull rolling of artillery wheels, as they passed, within a space of ten miles, thirty crosses that commemorated as many murders. It took them eight days to reach Camargo, but, regulars though they were, and veterans since Corpus Christi days, they felt well satisfied with their accomplishment.

For the volunteers — even the tough Baltimore Battalion, which was made up mostly of sailors, fishermen, and members of fire companies from the back streets of Baltimore and Washington — the march was hellish. They were routed over what was called the "Mountain Road," through a desert country where the only water lay in foul ponds and tanks built to collect the rainfall. Stifled by clouds of dust and tortured by thirst, all trace of such discipline as they had acquired since landing on Brazos Island left them. By each day's end they were a mere mob, organizations mixed together, officers powerless or without the will to exert their authority, the strongest in the van, all staggering on together toward the appointed halting-place, where water could be hoped for. And when they reached it, the water was never good, never adequate. Once it was a pool in which cattle had been standing for weeks to escape the heat. Its smell was appalling, but in their frenzy they drank it greedily. Next moment some fell in convulsions, frothing. All vomited. They, too, however, reached Camargo in eight days, having covered twenty-six miles in one of them.

They found the town, which was situated on low ground on the San Juan River a few miles above the junction of that stream with the Rio Grande, a dismal place. A large section of it had been devastated by the recent floods. The usual cathedral and a few of the usual low, flat-roofed, thick-walled stone houses surrounded the usual plaza, where the tents of American infantry and artillery had displaced the usual conglomeration of goats, fighting-cocks, stray mules, and burros. There was not a single shop, only a druggist, who plied his trade in one of the houses. Worth, who had returned to the army in June, much chastened in spirit by a bootless encounter with the authorities in Washington, Taylor had made military governor. His motto was now "a grade or a grave." Always a strict disciplinarian, he excluded all American traders and other unnecessary camp-followers from the place and had liquor-smugglers flogged.

Camargo had always been notoriously unhealthy, but if it had been a health resort it would have made little difference. The troops who had come by land brought diarrhea and dysentery with them. Germs were yet to be heard of, the boiling of drinking-water and placing guards over contaminated sources unknown. Those who escaped more serious maladies had doubtless to thank the immunity they had built up against the impure water supplies of their home towns. Among the Baltimoreans eighteen men in one company were soon too ill to be moved. Sickness reduced the 1st Tennessee Regiment from 1,040 to fewer than 500 effectives. In other volunteer organizations from one third to one half of their strength was on sick report. Hospital facilities were rudimentary, and many men died. "The graveyard" became the soldiers' name for Camargo.

Under a sun that, before midday, sent the thermometer to 112° in the scanty shade the troops had to clear from the areas assigned to them for camping the thorny, tough, and tenacious mesquite that covered all but the cultivated ground. For the army was camped in line of battle. A fine dust filled the air and coated everything with a thick white powder. Flies, from the great horse fly, whose sting raised a burning blister, to a variety so small that it penetrated mosquito netting and, in its self-immolated numbers, gave cooked food the appearance of having been sprinkled with coarse pepper, swarmed about the corrals, the latrines, and the kitchens.

At night a clammy mist enshrouded camp and town; venomous insects and a plague of frogs invaded the tents; and from time to time the stillness was shattered by the song of the "Mexican canary," the pack mule, of which large droves had now been assembled to make up for the lack of wagon transportation. For a while the rain fell every day: the men were so continually wet that a ration of whisky was issued. There were the rage and frustration over the shortcomings of the Quartermaster Department that are inseparable from all such situations. But even Taylor said that, if he waited for the Quartermaster to satisfy his needs, not only the enlistments of the volunteers but those of the regulars would have expired before he could advance. And that no annoyance might be lacking, the volunteer officers were now confronted for the first time with the maddening puzzle of War Department muster rolls that had to be made out in quadruplicate.

Even some of the Texans who had arrived with a good deal of éclat, with Albert Sidney Johnston at their head, cracked under the strain. To his disgust, their 1st Rifle Battalion, enlisted for less than a year, took advantage of the War Department's ruling, and forty-five out of every sixty of them went home. Those who remained were loud in their impatience for action, and the behavior of the Rangers was such that Taylor called them "licentious." When the neighboring town of Mier was raided by the Comanches, the Texans who were sent in pursuit of them failed to overtake them and, indeed, felt less unfriendly toward them than toward the Mexicans. There was a rumor in the camp, moreover, that the Comanches, having recently made a treaty with the United States, considered themselves to be acting against a common enemy.

Life at Camargo, however, had its ameliorations. The army fare could be varied with eggs, chickens, and fresh vegetables bought from the inhabitants, who, if not friendly to the invaders, had, many of them, been impoverished by the recent inundation and were eager to sell their produce, cattle, forage, and mules to the troops, who were easy victims of the Latin talent for bargaining. Horses were cheap here, as they had been at Corpus Christi, and soon it was a poor subaltern indeed who had not a mount for his pleasure, though his sense of fairness, if he was in the infantry, might prevent him from riding it on the march. As for those muster rolls, the mustering officer himself turned out to be both sympathetic and helpful.

By early August Taylor had a force of 15,000 at Camargo, and, in spite of everything, it was growing into an army that could be depended upon in battle. If the volunteers were learning the hard way, they were learning nevertheless. Homesick, weary, bored, and infested with disease, they were as confident as ever of being able to whip any number of the enemy. One of the most dispiriting features of the summer for them had been the frequent rumors that the war would end without their seeing action. Now they were delighted to gather from Mexicans who had or pretended to have reliable information from Monterrey that the forces gathering there would fight "mucho fandango."

Captain Blanchard marched in, with fifes and drums sounding at the head of his company, which he had named the Phœnix, since it contained all the Louisiana men who had resisted the temptation to go home. The Baltimore Battalion grew smart in their blue uniforms of regular infantry cut and color and looked down on the troops from country districts who wore hats and clothes "of a curious appearance." On August 17 Taylor reviewed the regulars in what one of their own officers described as "one of the most magnificent military displays we have had since the last war." Eight regiments of infantry and two batteries of horse artillery, they formed a line three quarters of a mile long.

Taylor, it was observed, had never looked in better health and spirits, though with him rode two of the President's new political generals. One of these was John Anthony Quitman, who was to demonstrate his courage on more than one battlefield, but whose principal qualification for the appointment would seem to have been his staunch adherence to the Democratic Party. The other was Gideon Johnson Pillow, Polk's former law partner, who was to become a major general in this war and, in 1862, deserve a court martial, which he did not get, for slipping away and leaving his troops behind him to be surrendered at Fort Donelson.

If a seer could have been present to read the roster of the officers in this army, he might have been moved to quote from the Gospel of Matthew: "Wheresoever the carcass is, there will the eagles be gathered together." In addition to Grant and Meade and Braxton Bragg, who was to fail to reap the harvest of his victory at Chickamauga, there was Robert Patterson, whose delusion in the Shenandoah Valley made possible the Confederate victory at First Manassas. There was Albert Sidney Johnston, whose death probably cost the South the Battle of Shiloh. There were William J. Hardee, who would be leading a Confederate corps that day; Don Carlos Buell, the arrival of whose troops turned the second day's fighting into a Union victory; and John Pope, who was to be routed at Second Manassas. And at the head of the 1st Mississippi Rifles rode Jefferson Davis. He had married one of Taylor's daughters against her father's will eleven years before. She had died not long after, and he had lately married again. But Taylor received him with friendly warmth at Camargo.

It seems a pity that Lieutenant George B. McClellan, who did not join Taylor's command until November, was not present to observe the way Old Rough and Ready made the best of what the War Department sent him, improvised the rest, and was now about to advance with the diminished force to which his transportation limited him against an enemy of unknown strength and a fortress defended by walls of solid masonry. The meticulous commander of the Army of the Potomac in 1862 might have moved less cautiously on the Peninsula or followed Lee swiftly after Antietam, and the whole course of the Civil War might have been changed.

As for Taylor, the poison of politics seems to have begun to work in his mind by this time. Whether or not he was taking his presidential possibilities more seriously now, he believed that Polk was doing so. He suspected Polk, Marcy and company of trying to ruin him. Had they not left him so short of transportation that he could advance with only some sixty-two hundred men, less than half of the troops he had managed to assemble at Camargo? Even for these there were many things lacking, from medical supplies to horseshoes. Tentage was still of the worthless muslin variety; and by way of a siege train with which to batter the permanent fortifications of Monterrey he could take with him only two 24-pounder howitzers and one heavy mortar. A hundred and forty miles of rugged plateau and mountain lay between him and his goal, and of these the first sixty were so arid that some of his precious wagons, all of which were needed to haul supplies, had to be turned to the transport of water. But if he did not advance, he would ruin himself. He must move, he said, "be the consequences what they may." Every day he waited, the enemy increased in numbers and their position grew stronger.

He organized his troops in three divisions, two chiefly of regulars and one of volunteers. In the First Division the Baltimore Battalion was brigaded with the 1st Infantry, since the 2nd Infantry had not yet arrived, and the Phœnix Company was given a place in the Second. Twiggs, now a brigadier, led the First, Worth the Second, and General William O. Butler of Kentucky the Third, which was composed entirely of volunteers. In command of the eight thousand, many of them sick, whom Taylor was compelled to leave at Camargo, he placed General Patterson.

Steamboats were moored in the San Juan River, and over a bridge laid across their decks marched Worth and the Second Division on the morning of August 19, their mission to establish a depot sixty miles southward across the desert waste at the town of Ceralvo. The troops marched in the highest spirits, confident that nothing ahead of them could be worse than what they were leaving behind. A recent scouting party had reported Ceralvo to be a charming place full of running streams and lemon and orange groves, and beyond that lay almost certainly a battle.

CHAPTER V

Iron Sleet and Washington Miasma

§1

IT WAS EASY for the smart young Topographical Engineers in Taylor's army, well read in military theory but without experience in the command of any unit larger than a platoon, to recognize their commander's shortcomings. But when some of them led armies of their own, they might have envied the steadfastness with which he staked success on his estimate of the enemy's strength, intentions, and fighting spirit and on the capabilities and courage of his own troops.

His errors were those common in his time. In the three decades that followed Waterloo the lessons of the Napoleonic Wars appear to have been forgotten in Europe, and in America to have been never learned. In attacking Garibaldi's Rome in 1849 Napoleon's old Marshal Oudinot blundered as seriously as Taylor did at Monterrey, and the movements of the Russian and Franco-British armies in the Crimea after the Battle of the Alma displayed a disregard of sound principles more inexcusable than anything of which Taylor was guilty.

It was as if the shadow of the moribund tradition of Frederick the Great had fallen once more across the military mind as it had done toward the end of the eighteenth century. Considering the shortage of transportation in Taylor's army, the allowance of baggage is reminiscent of the Duke of Brunswick's baggage train in the campaign of Valmy. One pack mule capable of a three-hundred-pound load was allotted to every eight men. The officers of each company had one for their baggage, and many of them bought another, which they were permitted to take along for the same purpose. Though the climate was such that Lieutenant Meade, who marched with the advance party, slept on the ground every night under his old India-rubber cloak without suffering from the cold or wet, tents were provided for all, shelter-halves being as yet unknown. Camp women had accompanied the troops to Camargo. Some of them went on with the army to Monterrey. One traveled luxuriously on an elaborate side-saddle. And all this when the siege train had to be so limited as to be entirely inadequate for the task before it.

The pack mules, with their attendant *arrieros,* could move less than half the load they could have hauled in wagons, but not one of the wagons ordered months before had yet reached Camargo. The intense heat made it desirable for the troops to march by moonlight. But the intricate business of loading the pack saddles could be accomplished only by daylight and by the few skilled *arrieros* with each train. Dawn came late; laden mules, made restive by waiting for their fellows, strayed off into the mesquite, bucked and tried to roll to dislodge their loads; and it would be after dark when they overtook the troops, who must then search among them for their belongings amid confusion worse confounded.

The *arrieros,* brawny and swarthy men in leather aprons and broad sombreros, found cause for merriment in the stampede of a mule or the spilling of a pack saddle. They laughed and sang through the hot waterless marches and managed to share their jokes with the soldiers of their escort, though they had hardly more than half a dozen words in common with them. Their gaiety was welcome. For in those first few days the road was deep with sand, the air thick with dust, and the water as bad as it was scarce. Nature, both animate and inanimate, seemed to produce nothing but thorns. Beyond the town of Mier, where the young officers rode in to inspect the scene of the Texans' gallant fight in 1842, there was hardly a ranch house until Punta Aguda was reached at the end of the fifth day. Many fell sick, and there was not a single ambulance with the army.

But as they left the Rio Grande Valley behind them the air

grew gradually better, the everlasting mesquite thinner. Great clusters of gorgeous morning glories appeared among the cactus, and from every hilltop they glimpsed misty mountain ranges blue with the promise of shady dells and clear cool water. Punta Aguda was a poor little place of thatched cottages, but at Ceralvo, one day's march farther, they found something more like what they had expected of Mexico. A substantially built town of sixteen hundred inhabitants, its low white houses shone amid pecan, peach, fig, pomegranate, lemon, and orange trees. A swift clear stream gurgled under fine stone bridges and was led away through channels to various private gardens. There was the inevitable unfinished cathedral on the inevitable central plaza, but it was a handsome structure as it stood, and the plaza was spacious and clean.

Upon Taylor's proclamation promising fair treatment by his troops the whole town turned out to sell them firewood, corn, and flour and to cut grass for their animals. No soldier who had hard United States cash and knew how to say *leche* and *pollas* went without milk and chicken. There were *vino de Parras* and *limonada* to be sipped in the shade of the trees or in the cool thick-walled houses. A lunar rainbow diversified the splendor of the moonlit nights. The local belles were not above accepting American officers as partners in the stately waltz, which was the step most used at the nightly fandangos, and there were several banks of monte for those who did not care to dance.

A marked improvement was noticeable in the behavior of the volunteers. Officers and men were acquiring march discipline — that most difficult of disciplines to inculcate in green troops. The Baltimore Battalion came in at the end of an all-night march at the standard three miles and a half an hour, and the false alarm of a night attack quickened their interest in mounting guard and outpost duty. From Ceralvo the mountains behind Monterrey were visible in the farthest distance. A chance copy of a month-old Mexico City newspaper that brought the army its first news of the fall of Paredes and the expected return of Santa Anna caused many of the regular officers to offer odds that the Mexicans would not put up a fight. But word came from Monterrey that Santa Anna had sent two thousand men and four guns to strengthen the garrison there and had placed Ampudia in command of the place with the promise of still further reinforcements. A spy, moreover, brought in such intelligence of the fortifications that when an engineer on Worth's staff drew them out on a map, they appeared to cover every approach to the city with direct, cross, and enfilading fire. So, upon Taylor's order warning the troops that thenceforward they might expect resistance to their advance, they took the road on the morning of September 12 with songs and laughter, though they were burdened with eight days' rations and forty rounds of ammunition, and the heat of the sun was withering.

§2

It had not been originally the intention of the Mexican government to defend Monterrey, although General Mejia, on reaching the city in August with the wreck of the army from the Rio Grande, had determined to make a stand there. But he had been supported with neither money nor men, and Santa Anna's initial orders to Ampudia were to destroy the fortifications and such matériel, military supplies, and public stores as could not be removed, and to retire through the Rinconada Pass to Saltillo, some fifty or sixty miles to the southwestward.

Against these orders Ampudia protested successfully. The demolitions alone would require a month, he urged, a large part of the supplies could not be moved, and the effect on the morale of the northern Mexican states, where, at best, the business of smuggling across the border made the people rather inclined to favor the North Americans, would be disastrous. On the other hand, the works defending the city were of great strength, and if he were permitted to fight there, he was confident not only of victory but of chasing the enemy across the Rio Grande.

By September 10 he had a force of more than three thousand regular troops and enough militia to bring his numbers to seventy-three hundred. If these were not enough to man all the fortifications, his numerous cavalry, which had lately been remounted, could be depended upon to distract and divide the efforts of the besiegers. It was true that he had no light artillery that could match the horse batteries of the Americans. But his works were well armed with cannon, and these not such obsolete pieces as had been lost at Resaca de la Palma but, many of them, fine English guns only two or three years old. The inhabitants of the city were aroused to fight in defense of their homes against a brutal and licentious invader. The defeats of May were made light of. To be sure, the North Americans, close to their base of supplies, had won on the Rio Grande; but they would find it a different matter here, at the end of a long and tenuous line of communications that was constantly harassed by Canales and his Ranchero horsemen. A certain Señorita Dosamantes put on a captain's uniform and rode out before the troops of the garrison, and their response to her Amazonian courage was enthusiastic.

It was Canales and his men who had caused the false alarm among the American troops on the night of the lunar rainbow. But that was the utmost of their accomplishment. He excused his ineffectual performance of the guerrilla role by explaining to his superiors that, since the enemy did not turn their animals loose at night, it was impossible to stampede them; that the roads were stony and therefore could not be broken up; that the absence of dry, grassy plains made it impossible to set the woods on fire; and that, since running streams abounded, the enemy's water supply could not be destroyed.

There were several rocky defiles where he might have fought delaying actions that would have cost the Americans valuable time, but he contented himself with flitting just ahead of their advance and — so they heard — "lariating" the wretched peons and dragging them off to work on the fortifications at Monterrey. One evening a timely warning was all that saved him from capture by an active scouting party that swooped down on a fandango at which he had been amusing himself. On another of those magnificent mountain nights Meade and a party of eighty men beat up his outposts but failed to lure him into pursuing them, although his command numbered eight hundred. The American "pioneer advance," which was composed of ninety pioneers for road-building, a hundred dragoons, and twenty-five Rangers and marched a day ahead of the rest of the army, offered him battle on the 14th. But the offer was refused, and on the next day it was only by the greatest effort that the Rangers got close enough to shoot two of his troopers, whose lances and carbines they brought in as trophies.

After that, Taylor took the precaution of keeping the road-builders at the head of the First Division, which he had placed in the lead at Ceralvo. Otherwise he held to his old arrangement of divisions following one another on successive days: Worth with the Second behind the First, and the so-called Field Division of volunteers bringing up the rear. Only now each division was accompanied by its own baggage and supply trains, which were kept closed up and furnished with strong rear guards, and the marches were made by daylight.

The heat continued to be great in the daytime. The ground was stony and hard on the feet. Frequent thunderstorms soaked the marching men. Gigantic Spanish bayonets studded the plain, some of them twenty feet high and a foot thick, and wolves prowled and howled about the camps at night. But the air was stimulating on the high plateau that the army was now traversing. The cinosa shrub covered the hillsides with white and pink blossoms. Mountains with fantastic crests and precipices that reflected the morning light in shades of lilac stood all about. At night the air turned cold enough to make campfires grateful to men chilled by fording the numerous mountain streams that intersected the road, and hot suppers of chicken and rice varied the routine of army rations.

The little town of Ramos, which they reached on the third day out from Ceralvo, was an oasis of grapevines, fig, pomegranate, and orange trees. At Marín, a place of two thousand inhabitants, which stood at the end of the next day's march, a mail from home overtook them. And, above all, there was the sight of their commander. For whatever the white-headed, rather slovenly-looking old man on his knock-kneed white horse might lack of the qualities that go to the making of a great general, he was a magnificent leader. One look at that calm, confident face and you knew that, as one young regular officer wrote, to Monterrey he was going, though twenty thousand men should oppose him. He might say "Nolus volus" for *nolens volens*, as Meade wrote that he did, but everybody knew what he meant by it and acted accordingly.

From a reluctant prisoner he squeezed the information that the force at Monterrey now numbered half again as many as the army he was leading against it. General Torrejón and a thousand Mexican lancers were just ahead of him. They had bivouacked in Marín the night before Taylor and the First Division entered the town, had shot a man in the graveyard for holding communication with the enemy, had carried off the local alcalde and the padre from both Ramos and Marín, and had driven the inhabitants to the hills. The pennons of their lances still fluttered three quarters of a mile ahead when the Baltimore Battalion, which formed the advance guard that day, marched between the barred doors and shuttered windows of the deserted street where the body of a dead man lay in a pool of blood across a threshold. But during the three days that Taylor remained there to allow his other two divisions to catch up with him, the wretched inhabitants, who had been visible in wistful clusters on the neighboring hillsides, began drifting timidly back to their homes, with babies and fowls in their arms and a train of goats and children following after.

Monterrey was only twenty-five miles distant now — two easy marches. In that clear mountain air you could see it distinctly from Marín church tower, with Mitre Mountain and the peaks of the Comanche Saddle behind it, and the Bishop's Palace looking like a castle on the hill to the west of the city. Leading up to it stretched a plain of singular sweetness, fifteen miles in width, with mountains springing straight up from it on every side and a little river curving through its length in Hogarth's Line of Beauty.

By the night of the 17th all three divisions were concentrated around Marín, and next morning the advance was resumed. Two companies of the Rangers led the way, fantastic in fringed leggings, shirts of red or blue, buckskin caps or broad-brimmed soft felt hats. They were armed with rifles, Colt revolvers, and bowie knives, and their quick tough horses and the bags of pounded meal on their saddles bore witness to their mobility and their ability to maintain themselves in the field. Behind them came the two regiments of mounted Texans, which had pushed off to the southeast as far as the town of China and had thus led the cynical to believe that they had taken their discharge like their comrades of the Rifles.

The Dragoons followed, and after them the First Division under Twiggs: Ridgley's battery, 3rd, 4th, and 1st Infantry, and the Baltimore Battalion. Worth came next, with the Second Division, which was composed of Duncan's and Mackall's batteries, the battalion of artillery acting as infantry, the 8th, 5th, and 7th Infantry, and Blanchard's Phœnix Company of Louisiana volunteers. Butler led the Field Division: 1st Ohio, 1st Kentucky Rifles, 1st Tennessee, and 1st Mississippi Rifles, and with them marched the travesty of a siege train, which was manned by gunners of the 1st Artillery.

Taylor's strength had been depleted by a considerable number of sick, whom he had been compelled to leave at Ceralvo, and by the detachment of two companies of the Mississippi regiment to guard them there. His army now consisted of 3,080 regulars and 3,150 volunteers: 6,230 in all, of whom 1,350 were mounted men; and his guns were so few and small that the sight of them sent the regular infantry officers to bed that night with the sober thought that if they wanted an adequate artillery, they must take it from the enemy.

Again the pennons of the enemy lancers flitted ahead of the advance. Again they did nothing more than that. But their proximity had become a terror to the *arrieros,* who had

lost their gaiety these past few days and turned glum with
the fear of what might happen to them if they were captured
in the service of their country's enemies. Now some of them
attempted to stampede, and it took all of Colonel Kinney's
vigilance, authority, and tact to hold them to their work. The
road was spotted, as it had been for some days past, with
copies of a proclamation by Ampudia, in which he called on
all good Christians in the American army to desert from the
service of a heretic country that was waging war on true be-
lievers and promised them protection, good pay, and rank in
the Mexican army equal to that they were holding in the army
of the United States. A few, mostly Irishmen, were restless
or pious enough to be lured away by these representations.
They formed the nucleus of the famous Company of San
Patricio, which was to be notable in several ways later in the
war. The Texans captured three lancers and that night at the
little village of San Francisco proceeded according to the custom of their old border war to "choke them a little" to extract
military information. Some, who were veterans of the Mier
expedition, caught a Mexican who had tortured them in their
captivity and would have beaten him to death if the regulars
had not rescued him.

There were only a few miles to go next morning, but the
going was tougher. The road, which now ran between fields
of corn and sugarcane, had been broken up by the enemy in
several places, in others flooded by dams in the little streams
that crossed it, and infantrymen were deep in mud, shoving
and hauling at the mired wagons, when three cannon shots —
heavy guns, by the noise they made — sounded from the head
of the column.

Taylor, who had marched with his advance cavalry that
morning, had topped the rise from which Monterrey was visible three miles in front of him and had ridden forward with
his staff until, at a range of about a mile, the guns of the
citadel had opened fire on him. By good luck nobody was hurt,
though one cannon ball passed through both the Texas regiments. Another ricocheted and missed Taylor by a mere ten

feet. The paymaster retrieved it as a souvenir, and the sight of it in his hands thrilled the Baltimoreans when they came up shortly after.

§3

The army pitched their tents about three miles northeast of the city, comfortably out of range of the enemy's guns, in a fine grove of tall live oaks and pecan trees shaggy with Spanish moss, where numerous springs of clear, cold water burst from a gentle slope. The place had been a favorite with picnic parties of the élite of Monterrey in peacetime. Bosque de Santiago was its name, but the Americans, doubtless with many a nostalgic memory of some fond spot on the outskirts of Louisville, or Memphis, or Cincinnati, called it Walnut Springs.

As soon as the camp was made they strolled out on the low rise of ground that lay in front of it to gaze at the city many of them had come two thousand miles and marched three hundred miles to capture. Set in a notch of the lofty Sierra Madre through which ran the road to Saltillo and the interior, it looked impressive in its extent, the white walls of its stucco houses gleaming like marble through the foliage of acacia and orange trees. The red, white, and green flag of Mexico flew from one of the tall towers of the cathedral and above the dark stone walls of the citadel — the "Black Fort," or the "Colored Gentleman," as the soldiers were soon to call it — which stood about five hundred yards forward from the northern suburb in such a position that its guns could enfilade any attack directed against the city to the east or west of it on that front. A strong redoubt with subsidiary defenses was visible at the northeastern corner of the city. On the slope of the hill to the northwest, where the houses ended, rose the old stone pile of the Bishop's Palace, and there was a redoubt on the hilltop above it.

From forts and city alike came the sound of bells, the roll of drums, and that continual bugling the Americans had learned to know so well. Fascinated, they strolled forward until the guns of the citadel opened fire on them. Even then a guard had to be set to check their curiosity. The Texan horsemen made a field day of it, galloping in circles almost up to the glacis of the fort and on their agile animals easily avoiding the slow flight of the projectiles of the time.

Afterwards Worth complained that Taylor arrived in front of Monterrey knowing no more about the place and its fortifications than he knew at Matamoros. But now, at all events, engineer officers, with little parties of horse or foot to protect them, pushed forward to right and left to feel out the enemy's strength and locate his defenses. It was risky work over a terrain partly cultivated, the rest pitted here and there with abandoned quarries and overgrown with bushes, and the whole overlooked by the bastions of the citadel. The long hours of the sunlit day were punctuated by cannon fire and the crackle of musketry as the Mexicans strove to keep the reconnaissance from finding out anything of value, while over cornfield and mesquite drifted the shadows of the powder smoke.

It was ten that night, and a great conflagration in front of the city showed where the enemy was clearing his field of fire, when the last report reached Taylor's headquarters with the return of Major Mansfield, who had ridden so close to the redoubts that defended the western end of the city and commanded the Saltillo road that the Mexicans had fired on his escort with grapeshot. He reported that the works thereabouts were strong, but such as could be stormed without great difficulty.

On the opposite flank Fort Teneréa, the redoubt that was visible at the northeast corner of the city, mounted six guns. Behind it, at about four hundred yards, stood Fort Diablo with four, and behind that in succession were two similar works with four and three guns respectively. All these were so placed as to be able to support one another with their fire. The intervals between them were closed with earthworks and walls loopholed for musketry. The fringe of detached houses, gardens, and orchards bordering the northern side of the city masked a small stream, the Ojo de Agua. Earthworks lined

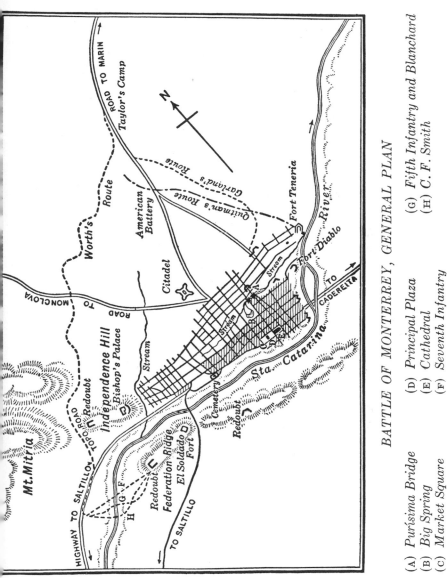

BATTLE OF MONTERREY, GENERAL PLAN

(A) *Purísima Bridge*
(B) *Big Spring*
(C) *Market Square*
(D) *Principal Plaza*
(E) *Cathedral*
(F) *Seventh Infantry*
(G) *Fifth Infantry and Blanchard*
(H) *C. F. Smith*

its farther bank, and a tête-de-pont armed with cannon defended the Purísima bridge, which crossed it.

In the central plaza, some two thousand yards south and west of this bridge, the cathedral had been turned into a great magazine. The streets leading to it had been barricaded, some of them with solid stone walls embrasured for cannon, and the parapets of every neighboring roof had been heightened with sandbags for infantry fire. Even the western, evidently the weaker, end of the city was stronger than Mansfield had been able to discover. Back of the hill that bore the Bishop's Palace and the redoubt and was known as Independencia, rose another, the Loma de Federación, with El Soldado, a work mounting two 9-pounders, at its eastern end and a small redan on the western crest. Between the two hills ran the main road to Saltillo and the little Río Santa Catalina, which separated Monterrey from the ridge behind it.

It was here that Taylor decided to launch his first attack, and at two o'clock the following afternoon (Sunday, September 20) the Second Division, with four hundred mounted Texans in advance, moved out to execute it. Their comrades watched their departure admiringly: the parti-colored Rangers; Worth on a fine horse, trim and soldierly in undress uniform, smiling and chatting with the members of his staff; the sky-blue ranks of the infantry; the artillery battalion in dark blue with the red stripe on their trousers; the Phœnix Company dressed and armed as each man chose but looking like the seasoned, resolute men they were; and two of the horse batteries, Duncan's and Mackall's, with uniforms, guns, caissons, horses, and harness so clean, smart, and shining that they reminded the Baltimoreans of Ringgold's battery on parade in the old days at Fort McHenry. They numbered about two thousand in all.

For seven miles they proceeded across the enemy's front, just out of range of his guns but in plain sight of General Ampudia, who rode to the top of Independence Hill to watch them. The movement was in flagrant violation of one of Napoleon's Maxims of War, but, like so many of Taylor's departures from textbook strategy, it went unpunished. The column bivouacked miserably that night a little beyond the range of the guns on Independence Hill, without fires, warm food, blankets, or shelter, in torrents of chilling rain, and about six o'clock next morning (Monday, September 21) resumed its advance under a dark and threatening sky.

In the gorge by which its road approached the Saltillo highway five hundred infantry and two thousand cavalry appeared to dispute its passage. Two hundred of the latter, gay with splendid uniforms, silver-mounted saddles, and pennons of red and green fluttering at their lance-points, charged the mounted Texans, and for a few minutes there was a brisk melee of lance, sword, pistol and carbine. But the fire of the light companies of the artillery battalion drove them back. The guns of Duncan and Mackall discouraged a second charge before it started. The Mexican infantry retired instead of advancing, and their cavalry streamed away: about twelve hundred of them up the Saltillo road, to be seen no more in this campaign, and the rest back to the city. At eight fifteen Worth sent to Taylor the jubilant message: "The town is ours."

He had, to be sure, captured the only road by which Monterrey could be reinforced and supplied. But even to hold what he had taken he must storm Independence Hill and also Federación, of which he now became aware for the first time. For a plunging fire from both of them forced him to retire at once up the road to Saltillo. Against Federación he immediately sent four companies of the artillery battalion and five companies of the Texans, dismounted, and, lest these should not be enough, reinforced them with the 5th and 7th Infantry.

They had to begin by fording the cold, swift, waist-deep Santa Catalina. Under the low clouds the hill looked about a thousand feet high to the men who struggled up the craggy slope, while five hundred infantry fired down on them and grapeshot from Independence Hill took them in flank and rear. Fortunately the guns above them could not be sufficiently depressed to bear upon them. At the last moment the enemy fled. The Americans swarmed over and into the fortifications, seized the cannon, and turned them on both the fleeing foe and the works across the valley.

Independence Hill was more difficult. The Mexicans believed it to be impregnable. Its peak was almost as high as Federación's summit; its sides were almost vertical; and La Libertad, the redoubt at its western end, was supported by the guns at the Bishop's Palace a little below and to the east of it. When darkness fell, the five hundred men whom Worth had sent against it — three companies of the artillery battalion, three of the 8th Infantry, and about two hundred Texans — were clinging part way up its precipitous slope. There for the most of the night they remained, hungry, cold, and drenched by a tempestuous rain that poured small rivers down the gullies where they kept a precarious foothold and loosened heavy stones that came plunging down upon them.

The whispered order "Forward" was welcome when it came at three o'clock in the black morning (Tuesday, September 22). Up they went through the thorny undergrowth, silently and as swiftly as they dared on the greasy slope, while above them the black sky turned slowly gray until the outline of the crest stood out against it. An outpost spied them close at hand and shattered the dripping stillness with a volley. They answered it with a rush and a yell. A brief musketry duel ended with the enemy in full retreat, the Stars and Stripes flung out above the captured ramparts, and the victors waking the mountain echoes with their cheers.

They were too much exhausted to pursue, however. The Mexicans, though only fifty or sixty in number, were by no means routed. In a last-minute effort to save their guns they dropped one of them down the hillside, but with the other and a couple of 6-pounders they presently opened fire on the redoubt from the Bishop's Palace. The two hundred and fifty men in that position joined in. Fifty dragoons reinforced them on foot; two hundred and fifty cavalry rode up on the slope below the palace. A counterattack appeared to be imminent.

Worth sent troops from Federación to threaten the palace from the flank and the 5th Infantry with a 12-pounder howitzer, which was disassembled and manhandled piecemeal up the steep hillside, to support the weary men on Independence. By noon shrapnel from this gun had knocked out the artillery opposed to it and was making havoc inside the palace walls, and in desperation the Mexican commander, who had thus far obeyed Ampudia's order to remain on the defensive, ordered a charge of horse and foot.

His troops responded gallantly, closing the gaps that the howitzer tore through their ranks and still advancing until a party of American infantry rose from ambush on their flank and poured upon them a deadly fire. Then they broke and fled, some as far as the city. But many rallied in the palace, where they fought on so stubbornly that the howitzer had to be trundled down to blow inward the massive gate. The batteries of Duncan and Mackall galloped forward in the valley and chased the fugitives with shell fire. The captured guns on Federation Hill joined in. It was four o'clock in the afternoon, and the western end of the city lay open to Worth's farther advance.

§4

Lying in the mud at the other end of the city, soldiers of the First Division watched the attack on Independence Hill through the murk of the early dawn. Weary, wet, and sore in body and spirit — for they had taken such a beating in the past twenty-four hours as few American troops had ever endured — they gazed with growing joy as the line of musket flashes, each like an electric spark, moved up the distant crest and the powder smoke shrouding the summit signified the success of the attack. Their efforts had had a far less happy outcome.

On Sunday afternoon, two hours after Worth's column had marched away to the westward, the long roll had called them to arms. With the volunteers and the batteries of Ridgley and Bragg they had formed line of battle about a mile in front of the citadel, and there they had stood until eleven that night, waiting in vain for the Mexicans to make a sortie, while the rain poured down on them in torrents and the city turned from darkness and sullen silence to a flashing of signal lamps, a glare of rockets, clanging of bells, the blare of military bands, and back to darkness and silence again.

Their fighting spirit was high, however, when, after a hearty breakfast, they fell in at eight o'clock next morning, about the time when Worth was sending off his optimistic message from the Saltillo road, and there were high words between at least one captain in the volunteers and his colonel when the former was told that his company was of those assigned — one company from each regiment — to guard the camp from the onslaughts of enemy lancers during the absence of the rest. The two 24-pounder howitzers and the mortar, which had been placed in battery in a depression about fifteen hundred yards from the citadel the night before, opened fire, but with no more effect than might have been expected of them. With the idea of pinning down any troops that Ampudia might be intending to move against Worth, the First Division and the volunteers were formed as if to attack, and to Lieutenant Colonel Garland, who was commanding the First Division that morning in the temporary absence of Twiggs, Taylor presently gave the order to lead the greater part of it against the northeastern corner of the city.

"If you think you can take any of them little forts down there with the bay'net, you better do it," he went on, and added that Major Mansfield would be found thereabouts and that Garland would do well to consult with the major when he got there.

Through brush and cornfields the 1st and 3rd Infantry and the Baltimore Battalion broke their difficult way to emerge about five hundred yards in front of Fort Teneréa. It immediately opened fire on them with grape and round shot and musketry, but they formed line and were pressing swiftly and steadily forward, though now under an enfilading fire from the citadel as well, when Major Mansfield appeared before them, waving his spyglass to direct them to the right, and Garland gave the order to change direction accordingly.

The result was disastrous. On the left of the line the Baltimore Battalion had been charging straight for the redoubt, confident that they could carry it by direct assault. Now they must take its fire on their left flank until, like the regulars ahead of them, they were enmeshed in a maze of lanes and alleys, gardens, orchards, and patches of corn. Mansfield's intention was to lead them under cover to the point where Fort Teneréa presented its open gorge to the eastern side of the town. But he could not find the way, and the way the Americans took, as one Baltimore officer observed, was exactly the one the Mexicans wished them to take. Musket balls pelted them from masked breastworks and housetops. Every street that led toward the center of the city was swept by cannon fire. Their mounted officers had their horses shot under them. Their trail was marked by their wounded, dead, and dying, for whom there was none to care.

Clustering behind angles and in doorways, they stepped out to fire and back to load, but they could not go forward. A section of Bragg's battery came tearing in and jammed in the narrow street, men and horses falling fast under a withering fire, and might have been annihilated there, unable to unlimber or retire, if the Baltimoreans had not manhandled the guns about so that they could be withdrawn. Untrained in street fighting, some officers and men followed a sound impulse, broke into houses, rushed to roofs and windows, and opened fire on the bridgehead and the breastworks lining the farther side of the stream. But officious superiors ordered them out as if they were skulking.

Only Captain Backus of the 1st Infantry, with about a hundred men, worked his way through far enough to escape this interference. When Colonel Garland gave the order to retire, as he presently did, this party remained ensconced on the parapeted roof of a building from which they could fire through the gorge of the redoubt at a range of a little more than a hundred yards. They could see its front strewn with the dead and wounded bodies of about a third of three companies of the 4th Infantry, which Taylor, sensing that the fight had grown serious, had ordered up to support the attack.

And now, behind the 4th, came Quitman's brigade. Jefferson Davis on his iron-gray Pompey, riding far ahead of his Mississippians, cried aloud: "Now is the time! Great God, if I had fifty men with knives, I could take that fort." He was right. The fire of Captain Backus's party was more than the Mexicans could stand. The cloth of the sandbags of their parapet had taken fire. Their commander, who had fled at Resaca, bolted again. Nevertheless they were forming pluckily for a counterattack when over the smoldering parapet, through the ditch, and in by the gorge poured a mingled tide of Mississippians and the men from Tennessee, overwhelming such as remained to fight and flowing on to capture the sandbagged and loopholed tannery that guarded the southern flank of the redoubt.

Attacking simultaneously on their right, the 1st Ohio swept past the wrecked section of Bragg's battery, where, amid the blood and foam of dying horses, the gunners were refitting teams and salvaging harness under a galling fire from the citadel. But, stalled like those before them in the suburb, they learned that they had come too late, that the attack had failed. They halted behind a hedge of pomegranate that shielded them from enemy observation but not from his canister and his skirmishers, who had pressed close to the retiring Americans.

Back in the open the troops of the First Division strove to re-form for a fresh attack. But again the guns of the citadel assailed them, and they were forced to seek shelter, some in the ditch of the Teneréa redoubt and some behind it. Taylor himself was on the scene by this time. Again the troops were sent forward. The captured guns in Teneréa were turned on the Diablo redoubt. General Butler led the 1st

Ohio in an effort to reach its gorge. The First Division was directed farther to the right, with orders to penetrate into the city. But again the musketry from barred windows, walls, and roofs swept the advancing columns, while once more the guns of the tête-de-pont blazed with deadly effect.

Some of the regulars succeeded in reaching the stream below the bridge only to find themselves under a storm of bullets from the opposite bank and the water too deep to ford. The 1st Ohio, the staff of their colors shot in two and the flag flying from a captured Mexican lance, got across farther down and had opened fire on the gorge of Diablo when volleys of musketry and a masked battery on their flank forced them to fall back. Ridgley led a section of his battery into the fight at a gallop, his head bowed forward, face to the right, as if it were sleet instead of a hail of lead and iron that tore past him; he unlimbered his guns and opened fire.

Here, there, and everywhere the magnificent voice of Albert Sidney Johnston, who was on Butler's staff, was to be heard above the din, encouraging and directing the men with sound common sense. Joseph Hooker, who was to lose the battle of Chancellorsville, was in the fray. Grant, whose duties should have kept him in camp, had ridden forward with that forlorn attack of the 4th Infantry on Teneréa and remained with them. A strong battalion of Mexican infantry that came down the street to reinforce the garrison of the tête-de-pont was driven back with loss. But the 6-pounders were without effect against the stone walls and heavier metal opposed to them, whereas the Mexican cannon balls tore through and through the houses from which the American infantry were firing. To advance farther was impossible, and again the order was given to retire.

To General Mejia, who commanded at the bridgehead, it seemed that now was the time to use his cavalry. Around by way of the citadel he sent the 3rd and 7th Lancers, and down they rushed upon the 1st Ohio just as it debouched into the plain. The regiment had never been taught to form square to repel cavalry, but they were in a mood of anger and frustration that was made uglier by the sight of Mexican horsemen spearing the helpless wounded on the ground and even leaping from their horses to murder them. There was a brush fence close by. The Ohioans lined it, drove back the lancers with their volleys, and proceeded to the rendezvous behind Teneréa, there to be cheered by the news that Worth's column had taken the works on Federation Hill.

It was still early afternoon: so much could happen in so few hours in those old battles of small numbers on a terrain limited by the short range of musket, rifle, and cannon. But Taylor attempted no more that day. His troops were exhausted, their cartridge-boxes almost empty, their spirits dampened, as well they might be, by the casualties they had suffered. Out of the four thousand under Taylor's immediate command that day, three hundred and ninety-four, almost ten per cent, had fallen dead or wounded. The loss among the officers was shocking. It included one general (Butler, wounded), eight field officers, seven captains, and eighteen lieutenants.

One of the 24-pounders was brought up to the Teneréa and joined the captured guns in the redoubt in a desultory bombardment of El Diablo and the works near it. The rest of the afternoon was spent in collecting such of the wounded as could be found and transporting them to the camp by such crude and often agonizing means as were available in the absence of ambulances. At nightfall most of the troops were ordered back to the Bosque de Santiago, their retirement mocked by the city's bells, which rang for joy at their discomfiture. Some of the officers found their mess table looking as if a feast of the anthropophagi had lately been spread upon it. It had been used for emergency operations, and the orderly had made a poor job of cleaning it by lantern light.

All night long the cannon thundered, and enemy rockets lighted the city and the surrounding mountains. The rain that drenched Worth's men as they clung to the side of Independence Hill poured down upon the survivors of the First Division, who shared with the Kentuckians the duty of holding the Teneréa redoubt. Without food, shelter, or blankets they wore out the hours of darkness, to be rewarded at dawn by the sight of their comrades' success at the western end of the city.

§5

Throughout that day (Tuesday, September 22) Taylor contented himself with firing on the Diablo redoubt with the guns at the Teneréa. His troops were in great need of rest and reorganization after their exertions and losses of the previous day, and he did nothing to co-operate with Worth's continued advance, though the men of Bragg's battery and the Baltimore Battalion, which he had placed in a depression in front of the citadel to guard against a sortie, could see clearly the fighting around the Bishop's Palace. They leaped to their feet and cheered again and again as the Mexican flag came down and the Stars and Stripes were hoisted in its place above the captured stronghold.

After the storming of the palace, Worth's men rested also, until the following morning (Wednesday, September 23), when Lieutenant Meade, who had worked his cautious way into the city, came back with the report that the enemy had retired on that side of the town to the fortified houses and stone barricades that made the area for two squares all around the central plaza an inner fortress. Then Texans and regulars together poured eastward down the long, straight streets with the deep roar rising to a falsetto scream that was to be heard on many an American battlefield less than twenty years later and to be known as the "rebel yell."

Thus far their losses had been as light as those of the troops under Taylor's immediate command had been heavy. "Taylor did the work, and our losses were Worth's gain," wrote a Baltimore captain afterwards. As Meade saw it: "With us . . . judgment and energy [were] quietly and surely advancing; on the other side [Taylor's] impetuosity and fearless courage . . . showed a determination at all sacrifice to carry everything before them." Whatever the merits of the case, it appears that among Worth's troops there was the greater ability to estimate the situation correctly and the greater aptitude to meet it. Within range of the barricades they wasted no lives in attempting to advance farther in the streets. Doors were battered down with planks, housetops scaled with ladders. The tactics were like those at Saragossa and Badajoz some thirty years before, or those used by the great-grandsons of these men in Italian and German towns a century later. Picks and crowbars tore holes through party walls; six-inch shells with sputtering fuses were tossed through the first small apertures; and through the widened opening leaped the assailants with bayonet or bowie knife to finish any bloody work the shell had left undone. The weapons changed, but the principles remained the same.

Through the fire and smoke, co-ordinating the various elements of the attack, galloped Captain John Pemberton — Pemberton of Vicksburg — who won a brevet that day; and George Kendall of the *Picayune*, who was paying off the old score of his captivity by serving as a volunteer aide to Worth. Bailie Peyton, whose Louisiana regiment Polk had refused, was also carrying Worth's orders. He paused to chat with Meade for a moment and shared with him the thought that their friend Henry Alexander Wise would have enjoyed himself had he been there. It would not have been the first time the fiery Virginian had hazarded his life for his convictions.

By nightfall Worth's men had the Mexican works under a blighting fire from windows and housetops from which they had driven the defenders. Worth had sent around for the 10-inch mortar that had been employed so ineffectually before the citadel and, setting it up among the graves of the Campo Santo, whose loopholed walls the enemy had abandoned without a struggle, began about eight o'clock that evening to lob its shells into the great square. These were dreadfully effective, for now the Mexicans were crowded in their restricted area. From six to ten of them fell at every

burst. At any moment, moreover, a lucky shot might send the
cathedral skyward by exploding the mass of ammunition
stored within its walls.

Meanwhile, at the other end of the city the struggle was
again more bitter. At daylight General Quitman's brigade,
which had taken over the Tenerea and its neighboring works
the previous day, discovered that the enemy had abandoned
El Diablo redoubt during the night. The Mississippians
promptly occupied it, and, above the drums that rolled for
"assembly," the troops in the Bosque de Santiago could hear
the firing as Jefferson Davis's men and a regiment of Texas
cavalry on foot began to advance into the city.

Again the troops from the camp marched to the attack,
the infantry swinging wide to the eastward, Bragg's battery
on the straight course at a gallop, to escape the fire of the
citadel. Again they rushed through the mazy suburb. They
knew their way this time and had learned their work at dreadful cost. Today the fight here also was from house to house,
with no busy martinets to treat them as skulkers. The artillery worked their guns craftily, loading them behind corners,
running them out to be trained and fired, and snatching them
back by a rope on the trail to be reloaded in shelter. With a
captured 12-pounder they swept the farther bank of the Ojo
de Agua clean of defenders.

But again progress was slow and bloody, and movements
were ill managed. Ammunition began to fail, and Lieutenant
Grant galloped back, clinging in Indian style to the safer
side of his horse, to bring up a fresh supply. Taylor, his old
Indian-fighter blood aflame, was on foot with his staff amid
the hurly-burly. He strolled across the street that led to the
cathedral, though down its length the Mexican bullets flew,
according to a regular officer who was with him, "as if bushels
of hickory nuts were hurled at us." But he might have done
better by remaining far enough in the rear to be able to direct
the entire operation.

He supervised in person the bursting in of a door. The

apothecary inside offered the intruders ripe limes and cold
water, of which some of them accepted the fruit only, fear-
ing there might be poison in the drink. The building on the
opposite corner housed a grocery, and the hungry soldiers
flung themselves on the bread and other eatables they found
in it. In another house five "rather genteel-looking women,"
some children, and a couple of men were on their knees before a crucifix, from which they turned with a cry of *"Capi-
tano!"* to beg for mercy from the officer who burst in upon
them.

By midafternoon eleven guns had been captured, and Ampudia, who now found himself confined to his defenses about
the central plaza on every side and cut off from his troops in
the citadel, sent a flag of truce to request a cessation of hostilities to enable him to evacuate the women and children
from the city. Taylor refused, relieved Quitman's men by
Hamer's, the other brigade in the Field Division, and sent
the rest back to camp. There, as darkness fell and the shells
from Worth's mortar in the Campo Santo began to trace
their fiery arcs across the smoky sky, he went to work on
orders for a concerted, simultaneous attack on both fronts
to be made the following morning.

At midnight, however, a Mexican bugle sounded the par-
ley in the darkness outside Fort Teneréa, and a Mexican
officer with an offer of terms on which Ampudia would evacuate the city was conducted to Taylor's headquarters. When
morning dawned, a white flag halted Worth's men as they
were about to renew the attack. Firing ceased, and in the
blessed stillness the Americans at the outposts sat down on
the bodies of dead mules to a gay if meager breakfast, while
the American commissioners, Worth, Davis, and Colonel
Henderson of the Texas troops, met with Generals Raquenna
and Ortega and Señor M. M. Llano to arrange the details of
a capitulation.

It was settled by ten o'clock that night. Next day (Friday,
September 25) the guns of the citadel fired a salute as the
Mexican flag came down, and the Mexican army marched

away up the Saltillo road to the tootle of their indefatigable buglers, with all the honors of war. They were permitted to take with them six of their best guns and all their small arms, and their officers retained their swords and such of their personal effects as had not been captured in the fighting. They did not look like a beaten army. Some of them were said to have rioted in protest against giving up the city. One lancer regiment was as fine-looking a body of men as one could wish to see, though their horses were small and poor by Northern standards. The infantry were wretchedly clad and marched in sandals, but they were brawny men and bore themselves truculently.

Not so their leader. Ampudia, crestfallen and nervous, seemed fearful lest some of the grimly watching Texans should take a pot shot at him. The Irish deserters drew jeers and hisses from their former comrades, and pitiable was the sorry train of camp women that followed, weary and draggled in so much of their cheap finery as had not been left behind in the captured baggage of certain officers, where it excited the derision of the victors.

The American troops marched into the city to the strains of *Yankee Doodle;* the American flag went up, while from the Bishop's Palace boomed a twenty-one-gun salute; and out to the Teneréa redoubt came the Mexican women, smiling ingratiatingly through their tears, to search for lost loved ones among the prisoners and the wounded. The Americans had a similar task, and it was a grim one. On roofs, in houses and walled gardens, and strewn amid the mesquite and cornfields on the plain their comrades lay where they had fallen or had been dragged into shelter and of necessity been left untended. Many had died of their wounds, some of thirst. Some, the horrid evidence seemed to show, had been gnawed by wolves while still alive. The task of identifying them was frequently gruesome. Recognition of the body of the commander of the Baltimore Battalion, who had been killed in the first day's fighting, depended chiefly on the new boots he had put on that morning. A few were still living after three days of neglect, with tongues horribly swollen from thirst, and wounds that crawled with worms.

But the city grew quickly bright and pleasant. It proved to be a charming place, well built and full of high-walled gardens rich with orange trees, pomegranates, grapes, and flowers. Fine houses, furnished with mirrors and excellent paintings, became the billets of the American officers. Arista's splendid palace, through whose umbrageous garden flowed a swift stream to feed a trellised marble bath, was taken over for the wounded. On the very day after the evacuation the market was crowded with men and women in gay colors, eager to sell their fruit and vegetables for American money. The streets were cleaned, the barricades demolished. Soon the shops reopened with bright displays of goods.

Within a week the cathedral had been cleared of its deadly store of powder and fused shells, and the Reverend Father Rey, one of two Jesuit priests whom Polk had sent with the army to combat the propaganda of the Church in Mexico, celebrated Mass at its high altar. And that nothing might be lacking to testify to the completeness of the American occupation, the rowdy element among the volunteers was soon keeping the provost guard busy, as they had always done when their living-conditions became so bearable as to make life dull for them.

The army, officers and men alike, were well satisfied with what they had accomplished, dearly though it had cost them. Flanking the handsome fountain in the central plaza, were ranged the captured cannon, some of those fine English 9- and 12-pounders among them bearing the date of 1842. They had been taken, together with a strongly fortified city, the strategic key to a great province, from an army of nine thousand men, with thirty-eight guns, by a force of two thirds that size, which was almost entirely lacking in siege artillery and was separated from its base by something like a hundred and fifty miles of desert and mountains. Officers of the Topographical Engineers, riding about the defenses and observing their strength, marveled that it had been done at

all. When those who had been with Worth had the opportunity to examine the eastern end of the city, they thought the
wonder was that any who had attacked there had survived.

As for the terms of the capitulation, there were few, if any,
who condemned them in these first days after the fighting,
none among the troops that had gone against the Teneréa,
El Diablo, and the Purísima bridgehead. Ampudia's army,
to be sure, had been permitted to go scot-free. But it had
been provided that the Mexican forces should evacuate
within seven days the entire state of Nueva León up to a line
running through the Rinconada Pass, the city of Linares,
and San Fernando de Presas.

Taylor, for his part, had consented to an armistice according to the terms of which the American troops were not to
advance beyond this line and hostilities were to cease for
eight weeks unless orders to the contrary were received from
either the Mexican or the United States government in the
meanwhile. But his reasons for doing so were well understood
by his troops. Exhausted physically and shaken by their
losses, the volunteers, Lieutenant Meade wrote to his wife,
had come near to a state of disorganization, whole regiments
holding back on that last dreadful day, individuals refusing
to advance, and the regulars crippled by their heavy loss of
officers. Some idea of his own state of mind can be gathered
from the fact that on the day of the capitulation he dated a
hasty note to her September 25 instead of the 24th. Doubtless it seemed impossible that so much could have happened
in only three days.

It was true that one more attack might have taken the
city by storm and captured Ampudia and all his men who
did not succeed in slipping away across the river and the
ridge behind it. But they would have had to be paroled —
to hold them prisoner would have been a physical impossi-
bility; and it was Meade's opinion that such troops would
surely have broken their parole. The citadel, moreover, with
its strong bastions and heavy, accurate guns, would have remained to be reduced by siege, and that by an army whose

fighting edge had been blunted for the time being like that of Grant's army after Cold Harbor, and whose supplies and munitions had been reduced to a dangerous minimum. Taylor admitted that the victory had cost him four hundred and eighty-seven killed and wounded, and the total of casualties reported by officers present with their organizations approached a thousand. There were, at most, not more than ten days' provisions in the camp at the Bosque de Santiago, and he had even now only the wagon train that had served him since Corpus Christi days with which to replenish them. It was November before any of the new wagons reached him.

These circumstances naturally disarmed any criticism of the armistice also. In urging a cessation of hostilities Ampudia pretended to have information that his government was actively engaged with the government of the United States in negotiations for peace. Taylor felt that these would be hindered rather than helped by a refusal to suspend operations; and his troops, like everybody else who had read the newspapers during the past summer, shared the knowledge of Polk's dealings with Santa Anna — a knowledge that did much to convince Taylor of the truth of what the wily Mexican told him.

§6

Meanwhile Kendall's fleet couriers galloped northward. As the news spread throughout the United States, public meetings, speeches, bands, and bonfires celebrated the victory. Professional soldiers might carp at the way in which it had been won. Professional Democrats might strive to minimize the importance of the Whig general's accomplishment. But Scott, with his characteristic impulsive generosity, called the Monterrey affair " three glorious days," and not even the casualty list could dampen the popular enthusiasm for Taylor as a great commander and the likeliest Whig candidate for the next presidential election.

Quite different, however, was the feeling at the White House. Never, probably, since kings ceased to lead their armies in person, and misunderstandings between governments and their generals became an inevitable consequence, has the news of so great a victory been received so shabbily. "Our troops fought well, though with some loss of officers and men," was the faint praise with which Polk damned it in his diary.

Compact of nervous energy though he was, the zealous little President had begun to suffer from the strain he had put upon himself in the past nineteen months. In mid-August — "considerably enfeebled by confinement to my office," as he explained to some future reader of his own record of himself — he had gone down to Fortress Monroe with his wife and her niece for a brief rest. But he was back at his desk a few days later to deal with the usual throng of important duties and small annoyances. The 3rd of September was a red-letter day, the first in his administration on which not one office-seeker called upon him. There was the matter of the new site for the Smithsonian Institution, which he had to help to settle. A letter from Monsieur Guizot, King Louis Philippe's Prime Minister, had to be answered: it appeared that the United States consul at Tripoli was having a dispute with the French consul about precedence.

A deputation of twenty Winnebago chiefs arrived with a present in the form of a five-foot pipe decked with feathers and beads and a silver band inscribed: "Wee-no-Shick, head chief of the Winnebagoes, to J. K. Polk." One chief lighted it with flint and steel, and the President and all the chiefs puffed it solemnly in turn — a ceremony that Polk appears to have found amusing. Mr. Bancroft took his departure for England to represent the United States at the Court of St. James's. Mason replaced him as Secretary of the Navy. But when it came to finding somebody to take Mason's place as Attorney General, Franklin Pierce declined the appointment, preferring to enlist for the war as a private in the volunteers. There was, moreover, always and increasingly, the prosecution of the war.

When the Adjutant General ushered Captain Eaton, the

bearer of Taylor's official report on the Battle of Monterrey, into the President's study in the early evening of Sunday, October 11, he found that the defeat of Ampudia's army, the evacuation of the city, and the capture of all the enemy's munitions and artillery — save the six guns he had been allowed to take with him — were as nothing, in the President's opinion, compared with the fact that the Mexicans had been permitted to march away with the honors of war.

As Polk saw it, Taylor had had them at his mercy, should have made them prisoners, paroled them, and seized all their arms. Instead, he had left them an army in being, completely organized, and soon capable of fighting again. As for the armistice, Taylor had violated his express orders in granting it. If he had been tricked into doing so — the only explanation that seemed possible — the armchair strategists who gathered hastily at the White House that evening were not disposed to excuse him on that score, though the Adjutant General ventured to speak in his defense.

Buchanan condemned the armistice heartily, and when the Cabinet held a formal meeting next day, the other members did likewise. They held that it gave the enemy invaluable time in which to reorganize and that Taylor had offered no adequate reasons for granting it. If the level-headed and fair-minded Bancroft had been present, he might have put forward the information that Captain Eaton must certainly have been able to give as to the perilous situation in which Taylor had found himself at the end of those three bloody days, and he might well have emphasized the fact that Taylor could hardly have put this into an official dispatch without risk of its soon becoming generally known in the United States and, before very long, in Mexico. For military secrecy was hardly more than an empty phrase in Washington, as the events of the next few months were to demonstrate.

Lacking such guidance, the Cabinet agreed to the drafting of a letter to General Taylor that, without indicating either approval or disapproval of the armistice, should order him to terminate it immediately.

CHAPTER VI

Easy Conquests and Difficult Politics

§1

T HE FACT IS that, as war presidents go, Polk was the spoiled darling of fortune and was as ungrateful as such people generally are. Since the end of August one bearer of great news after another had entered the White House. On September 1, through the courtesy of the British Minister, who had it from the British legation at Mexico City, he heard that Commodore Sloat had occupied Monterey in California without a fight and had issued a proclamation declaring that country to be in the possession of the United States. The same day he learned that Frémont had clashed with the Californian Mexican forces and defeated them in a skirmish. A month later dispatches from Kearny told of the bloodless capture of Santa Fe, of his proclamation of New Mexico as a conquered province, and of his intention to go on to California in September. But it was not in Polk to waste time in exultation, still less to dwell in imagination on the endurance, fortitude, and courage, both physical and moral, by which these successes had been won. He was already deep in plans for a new campaign.

The past record of Colonel Stephen Watts Kearny was, indeed, such as to inspire a confident expectation of success. At the age of eighteen he had fought against the British at Queenstown Heights and since then had served almost constantly on the Western frontier, pushing his explorations to the present sites of Des Moines and St. Paul and on to the distant Yellowstone.

From the grassy quadrangle of wooden barracks and officers' quarters, with the two blockhouses at its angles, which was Fort Leavenworth in 1846, he had set out late in June at the head of what Mr. Hone of New York called "a predatory force of military adventurers" and young Francis Parkman, who did not see them, described in his book as "the offscourings of the frontier." Actually Kearny's Army of the West included three hundred regular dragoons, Missouri volunteer infantry under the command of Colonel Alexander Doniphan, and a battery of St. Louis artillery whose men were to work their fine brass guns more like regulars than volunteers before they saw home again. In all they numbered about sixteen hundred.

Their route lay chiefly along the famous Santa Fé Trail, but here and there they deviated from it, and the country was rough. The road climbed steadily. Hardship began almost from the start. The heat was intense, the wind burning. Rations grew short, and water was so scarce and bad that out of the one hundred artillery horses sixty had died before the expedition had covered the six hundred and fifty miles to Bent's Fort on the Arkansas River. Two additional companies of dragoons caught up with it there, and Kearny took under his protection five hundred wagons laden with a million dollars' worth of goods belonging to certain merchants who had been halted at Bent's in their journey to Santa Fe by the news of the declaration of war. On August 1 he pushed southward and, with his "long-legged infantry" all but outmarching the dragoons, though they went on half-rations of flour that they stirred up with water and fried with a little pork, crossed the Raton Pass.

What lay ahead of them none could tell. The people of New Mexico had been reported to be discontented and restless under a government that oppressed them with heavy taxes, throttled their trade with enormous duties and onerous regulations, and gave them no protection from the forays of the Indians. From a housetop in the village of Las Vegas on August 15 Kearny reminded them of their wrongs, told them that he and his troops came not as enemies but as liberators, and absolved them of their allegiance to the Mexican government and to Armijo, their Governor.

He had already issued a proclamation promising the enjoyment of all civil and religious rights to those who went peaceably about their business. But word came in that the population had risen en masse to resist the invader and that the Apache Cañon, through which for seven or eight miles the road wound into Santa Fe, was held by several thousand militia and some regulars, with numerous guns.

For a day or two a grim tension reigned among the advancing Americans. To attack such a position and against such numbers seemed a desperate course. For to attack and be repulsed, with two hundred and fifty miles of desert behind them, where every hamlet and rancho would become a nest of lurking foes, would mean disaster. On the other hand, a retreat across that inhospitable waste, with supplies all but exhausted, could hardly be less fatal. On August 17, however, just as Kearny had made up his mind to try the doubtful expedient of turning the enemy's position by a long and difficult march over the mountains, a fat and jovial alcalde galloped up to him on a mule and announced between bursts of laughter that Governor Armijo and his regulars had "gone to hell" and the militia had spiked the guns in the canyon and disintegrated.

It appeared that Armijo, who was no general, was not even a courageous official. From the first he had been at cross-purposes with his military officers. A Kentucky Irishman, James Magoffin, who was a rich merchant, resident at Chihuahua, and who had been acting as Polk's informal agent, had been at work at Santa Fe convincing the men of substance there that they would be far more prosperous under the government of the United States than under the slack and corrupt rule of Mexican officials. And the warlike enthusiasm of the population, whipped up by their priests, had been deflated by tales of the deadliness of the American artillery, the size of the American horses, and the fierce strength of the American soldiers.

Kearny advanced through the pass, finding it even as the alcalde had said, and on the following afternoon entered the city. His reception was friendly. The chiefs of the Pueblo Indians came in to offer their submission. On a hill only six hundred yards from the town he planted his guns and began building a fort — Fort Marcy he called it — to guard against any change of heart by the inhabitants, and within two weeks of his arrival he marched off with seven hundred men to look for a Mexican force that was reported to be advancing from El Paso. No enemy was to be found or heard of, however, and he returned to Santa Fe.

All in all, the conquest had been almost disappointingly easy for a man of his experience. Fresh troops were on the way to reinforce his weary men: a thousand riflemen whom Secretary Marcy had authorized Sterling Price to organize at Fort Leavenworth after Kearny's departure, and a battalion of five hundred Mormons from the great emigration that was just then pausing at Council Bluffs. Kearny issued orders for the disposition and employment of these troops and for the pacification of the Eutah and Navaho Indians, and on September 25, with three hundred of his dragoons and a couple of mountain howitzers, set off for California.

Eleven days later, at Socorro on the Rio Grande, he met Kit Carson, the famous scout, who was bound for Washington with dispatches from Commodore Stockton and Frémont. The conquest of California was complete, Carson told him: every important town in American hands and a civil government about to be established with Frémont as Governor. On hearing this, Kearny sent two hundred of his men back to Santa Fe and continued to ride westward with the rest. But he persuaded Carson to send the dispatches on by another messenger and to return to California with him, and he kept with him his two howitzers. It was well that he did so, for at Agua Caliente on the California frontier he was met by a quite different account of happenings in the newly conquered territory.

§2

Up to the time that Kit Carson left for Washington with the reports of Frémont and Stockton, the California adventure had worked out as successfully and almost as bloodlessly as the conquest of New Mexico. Frémont had left Independence, Missouri, with Secretary Bancroft's particular approval, early in the summer of 1845. This time his mission was to discover a more direct route to the Pacific than the Oregon Trail. He had led his little party of hard-bitten frontiersmen by way of Utah Lake, the Great Salt Lake, over the Nevada mountains, and so for the second time into the Sacramento Valley.

At New Helvetia, as Captain Sutter had named his settlement there, the sturdy German Swiss still dominated the country from his bastioned fort, which was armed with cannon and garrisoned by his own company of uniformed Indian mercenaries, as he had done nearly two years before. But there were more American settlers in the neighboring country now, and the ardent little American brevet captain found them as contemptuous as ever of the indolent, good-humored, easy-going Californians and still more eager, as they expressed it, "to play the Texas game."

There were about eight hundred of them in California at the end of 1845. Of these, some were hard-working genuine colonizers. But most were rough and even vicious men, runaway sailors and adventurers of the mountains, many of whom had left their country for their country's good and wished only to live a life of lawless ease. A number of them had established themselves on the shores of San Francisco Bay. The great majority, however, had remained in the Sacramento Valley, which Indian raids made unpopular with the Mexicans, and where Sutter made them welcome.

Advancing southward through a country that in its whole extent from the Sacramento settlements to San Diego held only about ten thousand whites and fifteen thousand Indians,

Frémont arrived in January 1846 at Monterey to replenish his funds and supplies and to ask permission to rest his horses and men within the borders of the province. Things had hardly changed since he had passed along the western slope of the Sierra Nevada in 1844. The ranchers still led their lotus-eaters' life of gorgeous squalor, without benefit of wooden floors or glass in the windows of their houses, fleeting the time with gambling at monte or horse races with money borrowed at twenty-four per cent, while their womenfolk lolled at home in extravagant finery amid broods of children.

Herds of wild horses and cattle — almost half of them unbranded — roamed the country. Few of the farms were held by formal title. There were no police, no postal service, no courts of law. In one of its brief spasms of anticlericalism the Mexican government had ruined those seedbeds of civilization, the missions. There was not a school or a newspaper in the whole country.

Twice in the past decade — the second time as recently as the previous February — the Californians had expelled the brutal and rapacious troops sent to maintain the government of Mexico. Now a provincial Governor, Pío Pico, exercised a languid authority at Ciudad de Los Ángeles, while at Monterey, which — busy port though it was — consisted of only a hundred houses, José Castro, the commandante general, collected, with great profit to himself and other officials, customs duties amounting to from $80,000 to $100,000 a year.

Castro granted Frémont's request that he be allowed to remain in the country long enough to rest his men and replenish his supplies. But in March, on the pretext that some of the terms of the permission had been violated, he ordered him to leave, and set about raising the militia to expel him. The Americans might not be soldiers, and Frémont insisted that they were not, but one had only to look at the lean sun-dried stature of them in their fringed buckskins and fur caps, at their long twenty-six-pound rifles, and at the long hunting knives that hung at their hips to know that they

were fierce and crafty fighters and that, though they numbered only about sixty, they constituted the most efficient
military force in the province.

Resenting hotly the rude terms of Castro's order, Frémont
established his party in a log fort about thirty miles from
Monterey and would have initiated hostilities if the Mexicans
had not halted short of an ambuscade he had prepared for
their reception. But on hearing that Castro was about to attack him with cannon, he retired in the direction of Oregon.
He had, in fact, crossed the boundary and was encamped
near Klamath Lake when, on May 8, the very day on which
Taylor was winning his victory at Palo Alto, he was overtaken by that Marine lieutenant, Archibald H. Gillespie, to
whom the President had entrusted secret instructions for
Larkin, the consul at Monterey.

Gillespie's mission had proved to be a perilous one. Crossing Mexico in the month of the Paredes revolution, he had
been compelled to disguise himself as a merchant and to destroy his dispatches after committing their contents to memory, lest they should fall into the hands of the Mexican
authorities. Arrived at Mazatlán, he boarded the U.S.S.
Cyane, and while she made the voyage to Monterey via the
Sandwich Islands in order to conceal his mission still further,
he wrote out the dispatches afresh.

They informed Larkin that if the Californians should declare themselves independent of Mexico, he was to assure
them that they could count on "all the kindly offices in our
power"; that if they "desired to unite their destiny with
ours," they would be "received as brethren." And Larkin
was further informed that the United States "would vigorously interpose to prevent" any attempt of Great Britain or
France to make a colony out of California.

Gillespie carried also private letters to Frémont from
Senator Benton and, according to the belief of some, secret
instructions from the President directing his future course
of action. Whether this was so or not, Frémont, who found
that deep snows lay ahead of him to the northward, and who
on the night of Gillespie's arrival narrowly escaped being

wiped out by a treacherous attack by Indians, promptly returned to the valley of the Sacramento.

There he found the settlers in a ferment. The rumor was abroad among them that Castro was gathering a force with which to expel from the country all but the few of them who had taken the trouble to become naturalized citizens. They believed that a herd of horses that he was moving southward from Sonoma had been collected for that purpose and proceeded to capture it. Then, sure that he would retaliate, they advanced on Sonoma, a somnolent Californian town fifteen miles north of San Francisco Bay. They seized it and, with it, eight field guns, two hundred stands of arms, and a hundredweight of powder. They made prisoners of a number of important Californians whom they found there and, under the leadership of William B. Ide, proclaimed a government of their own, hoisting a flag that bore on a piece of white cotton cloth, with a strip of red flannel sewn to its lower edge, a red star, a bear, and the words "California Republic."

Frémont refrained from taking part in this action, but when the prisoners were brought in, he compelled Sutter, who viewed the movement askance, to lock them up in his fort. And when Castro marched against the insurgents, Frémont not only joined them and accepted command of their forces but also led a kind of preventive foray against the Indians, whom Castro was believed to have incited to burn the Americans' wheat and barley as it stood in the fields, dry and ready for harvest. By July 10 he was heading an advance against Castro's forces when a courier from Monterey brought him word that the United States and Mexico were at war at last and that Commodore Sloat had seized that port and occupied the town.

Back in March, upon the first clash of wills between Castro and Frémont, Larkin, in a state of great uneasiness, had sent an urgent message to the Commodore, who had caused the U.S.S. *Portsmouth* to arrive at Monterey in April. But it was not until the first days of July that Sloat appeared there. Sloat had served under Decatur on the *United States* in her action with the *Macedonian* in the War of 1812, but he was sixty-five years old now and only waiting until his request to be retired should be granted in order to go home. Lying at Mazatlán, he had news of Palo Alto and Resaca and of the capture of Matamoros, but only on intelligence of the blockade of Vera Cruz did he set sail for Monterey.

His orders were clear. Cautioned to avoid any and every act that might be construed as aggressive, he was, however, directed to seize Yerba Buena, the settlement on San Francisco Bay, and to capture or blockade such other ports as he was able, if he should hear positively that war had been declared. But no word of a formal declaration of war had reached him; he had a daunting recollection of how Ap Catesby Jones's rashness at this very port in similar circumstances in 1842 had come near costing that officer his commission; and even after he had dropped anchor before the dilapidated and extemporized fortifications of Monterey he hesitated until word of Frémont's doings in the north convinced him that the explorer must be acting on definite orders from Washington.

Then from the *Savannah*, his flagship, and from the *Cyane* and the *Levant*, which he found at Monterey when he arrived there, he landed eighty-five marines in the tail-coats and white crossbelts of the time and a hundred and sixty-five sailors armed with muskets and bayonets, and the Stars and Stripes went up over the customhouse to a salute of twenty-one guns. The marines, with their customary versatility, proceeded to organize a company of dragoons composed of some of their own men, sailors who knew enough to board a horse on the port side, and civilian volunteers. With these they established a courier service to San Francisco Bay, where the *Portsmouth* had been busy supplying Frémont and the Bear Flag forces with arms and ammunition. On orders from Sloat, her commander put a landing party ashore at Yerba Buena, hoisted the American flag, and established a garrison of fourteen marines.

The couriers found Frémont at the Mission of San Juan. He promptly led his force, which now numbered a hundred and sixty tough frontiersmen, to Monterey and desolated the nervous Sloat by telling him that he had no specific orders for what he had done. But events soon proved that Sloat had acted none too soon to carry out the spirit of his instructions. A few days after his landing, Admiral Seymour on Her Britannic Majesty's powerful man-of-war *Collingwood* arrived at Monterey, and he was reported to have said to the American commodore: "Sloat, if your flag was not already on shore, I should have hoisted mine there."

On July 15 Stockton arrived at Monterey on the *Congress,* and on the 23rd the tired old man turned over the command to him and sailed for home. Stockton, like Sloat, was a veteran of the War of 1812: he had served under Rodgers on the *President* in her action with the *Little Belt* and in the defense of Baltimore, and on the *Spitfire* in the War with Algiers in 1815. But he was fifteen years younger than Sloat, possessed large private means, and had been so much of a figure in politics that President Tyler had offered him the appointment of Secretary of the Navy. Completely recovered from the injuries he had received from the explosion on the *Princeton,* thoroughly in sympathy with the administration's policy of expansion, well informed as to its intentions when he sailed from Norfolk the previous November, and of an adventurous and impetuous disposition, he suffered from none of the fears and hesitations of his predecessor in command on the California coast.

He mustered Frémont's men into the service of the United States as California Volunteers, with Frémont as major and Gillespie as a captain, and sent them off by sea to San Diego, of which they made an easy conquest. He hoisted the American flag over Santa Barbara and, anchoring at San Pedro, where Los Angeles was only an eighteen-mile march away, demanded of Castro that he accept independence under that standard, though even now positive information of a formal declaration of war was still lacking.

At Los Angeles Governor Pico, a fat, good-natured, hardly literate farmer, had issued a proclamation late in June in which he called upon his compatriots to imitate the conduct of the "citizens . . . at the Pass of Termopyle . . . under General Leonidas." He had got together some eight hundred men and ten cannon. But his classical allusion fell upon ears untrained to appreciate it; there was an old feud between him and Castro over the division of spoils from the customs duties at Monterey; and in the north the people were apathetic and gave him no support. On August 10 Castro retired hastily toward Sonoma: Frémont was again close at hand with his dreaded volunteers.

Two days later Stockton led his marines and sailors into Los Angeles with a brass band at their head. On the 17th he received the tardy news of the declaration of war and proclaimed California to be a part of the United States. Californians who had been made prisoner were released on parole. By September a school was opened, a newspaper started. Municipal elections were held with excellent results, alcaldes were appointed, and Kit Carson was dispatched overland to carry the good news to Washington.

Suddenly possessed by the fantastic scheme of marching to Mexico City from the Pacific coast of Mexico, Stockton sent Frémont to the north to raise troops for that purpose and himself set sail for San Francisco Bay soon after upon a report that a thousand Indians were about to attack the settlements in the Sacramento Valley. There followed immediately a complete reversal of fortune in the south. At Los Angeles, where pro-American sentiment was weakest, an uprising forced the little American garrison to capitulate and embark on a merchant ship at San Pedro. Santa Barbara had to be evacuated; the garrison at San Diego was besieged; and an attempt to retake Los Angeles was unsuccessful. The California legislature declared martial law and made the leader of the insurrection provisional governor and commandante general.

When Kearny reached Agua Caliente early in December,

he was informed that an enemy force was close at hand. He asked for and received a small reinforcement from the few troops at Stockton's disposal. But it was only after a sharp fight at the Pass of San Pascual, in which the animals carrying the mountain howitzers stampeded and Kearny himself and fourteen others were wounded and eighteen of his men were killed, that he managed to reach San Diego.

In general, however, things had not been going well for the insurrectionists. They lacked money and ammunition. Popular support was wanting. Their legislature failed to obtain a quorum. Monterey was held fast by the Americans. Soon Stockton's forces outnumbered theirs, and two days before Kearny fought his way into San Diego the malcontents had thrown their leader into prison. By the 1st of December Stockton had reoccupied San Pedro and relieved San Diego. On the 29th his four hundred sailors and marines, together with Kearny's dragoons and with that experienced fighter as executive officer, advanced up the hundred-and-forty-mile-long sandy road that led to Los Angeles.

A force of about four hundred and fifty poorly armed Californians attempted to stop them at the San Gabriel River on January 8. But the Americans charged with the cry of "New Orleans" — it was the anniversary of Jackson's defeat of the British in 1815 — and two days later the same flag that Gillespie had been compelled to haul down was hoisted once more above the City of the Angels. Frémont arrived in the neighborhood simultaneously and arranged a capitulation on liberal terms — the so-called Treaty of Cahuenga — with such of the California troops as had not disintegrated after their defeat.

A mere brevet captain, who had yet to receive his commission as lieutenant colonel, Frémont grossly exceeded his authority in doing this when a commodore and a brigadier general in the persons of Stockton and Kearny were close at hand. Stockton confirmed the capitulation reluctantly, for a good many of the Californian officers had broken their parole and thereby made themselves liable to the death penalty. But the arrangement had been a wise stroke of statesmanship. The Californians were disgusted with the Mexican government for its failure to support them and were convinced of the hopelessness of contending longer against the Americans. They had satisfied their honor by the resistance they had made; they appreciated Frémont's maganimity, and by far the greater number of them were satisfied to observe the terms they had accepted.

At San Francisco Bay a "California Legion" arrived from New York, their blue shakos, blue frock coats, and white crossbelts somewhat tarnished by their months at sea. They called each other "mister," snubbed their officers, and proceeded to avenge themselves for the hardships of their long voyage by painting little Yerba Buena red. But in due time the hard work of building a battery brought them into the traces. At Los Angeles, by midsummer, relations between Americans and Californians had become so friendly that Señora Pico was among the many Californian ladies who attended the Fourth of July ball given by the officers of the United States army and navy.

The cessation of hostilities brought discord among the conquerors, however. Kearny laid claim to the governorship of the country on the strength of the instructions he had received from Washington before he set out from Fort Leavenworth. Stockton and Frémont maintained that the course of events had made these of no effect. Stockton kept Frémont in office, and the wrangle came to a sorry end more than two years later in one of the several courts-martial, official inquiries, and investigations that clouded the arrival of peace.

Had Kearny been at Santa Fe in the latter half of January 1847, he would have had something more important to occupy his time. In New Mexico the harmony between the inhabitants and their conquerors was almost as shortlived as it had been in California. Discipline among the American volunteers was worse than lax. A British observer called them "the dirtiest, rowdiest crew" he had ever seen. The native population began to fear for their property. In December

Doniphan marched off with some eight hundred men to the conquest of Chihuahua, and on January 17 the New Mexicans rose in arms. At Taos and at several isolated ranches they murdered fifteen Americans with singular barbarity, Charles Bent, the civil governor, being one of the victims. But Sterling Price, who was to come near winning Missouri for the Confederacy by his victory at Wilson's Creek in 1861, restored order, rounded up the guilty, and hanged fifteen who were convicted of murder. The rest, who were charged with treason, President Polk pardoned on the ground that Mexican citizens could not be held guilty of treason against the United States.

§3

Santa Anna, Santa Anna,
Tell us by what secret juggling
Cam'st thou in by Yankee smuggling
Like a contraband Havannah.

Thus in October 1846 did the *Illustrated London News*, in its devotion to what Dickens gibed at as the "gentlemanly interest," vent its anxiety as to the soundness of Mexican bonds. The Yankees, it said in its "Gossip of the Week," had begun the war "in a spirit of the most shameful rapacity" and were now "desirous of compounding it in a spirit of the most dirty huxtering" that was "generally characteristic of Yankee heroism." They were not, the writer observed, attacking San Juan de Ulloa but were "pouring a force, half emigrant, half military, into California," and he had no doubt that Santa Anna would "do President Polk's dirty work."

In November, after Taylor's success at Monterrey, the *Illustrated London News* became more respectful. It likened Taylor's informal habit of dress to the broad-brimmed straw hat and cudgel with which Commodore Napier of the Royal Navy had led an attack in Syria. There was less and less talk of intervention in Mexico's behalf in the British press generally, though its tone continued to be hostile, and by the beginning of winter Bancroft was able to report that "England sees that California must be ours, and sees it with regret, but remains 'neutral.' "

In Washington Mr. Fox, the former Minister from Great Britain, who had lingered there, continuing to turn night into day, died a death that was said to have been hastened by the too free use of opium. The President had to attend the funeral, but, the sooner to get back to work, he did order his coach out of the cortege as it passed the White House. The Portuguese Minister called to announce officially the birth of still another child to Queen Maria II and her consort. She had one every year, and Polk was sourly amused by the diplomat's detailed account of the royal obstetrics.

But what seems to have given him the greatest satisfaction was his dealing with a Presbyterian minister who called to request, or rather to demand, an appointment to a chaplaincy in the army. A truculent reference to the Roman Catholic priests already with Taylor's troops and a thinly veiled threat to make serious trouble for the administration at the approaching election if he were not given what he wanted caused Polk to explode. Keen politician though he was, considerations of religious faith raised an issue that he would not palter with. The navy had chaplains, he explained, but the army had none; the status of the priests with Taylor was that of civilian employees; they spoke Spanish, and their mission was to counteract the anti-American propaganda of the Church in Mexico. He ended by giving the reverend gentleman to understand that he was not to be blackmailed into giving him any appointment whatsoever.

On the more serious side was the condition of the Treasury. The gibe in the London *Times* to the effect that the United States lacked both money and credit was not without foundation. Owing to the new tariff, the receipts from customs duties had fallen sharply, and in October Secretary Walker returned unsuccessful from an attempt to arrange with the Wall Street bankers for the flotation of six-per-cent notes redeemable in twelve months. More serious still was the political situation, especially after the numerous Democratic defeats in the elections in November.

Buchanan held the tariff responsible for them in Pennsylvania. Polk blamed the Old Hunkers in New York, whence William Cullen Bryant wrote to his friend the Reverend Doctor Dewey that "we Democrats" had been "beaten small, ground to powder." Whatever the cause, the consequence was that, between Whig gains and lukewarm support in his own party, Polk had to regard his majority in Congress as merely nominal and was set to defending the war itself in a lengthy message when that body convened in December. He maintained that the Rio Grande had been the boundary between Texas and Mexico at the time of the cession of 1803, that it had remained the boundary of Texas after the cession of that territory to Spain by the United States in 1819, and that it had been so recognized by Santa Anna in his treaty with the Texans after San Jacinto. He accused the Whigs of giving "aid and comfort" to the enemy by the attitude they were taking.

The Whigs called the war unnecessary and unjust, a squandering of blood and money actuated by "a quenchless thirst for conquest" and the desire to extend slavery. If this were not so, what then was the purpose of the war, they asked. They attacked the blockading of the Rio Grande before hostilities had begun and accused the President of trampling on the rights of Congress and violating the Constitution by sending an army into a country with which the United States was at peace. Alexander Hamilton Stephens was the leader of the attack upon him. Andrew Johnson defended him. So strangely were these two opposed fifteen years before the one became Vice President of the Confederacy and nineteen years before the other was to succeed to the Presidency of the United States in the Black Republican era. The war, the true-blue Democrats explained, was being fought, first, to defend Texas, secondly, to secure the just claims of United States citizens against the government of Mexico, and, thirdly, to get back the cost of the war. As for its offensive character, the act of May 13, 1846 had taken the war out of the President's hands, and it was by that act that it became offensive.

There were not enough Democrats, however, who could be relied upon to support the administration's policy. After a New Year's Day when Polk was worn out by shaking hands steadily from half past eleven in the morning until three in the afternoon, Buchanan told him that he thought the armies should advance no farther but should merely hold what they had taken, while efforts were made to stir up revolt in the northern states of Mexico. The rest of the Cabinet appeared to concur in this, and Calhoun had expressed the same opinion a few days before. It was discouraging to the ardent little Polk, who, though he was no soldier, knew at least that the cheapest way to win a war was to prosecute it vigorously.

But worse was yet to come. On January 4 Mr. Preston King, Democrat from New York, introduced in the House what Polk called a "sensational bill." Polk in his December message had asked once more for the two million dollars with which to facilitate peace negotiations with Mexico. King's bill was for an appropriation for this purpose, with the stipulation that slavery was to be excluded from any territory that should be acquired from Mexico.

Polk heard of it with deep misgivings. "The slavery question," he wrote in his diary that night, "is assuming a fearful and most important aspect. The movement of Mr. King today, if persisted in . . . cannot fail to destroy the Democratic party, if it does not threaten the Union itself." The slavery question, Polk held, had been adjusted in one of the compromises of the Constitution and could have no legitimate connection with the war with Mexico or with the terms of peace.

The Cabinet believed the matter could be settled by extending the Missouri Compromise to the Pacific. Webster agreed with Polk that slavery was economically impossible in New Mexico. In December Calhoun had told the President that he would support the two-million-dollar bill if no anti-slavery strings were attached to it : not, he explained, that he wished slavery to be extended, but as a matter of principle. Half the session went by, and the fierce and violent debates on the subject continued, to the exclusion of pressing business. By the end of January Polk saw the Democrats in both houses so intent on the 1848 elections that the administration had practically only a minority in Congress, and he had begun to regard Calhoun as an opponent.

Hannibal Hamlin — at this time a Democrat, though he was to become Lincoln's Vice President in 1861 — had spoken against an increase of the regular army for the duration of the war. In a joint committee of both houses Calhoun and some whom Polk described as Calhoun's "peculiar friends" voted with the Whigs to reject the administration's bill to provide ten new regiments of volunteers. They joined the Whigs again to exclude from the privileged seats in the Senate Chamber the editor of the *Union* newspaper because he had published a letter that condemned the rejection of that bill, and Polk's blood boiled in behalf of the freedom of the press.

He told senators and congressmen who called on him that he considered their delays in passing his war measures inexcusable. He, for his part, stayed home from church on Christmas Day in order to work, and he wrote of himself rather ruefully at the end of January : "Though I occupy a very high position, I am the hardest working man in the country" — which was probably true. About the only bright spot in his life during these weeks was a call by Senator Crittenden, who, though a Whig, concurred in his ideas on the two-million-dollar appropriation, the prosecution of the war, and the slavery question as related to it. On February 10, however, the ten-regiment bill was passed, and the President sought a little recreation on Washington's Birthday by attending the birthnight balls at Carusi's Saloon and Jackson Hall. He squired Mrs. Dallas at supper and did not get home until midnight.

§4

Secretary Marcy, now heart and soul in the prosecution of the war, was overwhelmed by the business of his office. For, to the President's eye, the army officers at the War Department were either indifferent — grown soft in their soft jobs — or hostile to the administration. In order to help out, Polk had taken on himself such details as the purchase of two additional steamers to transport troops across the Gulf of Mexico. The mere prospect of the ten new regiments had brought down upon him a fresh swarm of commission-seekers, and long before those regiments were authorized a question had been raised in the Cabinet as to the advisability of calling upon doubtful Massachusetts for one of them. Polk settled it trenchantly: let Massachusetts be asked, and if she refused, as she had done in 1812 and 1814, the whole country would hear of it.

Back in September Polk had become convinced that the war could not be won by Taylor in northern Mexico and had begun to plan a seaborne expedition against Tampico. On the day before Captain Eaton arrived with Taylor's report of his success at Monterrey it had been decided to extend this operation to include the capture of Vera Cruz, and Polk had summoned to Washington a former consul at that place to enlighten the dense ignorance of himself, the Cabinet, and the War Department on the nature of the adjacent country.

But who was to command this new invasion force? Polk had come to the conclusion that Taylor, though brave enough, had not the grasp of mind for such a task. By mid-November, moreover, he was convinced that Taylor had become a bitter political partisan, completely under the influence of Bailie Peyton, Kendall of the *Picayune*, and Bliss, his Adjutant General, all of whom were more intelligent than he was. A weak man, turned giddy by the idea of the Presidency, Polk thought him, when Taylor wrote an ill-tempered protest against the Tampico project as an interference with his conduct of the war.

The Cabinet agreed with the President in feeling that Taylor had striven continually to throw upon the administration the blame for any possible disaster, and the fact that conditions in the service of supply on the Rio Grande had become so bad that Quartermaster General Jesup had been sent there at his own request seems to have done nothing to make them think otherwise. Polk favored Butler for the command of the Vera Cruz expedition, but Marcy opposed his appointment. Patterson the Cabinet held to be too lacking in experience. Marcy felt that Scott was the man for the place, and it did seem as if there was nobody else who was fitted for it. Anybody would be better than Taylor, Polk decided. But he had considered Scott to be so much more embarrassing than helpful during the past few months that he thought of ordering him to some other post. He could not forget Scott's impulsive letters of the past May, and when Scott, who was frankly eager for the command of the expedition, stated that twenty-five or thirty thousand men would be required for it, Polk suspected him of wishing to embarrass the administration.

Polk had another candidate in mind, but was not yet ready to bring him forward. So, on November 19, with the approval of the Cabinet, he had Scott summoned to the White House and gave him the command. Scott was much moved — "almost shed tears," Polk noted — protesting his gratitude, his confidence in the administration, and his willingness to cooperate with its wishes even to the point of taking with him any of the volunteer generals whom the President might choose to designate. It was something of an undertaking for a professional soldier like Scott, that galaxy of political warriors, all Democrats — Butler, Pillow, Shields, Hamer, Patterson, Marshall, Henderson, Persifor Smith, and Quitman — but Polk was not the man to appreciate it at its true value.

The next week saw the two men conferring together twice a day. They parted with every sign of cordiality and mutual confidence. Scott sailed from New York on the steamer *Union* on the last day of the month, and when he dined with Henry

Clay in New Orleans three weeks later, he was warm in his
praises of Polk's treatment of him. Polk was less satisfied.
The general's ship had been delayed by storms, and the President and the Secretary of War grumbled that he could
have reached New Orleans in seven days by traveling overland. The New Orleans *Patria*, a Spanish-language newspaper, published a long though badly garbled account of the
plan of the new campaign, and Polk jumped to the conclusion that Scott's "inordinate vanity" had led him to babble
and boast. In point of fact, all that the *Patria* printed had
been known in New Orleans for some days before Scott's arrival. Not even the simplest precautions were taken by the
War Department to ensure secrecy. No ciphers were used;
dispatches were often entrusted to civilians and were frequently lost; and the New York newspapers announced that
Scott had left Washington to conduct an attack on Tampico
four days before he sailed from New York.

Politically, however, Polk had struck a shrewd blow by appointing Scott. With two Whig generals winning military
glory, the Whigs might well be divided when the next election came around. He now proceeded with a scheme that
promised to accomplish much more than this. On November 6
Senator Benton had come to him with a proposal that, after
taking Vera Cruz, the army should march on Mexico City,
that three peace commissioners should accompany it, and
that one of them should be Benton himself. When Polk consulted him four days later in his dilemma over appointing a
commander, Benton agreed that Taylor would not do, added
that he had no confidence in Scott, and ended by stating that
he himself would accept the appointment if Congress would
authorize the grade of lieutenant general for him so that he
should be superior to Scott and Taylor.

Polk was delighted with the suggestion. Had not Benton
raised and commanded a regiment of volunteers under Jackson in 1812? To be sure, he had seen no fighting, but later in
that war he had held a commission as lieutenant colonel of
regulars that had given him seniority over both Taylor and

Scott. The proposed appointment would prevent those two Whigs from winning more glory and would conciliate the Van Buren Democrats, with whom Benton was affiliated.

Untroubled by the implications of his dealings with Scott, Polk set to work. But he immediately encountered opposition. Congressmen from Georgia, Illinois, Kentucky, and Tennessee assured him that no lieutenant general's grade would be authorized if it were to have the effect of superseding Scott and Taylor. Cass told him that the irascible and imperious Benton was so unpopular in the Senate as to make his appointment impossible, and Calhoun was against it. But it became evident that Benton would be dissatisfied if Polk did not go on with the project, and the bill had actually been passed by the House when it was defeated in the Senate through the efforts of Marcy, Buchanan, and Walker.

Benton then told Polk that if he were made a major general and placed in chief command, with plenary powers to make peace, he would end the war before July. But even Polk could not see his way to putting him over four major generals who would be senior to him, and Benton — to his great loss in public esteem, according to Franklin Pierce — declined the appointment on any other terms.

Polk was much disappointed. He was more than ever annoyed by the behavior of Scott and Taylor by this time. Already convinced of the indiscretion of the former, he received late in February an incomplete account of a court-martial that had sentenced Colonel Harney of the dragoons to a reprimand for disobedience of orders. This had been Worth's doing. He could hardly have done less, for the offense appears to have been flagrant. Scott remitted the sentence. But it was Scott whom Polk blamed, holding that both Scott and Taylor acted in the same "proscriptive spirit" toward gallant officers who were Democrats. He directed Marcy to write to Scott expressing his disapproval, though the Cabinet did not favor such action.

Taylor's camp Polk believed to have become "a political arena." Old Rough and Ready had written General Gaines a letter assailing the administration, uttering unfounded complaints, and giving out the secret plans of the forthcoming campaign, and the egregious Gaines had given it to the newspapers. Polk had Marcy write to Taylor condemning his letter as both unmilitary and contrary to his duty as an officer. He caused the House to pass a resolution calling for the correspondence between Taylor and the War Department, and was thus able to bring the facts to the attention of the public.

In his own Cabinet he was not being served, he discovered, with the efficiency that he desired. When somebody remarked at a Cabinet meeting on February 20 that, according to General Scott's letter of January 12, he was probably attacking Vera Cruz at that moment, Secretary of the Navy Mason expressed surprise. He had not heard of the letter, he said, and the U.S.S. *Ohio* and the bomb vessels that were to participate in the attack had not yet entered the Gulf of Mexico. The President remarked that he had supposed the Secretaries of War and Navy to be continually in conference to co-ordinate the movements of their respective forces, and Secretary Mason, much mortified, left the room to issue orders to hasten the movement of his ships.

That night the weary Polk set it all down in his diary, without comment, which he doubtless thought would have been superfluous.

§5

Scott heard of the Benton intrigue on December 23 just as he was sailing from New Orleans for "the Brazos," the region about the mouth of the Rio Grande. It was exactly the fire on his rear that he had feared in May, but now, completely deceived by Polk's recent manifestation of confidence in him, he simply refused to believe it, wrote Marcy to that effect in a private letter, and added that he had "laid down *whiggism*, without taking up *democracy*."

The task of organizing the expedition against Vera Cruz was more than enough to occupy his entire attention, and the conditions that he found prevailing among the troops along the Rio Grande were the reverse of satisfactory. At Baltimore *Niles' Register* had already reported that duels were expected to take place between some of the officers at Camargo. Lieutenant George B. McClellan, who had arrived at that unhealthy place in November in company with Lieutenant Gustavus W. Smith, later his opponent at the Battle of Seven Pines, had found the volunteers "dying like flies" and the quartermaster service such that he wrote: "Never trust anything to that Department."

Even in distant London it was understood that there was "a painful reaction in Taylor's army after the excitements and fatigues of the campaign." At Monterrey half the troops came down with chills and fever, and there was a sore lack of medical officers. The gallant Ridgely, who had seemed to court death throughout the fighting, had been killed by the fall of his horse soon after. The death of the brave and able Ohioan General Hamer caused Taylor to exclaim that he had lost the balance wheel of his volunteer army. In spite of the vigilant activity of Worth's provost marshal, "striped tigers," which were gambling-dens, and "spotted pigs," which were drinking-places, plied an active trade in the chaparral thickets, and at Camargo the *fonda* of Hindoo John did nothing to improve either moral or physical welfare. Desertions became frequent — some fifty — among the regulars, but none from the volunteers, according to one of their own officers. Those who departed now were not Irishmen, it was observed, but Englishmen and Germans. All found their way, however, into the hard-fighting Mexican corps of San Patricio.

The Texas troops had availed themselves of their right to discharge and had gone home, all but McCulloch's and one other company of Rangers. Regret at their departure was mitigated by relief among the rest of the troops, for their outrageous behavior to the inhabitants of town and countryside had brought about reprisals in the form of assassinations by knife and lasso from which none who wore the

American uniform was safe. Father Rey, the excellent and devoted priest, together with a soldier who had been detailed to assist him, were among the victims. They were murdered on an open road in broad daylight by some who evidently hated an *Americano del Norte* even though he was in holy orders. The misconduct of the Kentuckians came close to equaling that of the Texans until Taylor put a stop to it by assembling their officers and threatening to send the regiment to the rear in disgrace if its members did not mend their ways.

Scott's chivalrous nature was "agonized," he wrote to Marcy in mid-January, by what he heard from regulars, seven out of ten volunteers, and steamboat men alike about the crimes committed by some of the volunteers against the inhabitants along the Rio Grande: "Murder, robbery, and rape on mothers and daughters, in the presence of the tied up males of the families . . . sometimes in the presence of acquiescing, trembling volunteer officers." He determined to take to Vera Cruz as few of such troops as possible, and the alternative was to draft from Taylor all of his regulars, except the dragoons and the light-artillery batteries, and most of his volunteers who had seen fighting. The list of officers of whom Taylor was thus deprived becomes impressive when read in the light of events that were to take place less than twenty years later. It included the names of Lee, Grant, Meade, Patterson, and Pillow.

Before leaving New York, Scott had endeavored to prepare Taylor for something of this kind by writing to him that although new troops were being raised, they would not be ready for service before the season of yellow fever would prevent operations in "the new field." He continued: "I will have to take most of your troops; your victories, however, have placed you on such an eminence that you can afford to act on the defensive for a time." And he expressed the desire to consult with Taylor when he arrived at Camargo.

Last spring Taylor had been prepared to welcome Scott as his immediate commander in the field. But political ambition had soured him since then. Convinced that Scott had joined the conspiracy he believed to have been organized at Washington to ruin him, he had already changed the name of the hated firm of Polk, Marcy and Company to Scott, Marcy and Company. Of Scott's courteous and kindly letter he wrote that "a more contemptible and insidious communication was never written." He ignored the request for a meeting at Camargo, which he ought to have taken as an order, and replied coldly that he expected to be busy at Victoria until early in February, when, unless otherwise instructed, he would return to Monterrey, though he would at all times be happy to hold himself and his troops at Scott's disposition.

Communications between Camargo and Taylor's headquarters were uncertain and difficult; between Monterrey and Victoria still more so. Both Scott's letter and Taylor's reply were greatly delayed. Scott knew that Taylor had already been deeply angered because Marcy, in order to save time, had issued orders directly to Patterson for the occupation of Victoria instead of sending them through Taylor's headquarters. But he had only a limited time to spend on the niceties of military courtesy and was presently compelled to issue his orders over Taylor's head. He did what he could to palliate this rudeness by sending copies of the orders and a complete plan of his forthcoming campaign to Taylor's headquarters at Monterrey, and returned to the mouth of the Rio Grande, there to await, for what he described as "six weeks of cruel uncertainty," the arrival of ships to take his troops to their destination.

The *Washington Union* had credited Taylor with having 20,000 men. His own staff reckoned them to be 14,000, though at least one young line officer in the regulars doubted that he could put more than 10,000 into battle. With these, and his superb confidence in himself and his soldiers, he had planned to hold a line that was about 800 miles long, including his communications, with a front extending from Tampico through Victoria and Monterrey to Saltillo, in spite of reports that Santa Anna was gathering an army of 30,000 men at San Luis Potosí.

After his own fashion he had complied with Marcy's order and occupied Victoria in the state of Tamaulipas in December. In flat disobedience of instructions from Washington that he should not advance beyond Monterrey and such adjacent points as were necessary to the defense of that city, he had, immediately upon the revocation of the armistice, pushed Worth's brigade sixty-eight miles southwestward to occupy Saltillo, a city of 20,000 inhabitants and the capital of the state of Coahuila. During his correspondence with Scott he had been distracted by the necessity of supervising the Victoria movement and at the same time guarding against a false alarm of an advance by Santa Anna against Worth's exposed position.

But early in January he saw to the departure of Twiggs's regulars and Patterson's and Quitman's volunteers over the two hundred miles of atrocious mountain mule tracks to Tampico, which the Mexicans had evacuated and the navy had occupied in November without firing a shot. Worth's brigade marched back to Camargo and so down the river to await its transports at Point Isabel. Victoria was abandoned to Urrea's cavalry, who swooped down from the mountains to make the inhabitants pay dearly for their collaboration with the invader.

"I must ask you," Scott had written to Taylor, "to abandon Saltillo and make no detachments, except for reconnaisances and immediate defense, much beyond Monterrey." It was an order — as Scott thought orders should be phrased between generals and gentlemen. But Taylor wrote Marcy that he considered it no more than advice and replied to Scott that he would "do no such thing without orders to that effect from proper authority." Instead, he pushed still farther southward, threaded the defile of La Angostura, and by Sunday, February 14, had established his camp at the hacienda of Agua Nueva, seventeen miles out on the Saltillo road to

San Luis Potosí, where, he said, he would have more room to train his troops.

At the same time he was appealing to high heaven to witness how he had been robbed of his army and exposed to ruin by an administration that would stop at nothing to gain a victory at the next election. But actually Scott had left him with between 6,000 and 7,000 volunteers and about 800 regulars to maintain a purely defensive position. For in November General John Ellis Wool, with what was known in Washington as the Army of the Center, had arrived at Monclova in the state of Coahuila, had advanced to Parras, 110 miles west of Saltillo, as soon as the armistice was terminated, and had been placed under Taylor's command.

Wool had left San Antonio late in September, crossed the Rio Grande at Presidio del Rio Grande, and marched eight hundred miles over deserts and mountains. His force had set out as a heterogeneous, half-rebellious collection of individualists. But Wool was a martinet. He had fought at Queenstown Heights and Plattsburg in the War of 1812. It was he who would save Fortress Monroe from the Confederacy in 1861. And he had enough regulars with him on this occasion to enforce discipline to the point of compelling every man in his command to shave every day, whether he was old enough to raise a beard or not. When Taylor called them in to Saltillo to replace Worth's brigade, they came in four days, covering thirty-five miles in one march, though they brought with them 350 wagons laden with sixty days' provisions, 400,000 rounds of small-arms ammunition, and 200 for their cannon. They had not been in action, but almost five months of hardship had seasoned and toughened them, and Taylor sent them to his advance position at Agua Nueva.

Their arrival gave him a strength of about 4,650 at that place. His regulars comprised two companies each of the 1st and 2nd Dragoons, and Bragg's, Thomas W. Sherman's, and John M. Washington's batteries — fifteen guns in all. The volunteers were the 1st Kentucky Cavalry, 1st Arkansas Cavalry, 2nd Kentucky Infantry, 2nd and 3rd Indiana Infantry,

1st and 2nd Illinois Infantry — all of which had profited from months of drilling and association with regulars but were still to be tested in action — and the veterans of the Monterrey campaign: the Mississippi Rifles and the two companies of Texas Rangers.

Taylor was to be bitterly criticized in administration circles for exposing this small force to defeat by the overwhelming numbers that Santa Anna was gathering at San Luis Potosí; but, granted the validity of his confidence in his men and his estimate of his enemy, his reasoning was not unsound. Saltillo was the key of all that country. He who held Saltillo commanded not only the road to San Luis Potosí, the only road from the north to Mexico City that was practicable for wagons and guns, but also the roads eastward to Victoria and westward to Chihuahua. If he abandoned Saltillo, he must retire to Monterrey, where he would be besieged; the population of the surrounding country would rise in arms with the return of the Mexican army; his communications, uncertain at best, would be destroyed along with the little garrisons that defended them; and he would be starved into surrender. To retire, moreover, would be to expose to Santa Anna the little force under Colonel Doniphan that had left Santa Fe in December with the purpose of joining Wool in his attack on Chihuahua. It had made an easy prize of El Paso and now, though only nine hundred strong and encumbered with more than three hundred wagons and as many civilians, should be not far from its objective.

On the other hand, if Taylor remained where he was or, to be exact, fell back a few miles to fight where the Saltillo road came down from the hacienda of Buena Vista to the Angostura Pass, the Mexicans would be compelled to attack him as they emerged from their three-hundred-mile march across the desert from San Luis Potosí without either the time or the opportunity to recuperate from its hardships. Taylor, however, was convinced that Santa Anna would not move against him at all, a conviction that Scott shared with him. For the messenger who had been entrusted with copies of Scott's orders to Taylor's troops and Scott's letter describing to Taylor his projected campaign had been ambushed and murdered, and it seemed unlikely that Santa Anna was not by this time well aware of Scott's intentions. In that case he would waste no time on Taylor, they reasoned, but would hasten at once to oppose the new invasion on the beach at Vera Cruz.

Down at Tampico Scott pooh-poohed the anxiety for Taylor's safety that numerous rumors of Santa Anna's advance northward raised among his former troops as they waited for their transports. "Men of straw!" he scoffed. "Men of straw!" But the sagacious young Meade saw it otherwise: let Santa Anna strike and annihilate Taylor, and Scott would have to abandon the Vera Cruz enterprise and speed to the defense of the Rio Grande frontier.

Such, in fact, was Santa Anna's intention. To him it may well have seemed that the destruction of Taylor's army would end the war. The Mexico City newspapers were printing accounts of strong speeches by Daniel Webster and others against its continuation. One editor even believed that the peace party in the United States would "pronounce" against President Polk before very long. And Santa Anna had need to draw encouragement from any source where he could find it. Since his reception at San Luis Potosí in October, with its flags and flowers, bells, and salutes of cannon, his support had become lukewarm. Enough of his intrigue with Polk had become known to cause his patriotism to be suspected. The northern states of Mexico hated him for his treatment of them in the past, and throughout the country the Federalists were against him. The newspapers attacked him with increasing bitterness as time went on. He lacked money and could get little by legitimate means.

But he worked with enormous energy and surprising success. He established factories for the manufacture of uniforms, shops for the repair of arms. By January he had built up an army of twenty-one thousand men, with seventeen guns that ranged in size from 8-pounder field-pieces to 24-pounder siege guns. His cavalry numbered six thousand and were, as was usual in the Mexican armies, excellent. All in all, it was the best-equipped and most resolute army that Mexico had put in the field in this war. Among the officers, however, all the old names appeared once more. At first Santa Anna had determined to court-martial Ampudia and some others for their conduct at Monterrey, but he had finally decided to accept at its face value that accomplished liar's report of what had happened there and had placed them again at the head of divisions and brigades.

On January 23 he set the mint to coining for his military chest ninety-eight bars of silver of which he had made forcible seizure. Five days later he began his advance, with eighteen thousand men, himself in a coach drawn by eight mules and followed by his customary entourage of fighting-cocks and women, and on February 17 his troops began to arrive at La Encarnación, a hacienda about fifty miles south of Saltillo and thirty miles from Agua Nueva. His cavalry thoroughly screened this movement. He had taken every precaution to keep any word of it from reaching his enemy. Nobody was permitted to go to Saltillo unless he had a pass bearing Santa Anna's own signature. But had he known the spirit that prevailed in the American army he might have spared himself the trouble.

Late in January two parties of Kentucky cavalry, one of which included Captain Cassius M. Clay, whom Lincoln was to make United States Minister to Russia in 1861, had been captured at La Encarnación, all of them sound asleep in the disregard of discipline and contempt for their adversaries that were general among the American volunteers.

There seems to have been little if any other scouting by Taylor's troops until several days later: such was his disbelief of, or indifference to, numerous and persistent rumors of Santa Anna's approach. A remark to the *New York Herald's* correspondent at Agua Nueva epitomized his feeling: "Let them come; damned if they don't go back a good deal faster than they came."

But back at Monterrey, where, with his usual care for his bases, he had garrisoned both town and citadel with eight hundred veterans of the 1st Ohio and 1st Kentucky regiments, there was less confidence. They, too, heard the rumors, and they lacked the inspiring presence of their general. By mid-February nobody undressed or even took off his boots at night, for enemy signal fires blazed on the mountaintops; General Urrea, with two thousand cavalry, fifteen hundred infantry, and a large body of rancheros under the command of their old enemy Canales, was said to have turned Taylor's position by way of the Tula Pass, west of Victoria, and to be advancing against the American line of communications, on which the 2nd and 3rd Ohio and the 1st Indiana regiments, which garrisoned Marín, Ceralvo, Punta Aguda, Mier, and Camargo, seemed likely to become his easy prey.

Still more disquieting was Monterrey itself, as the lately ingratiating inhabitants turned sullen or surly and from day to day more and more of them took their quiet departure. Schools, shops, and houses were closed. The streets became empty and silent. By February 22 the city had become like a city of the dead. The garrison moved all public property to the citadel and in their turn built barricades around the Plaza Mayor. Couriers ceased to arrive either from Taylor or from the north. On the 23rd an officer on the mountaintop south of the city heard the faint sound of two cannon shots from the direction of Saltillo. A sharp-eared sentinel at the citadel heard them, too. But according to the latest reports, Taylor's army had been fifty miles away by air line, eighty by road. Could it be that he was falling back and had been compelled to fight to make good his retreat?

CHAPTER VII

Victories Dear and Cheap

§1

IF THOSE TWO cannon shots that were heard at Monterrey on February 23 were not the product of the strained nerves of the listeners there, it was strange that more of them were not audible. For all that day the guns had thundered from the Angostura defile back to the hacienda of Buena Vista. Once the heavier pieces that guarded Saltillo had joined in. Nature's thunder swelled the chorus; lightning flashed above the battlefield, rain and hail poured down. But the firing did not cease.

On February 21 May and his dragoons, who had been scouting to the eastward, rode into Agua Nueva with information that Santa Anna's cavalry division under General Vicente Miñon was at La Hedionda, only twenty miles away, whence by mountain roads it could assail the American rear. McCulloch's Rangers reported the Mexicans in great force at La Encarnación, and tall dust clouds on the roads to the southward showed that the enemy was not far behind the news of his advance.

Taylor could not fight where he was. There was a strong position a little to the south, but it could be easily turned by a road that came in to Agua Nueva from the east. He immediately ordered Wool to destroy such of the stores accumulated at Agua Nueva as could not be removed and on the 22nd fell back twenty miles to the Angostura defile and the clay-roofed buildings of the sheep ranch of Buena Vista about a mile to the north of it. Here the mountains closed in on a dull gray plateau studded with cactus and Spanish bayonet and intersected by deep ravines in such a way as to give his army at least a fighting chance against the greatly superior numbers that were evidently advancing to attack him.

It was a regrettable movement to be compelled to make, discouraging to troops that had never been tried in battle, this retirement in the face of the enemy, with the smoke of their burning supply dumps rising behind them. But if they made it with more than the necessary haste, their bands played them up the long road with the strains of *Hail Columbia;* "Honor to Washington" was the password in recognition of the day; and while the Mexican troops spread out below them, they took their positions with high confidence that what their compatriots had done at Resaca and Monterrey they could do here, though they knew that they were outnumbered three to one and that Miñon's cavalry had already been seen behind them.

A combination of ravine and mountain made their right too strong for any serious attempt upon it. In the center, at La Angostura itself, where the road threaded the defile, five guns of Washington's battery grinned above a ditch and parapet with an impassable network of ravines on its right and on its left a bold eminence that was hastily fortified. But thence the line stretched away for three thousand yards to the mountains, and there lay the position's weakness. For if the enemy could break through there, he could sweep along the margin of the plateau and assail the Americans in flank and rear, and Taylor, after providing for a sufficient reserve and a small guard for his train, which was parked at Buena Vista, lacked troops enough to hold the plateau and the adjacent mountain slopes with adequate strength.

To Santa Anna, however, who had misinterpreted the signs of the Americans' hurried departure from Agua Nueva and came tearing up at the head of 2,500 cavalry with the idea of overwhelming a disorganized enemy by mere weight of numbers, the position looked too strong. Like Pico in California he recalled Thermopylæ — only the enemy seemed to have the part of "General Leonidas" in this situation. But attack he must. For although he had come through the arid waste with 15,000 of the 18,000 troops with which he had set out from San Luis Potosí, he was in almost immediate need of supplies. McCulloch, who had sneaked close enough to the Mexican camp on the morning of the 21st to be able to listen to the reading of the orders for the day, reported that the Mexican troops had been told they must take their food from the enemy, that their general had none to give them.

To gain time for the arrival and deployment of the rest of his forces Santa Anna sent his surgeon general to Taylor under a flag of truce to inform him in the name of God and Liberty that resistance was hopeless, since he was surrounded by an army of 20,000 men, and to offer him the opportunity to surrender on liberal terms. The offer was, of course, refused — orally by Taylor in language that delighted those of his soldiers who were within earshot, and in writing by Bliss in parliamentary form. For the waiting Americans the hours dragged while the Mexican forces took up their positions for attack. Finally, late in the afternoon, a howitzer boomed its signal from the enemy lines, and off to the left the Mexican light infantry under Ampudia advanced against the dismounted troopers from Kentucky and Arkansas and the rifle companies that held the slope of the mountain. They made little progress, but even after darkness had fallen the troops on the road could see the sparkle of the contending musketry.

Taylor, satisfied that the able and energetic Wool could be relied upon to deal with the situation during his absence, and concerned as always for the safety of his base, rode back to Saltillo, taking with him the Mississippi Rifles and the 2nd Dragoons. For he had left only four companies of Illinois volunteers, with two 24-pounders in an unfinished redoubt, to defend the city, and he did not underrate the reports he had received of Miñon's cavalry. He spent the night at Saltillo, strengthened the garrison with two companies of the Mississippians, and, marching back with the rest of them and the dragoons next morning, arrived on the battlefield in the very nick of time to prevent a crushing defeat.

That night of February 22 was cold and drizzly. While President Polk at Washington was squiring the Vice President's lady at supper at the Birthnight Ball, the soldiers on the plateau and along the road between La Angostura and Buena Vista huddled together for warmth under their blankets, without tents or fuel for fires. With the coming of daylight there was a grand parade in the Mexican lines to the music of the massed bands of the entire army. A military Mass was celebrated, and priests in gorgeous vestments blessed the troops as they marched into action. On the American side there was an issue of fresh flints and ammunition. There the devotions, of which there were doubtless many among the untried volunteers, were strictly private.

The Mexicans assailed the American center only to be driven back by the fire of Bragg's guns on the mountain to the right, by Washington's at the defile, and by the musketry of the troops supporting them. Ampudia renewed the attack on the mountain slope on the left, while between La Angostura and the mountain two full divisions of Mexican infantry debouched upon the plateau, formed column of brigades, and advanced at parade step, their belts white with pipe clay, polished arms and brazen buckles flashing, and a band playing their national anthem.

Three of Washington's guns and three hundred and sixty men of the 2nd Indiana, who were the first to meet them, opened fire at a hundred yards and — such was the effect of musket cartridges charged with a bullet and three buckshot each — brought them to a stand. For half an hour the Indianians, though enfiladed by five Mexican cannon, not only held their ground but were about to advance when their colonel, appalled by their losses — ninety of them had fallen dead or wounded — ordered: "Cease fire — retreat."

What followed corresponded more closely than most battles do to the prophet Isaiah's opinion that "every battle of the warrior is with confused noise and garments rolled in blood." The retreat quickly degenerated into a rout. Of the guns one was lost — every man of its crew and every horse of its team either killed or wounded — and the rest were saved only with great difficulty. The 2nd Illinois, which was echeloned in the rear of the Indianians, its flank uncovered by their flight, had to retire and change front. The troops on the mountain, cut off from their comrades, could only fall back and, chased by Ampudia's men and Mexican cavalry, which now swept along the base of the mountains, were fortunate if they reached safety at Buena Vista, three miles from where they had begun to fight. "One charge more!" the Mexicans were shouting when Taylor, about nine o'clock, arrived upon the field.

To almost any other general the battle would have appeared to be lost. His line was broken, his whole position outflanked, his rear in immediate danger. By rising in his stirrups he could see the glitter of Mexican lances on the Saltillo road behind him. But the arrival of a thousand regulars would not have done so much to save the day as did the sight of his imperturbable countenance as he rode forward to the high ground to the southeast of the defile. During the weary weeks of boredom and homesickness since Monterrey, while rumors of peace and going home alternated from day to day with stories of Mexican advances in overwhelming numbers, his men had come to swear by him. They called him "the Old Man," and loved him for his easygoing ways, his dislike of military pomp and ceremony, his "old oil cap," dusty green coat, and "frightful" trousers, his slouching seat in the saddle, and the manly tears they had seen him shed at Ridgely's funeral. Scott's stripping him of his regulars and battle-tried volunteers had made them his ardent partisans.

When he had passed, the fugitives from the mountain turned on their pursuers and, with the little guard of the wagon train, blasted them from the walls of the hacienda. The dragoons and mounted Kentuckians routed the cavalry that followed, sent part of them flying over the western ridge and the rest back whence they came. The Mississippians, their red shirttails flapping outside their white duck pantaloons, went against Ampudia's men and, assisted by about half of

"OLD ROUGH AND READY"

General Zachary Taylor in the field. From an engraving by Wellstood of a painting by Alonzo Chappel, as reproduced in Battles of the United States, *by Henry B. Dawson (1858)*

THE BATTLE OF BUENA VISTA, FEBRUARY 22, 1847

From a lithograph of a painting by Carl Nebel, as reproduced in The War between the United States

the 2nd Indiana men who had rallied under their lieutenant colonel, drove them from the field. The 2nd Kentucky, backed by guns from Bragg's and Sherman's batteries, reinforced the hard-pressed 2nd Illinois. They were played upon by a strong Mexican battery manned by the San Patricio Corps of American deserters, but between them they sent a large part of the enemy's heavy column of attack reeling back to the mountains, and with it went Santa Anna himself, whose horse had been killed under him.

The remainder of the Mexican column swept onward. It might capture Buena Vista and the train or join Miñon and seize Saltillo. Taylor sent against it the Mississippians and the 3rd Indiana, which had been held in reserve at the defile. The Mexicans — magnificent cavalry, all blowing plumes and fluttering pennons — charged them gallantly, making small circles in the air with their shining lance-points as they came. But a volley stopped them, and the Indianians with their bayonets, the Mississippians with their eighteen-inch bowie knives, fell upon them, tore many from their saddles, and sent the rest galloping to the rear.

Now it was that the rain came down, the thunder rolled. But the American guns kept firing, blasting the dense masses of the broken foe that huddled at the foot of the mountains until it seemed that they must either surrender or be annihilated. Mexican officers galloped up to Taylor and asked in Santa Anna's name what the American general wanted. Taylor sent Wool forward under a white flag to seek an explanation of the amazing query, only to return when the Mexican guns continued to fire. It was a simple ruse, but it served. For in the interval, in which the American artillery had ceased firing, the cornered enemy had slipped swiftly away to shelter behind the San Patricio battery.

A golden opportunity had been lost, but it appeared to Taylor that something might be retrieved by an attack on troops that must still be shaken. He ordered the 1st Illinois to charge them. The Mexicans, however, met the attack firmly. He sent the 2nd Illinois and the 2nd Kentucky to

support it. Two of Bragg's guns and two of Sherman's under
George Henry Thomas, who was to rob Bragg of the fruits
of his victory at Chickamauga, galloped into the fray. But
now over the rim of the ravine on the attacking Americans'
right poured a storm of Mexican infantry. In that quiet interval Santa Anna not only had extricated his troops from
the trap against the mountain but had assembled every available man and gun for what he meant to be a crushing final
blow.

Under it the regiments from Illinois and Kentucky broke
and fled. Their colonels fell fighting, sword in hand. For this
time the Mexicans shot straight and low. The right wing
swept on toward the American center, where there was next
to nothing to meet it. On their left the Mexicans, pausing
only here and there to kill the wounded and plunder the dead,
poured in a torrent after the broken regiments down a broad
ravine that led to the road below Washington's battery at
the defile.

But by this time the rest of Bragg's and Sherman's batteries were coming down from the north, their weary horses
galloping under whip and spur. Unsupported, they swung
into action with the muzzles of their guns a mere few yards
from the charging enemy. Behind them, at a run, came the
Mississippians and the men of the 3rd Indiana, with Jefferson Davis, wounded but still in the saddle, at their head, and
fell upon the Mexican right flank and rear. At the defile
Washington's gunners let the fugitives pass, then blasted
their swarming pursuers with such a storm of grape shot that
young Lew Wallace, who visited the ground three days later,
wrote in his old age that not even in the Civil War had he
seen evidence of such carnage as that ravine presented: "the
dead lay in the pent space body on body, a blending and in-
terlacement of parts of men as defiant of the imagination as
of the pen."

And all the while old Taylor sat there on Old Whitey, a
shining mark for every Mexican gun and marksman, his
arms folded, one leg hooked negligently over the pommel of

his saddle, though one bullet ripped the coat across his breast and another tore through the inside of his left sleeve above the elbow. If he did not say, as the story ran about the country afterward: "Give them a little more grape, Mr. Bragg," it was: "Double shot your guns and give them hell!" For he was within easy speaking-distance of Bragg's guns when they went into action. And when the Kentuckians rallied, he rose in his stirrups, shouting: "Hurrah for old Kentuck! That's the way to do it. Give 'em hell, damn 'em!"

Under such a leader infantry that simply did not know when it had been thrice beaten and artillery that moved with the speed of cavalry, fought with the recklessness of skirmishers, and fired two hundred and fifty rounds per gun in a single battle were too much for even the resolute army of Santa Anna. They had been fighting since daylight. It was after four in the afternoon when the Mexicans launched their last attack. By five their heavy masses were reeling back into the great ravine from which they had emerged.

The battle was won, though the victors did not dare believe so. They had lost 673 in killed and wounded out of a total strength of 4,757, and those who remained unhurt were ready to drop in their tracks from fatigue. The Mississippi companies that had been left at Saltillo marched back to Buena Vista that evening with the good news that an attack on the city by Miñon's cavalry had been completed routed. But Taylor spent the night wondering whether the Mexicans were turning his flank under cover of the darkness or organizing another frontal attack for the morning, and Wool went about beating exhausted officers with the flat of his sword in his efforts to prepare for either eventuality. For the Mexican campfires burned in undiminished numbers and their mounted patrols kept moving in front of the American outposts. When daylight came and, with it, evidence that the enemy was in full retreat, the two generals fell into each other's arms.

Some 1,800 Mexican dead and wounded lay among the cactus and chaparral on the battlefield. But how thoroughly the enemy had been defeated became evident only when the American cavalry pushed forward to find the road south of Agua Nueva strewn with the debris of a demoralized army and La Encarnación filled with wounded who had been abandoned there. It had been, however, as Wellington said of Waterloo, "the nearest run thing you ever saw in your life." There was only one regiment in Taylor's army that had not turned its back to the enemy at one time or another during the battle. Of the strength he had possessed at Agua Nueva ten days before, he had lost close to fifteen per cent. Once more, as at Monterrey, the loss among the officers had been shocking. And defeat would have meant mere ruin, for Urrea's cavalry were sweeping through the country northward, wrecking supply trains and driving the garrisons at Marín, Ceralvo, and Punta Aguda to seek hard-won safety at Monterrey.

Ten days after the battle, conditions in the rear were such that the *Picayune's* messenger had to make a detour of five hundred miles to bring the news of the victory to Camargo, and the bearer of Taylor's official dispatches was forced to travel with a strong convoy that had to fight hard to reach its destination. It was more than a month before Washington heard of the victory. But down at Vera Cruz, where Scott's army was by that time preparing to bombard the city, word came in about three weeks that "Old Wooden Leg's" army had been "licked up like salt" at Buena Vista, and the trenches rang with the cheering.

§2

Scott had finally sailed from the Brazos on February 15. He still lacked most of the ordnance and supplies, many of the troops, and about half of the surfboats — the infantry landing craft of that day — that he had asked for and been promised. But if he were to take Vera Cruz and march into the interior before the yellow-fever season began, it was more than time for him to go. Owing to a misunderstanding between him and Jesup on the one hand and Marcy on the other and to a dearth of ships and sailors at New Orleans, he lacked transports, and when they came, they were mostly little schooners and brigs that were hardly seaworthy, and a succession of northers kept them pitching "like mad" on that "terrible coast" for days before the troops could be crowded into them.

Meanwhile the regiments that had marched across the mountains from Victoria enjoyed at Tampico recreations that seemed fairly metropolitan after their long months in the interior. In order to assemble an army large enough to drive Taylor beyond the Rio Grande, Santa Anna had withdrawn the garrison from Tampico, and ships of Commodore Conner's squadron had captured the place in the previous November without firing a shot. The town was clean and attractive, the inhabitants not unfriendly to the "Llanquies," as they called the invaders. American enterprise followed the flag, as it had done at Matamoros, and to the pleasures of the Mexican cafés, shops and dance halls and the society of a hospitable foreign colony were soon added those of an American theater and an American newspaper.

Officers and men alike, however, chafed at the inaction forced upon them by the want of transports. They could have captured Vera Cruz in the time they were kept waiting, they believed. They were disgusted at what they learned through the Mexican newspapers of Daniel Webster's speeches against the war and were pleased by Senator Crittenden's support of it. They were eager to march to the rescue of two hundred Louisiana volunteers who were shipwrecked near Tuxpán, and when the transports finally arrived, but without space for the horses of the Tennessee cavalry, the men voted unanimously to leave their beloved animals to be sent after them rather than risk losing the chance to fight.

As a rendezvous of the expedition, which was gathered from points that ranged all the way from Tampico along the Gulf coast and on up the Atlantic seaboard to New York, Scott named the islands of Lobos, which lie about fifty miles south of Tampico and a hundred and seventy north of his objective. Northers made the voyage difficult. It was miserable for some troops who, crowded into little ships from Mobile and still farther away, were on short rations of food and water before they reached their destination. The new regiments were composed of volunteers who had answered the call in November. Some still had no uniforms. They were unseasoned in mind and body for what they were called upon to suffer. Seasickness raged among them. The risk of collision and shipwreck, often only narrowly avoided, added terror to their misery.

In the broad safe anchorage at Lobos, however, their spirits revived. They were put ashore on the low sandy islands, where the water, though warm and brackish, was at least drinkable, and set to drilling and clearing the brushwood from their camping-grounds, while each day more and more ships arrived, until by February 27 a hundred lay waiting for Scott's signal to sail. They embarked singing:

> *We are bound for the shores of Mexico,*
> *And there, Uncle Sam's soldiers, we will land, ho, ho!*

But Scott still delayed, expecting daily the arrival of the vessels that carried his siege train and supplies, and one bored shipload of Pennsylvanians passed resolutions in which they demanded to be sent either to "the seat of war" or home.

It was March 3 before the expedition, though still without its siege guns, finally set sail. The steamer *Massachusetts*, with the red-centered blue flag of the Commander-in-Chief at her main truck and Scott in full uniform towering bareheaded on her quarterdeck, led the way amid the cheers of the soldiers on the ships that followed her. A norther sent them flying southward so fast that in the afternoon two days later the cruisers of Conner's squadron off Vera Cruz sighted their topsails. Presently soldiers who were not too seasick could count the sixteen domes that rose above the long white wall of the City of the True Cross and observe the dark sixty-

WINFIELD SCOTT

Commander-in-Chief of the Armies of the United States, at the period of his commanding in Mexico. From an engraving of a painting by Alonzo Chappel, as reproduced in Battles of the United States, *by Henry B. Dawson (1858)*

THE NAVAL BATTERY AT THE SIEGE OF VERA CRUZ, MARCH 1847

From a lithograph of a painting by Carl Nebel, as reproduced in The War between the United States and Mexico, by George Wilkins Kendall (1851)

foot ramparts of San Juan de Ulloa frowning upon the reef-infested waters that surrounded them.

By the evening of the next day the whole fleet, now numbering two hundred sail, lay snugly behind the island of Anton Lizardo, within twelve miles of its objective. On the decks of the various ships the regimental bands played such favorites as *Love Not, Some Love to Roam, Alice Gray*, and *Oft in the Stilly Night*. Ammunition and three days' rations were issued, and swift boats sped from ship to ship with orders for the landing, which was planned for the next day.

§3

The officers and men of Commodore Conner's squadron — the Home squadron officially — were delighted by the arrival of the expedition. Some of the ships had escorted it through Mexican waters. For almost a year now they had maintained the blockade along that dangerous coast, scorched by the burning suns of summer and in the winter chilled by northers whose sudden onslaught had sent more than one of the smaller vessels to the bottom. Some of the ships had lain off Galveston in company with French and British men-of-war in the days when the Texan Republic was coquetting with the idea of a European protectorate. Some had guarded Taylor's little force in its voyage to Corpus Christi and had watched while the Mexicans set the customhouse and other buildings burning at Point Isabel to keep them from falling into American hands on the eve of Palo Alto.

Thanks to the labors of Secretary Bancroft and Secretary Upshur, it was an admirable squadron to have been assembled by the goverment of a young, commercial, and aggressively peaceful nation. In it the fine paddle-wheel *Mississippi* and the propeller *Princeton* represented the recent application of steam to naval warfare. There were five frigates and five twenty-gun sloops-of-war, and there had been five ten-gun brigs until the winter storms wrecked three of them. The armament was reasonably up to date; the recently invented shell guns and smooth bores of large caliber were on many of

the gun decks. Ship for ship the United States had nothing
to be ashamed of in comparing them with the British, French,
and Spanish warships that lay in observation at anchor off
the near-by island of Sacrificios.

The grinding service against the slave traders on the coast
of Africa and the suppression of the pirates in the Caribbean
had kept American naval standards high during the thirty
years since the Treaty of Ghent. The crews were well disciplined and efficient, and a group of able and enlightened officers was rising to replace the tarry old stick-and-string commanders who clung to ancient abuses of the service as they
did to everything else that belonged to the glorious days of
Hull and Decatur.

This blockading duty was bitter hard, however, and it had
been necessary to hang one man at the yardarm for striking
an officer. Since the ships were cut off from every near-by
port and Congress in its wisdom had provided neither store-
ships nor tenders, the crews had to be fed on salt rations.
When these were exhausted, each ship in its turn had to sail
across the Gulf to Pensacola to replenish its supplies. There
was a good deal of scurvy and so much yellow fever on some
vessels that they had to be sent far up the Atlantic coast in
order to get rid of it. Many died and went to graves in the
warm sand of Anton Lizardo. The pitch in the planking of
the ships at anchor there bubbled in the summer sun. The
only recreation was to row ashore evenings and bathe in the
tepid sea. Officers smoked a quiet cigar on the beach or had
themselves rowed across to Sacrificios to call on the officers of
the foreign warships and listen to the news from Mexico that
the British officers had picked up on shooting trips on the
mainland.

Aside from the frequent northers in winter and the fierce
and sudden summer squalls, about all that broke the unend-
ing monotony were the occasional chase and capture of a
blockade-runner and the regular monthly arrival of the British mail steamer, which was exempted from the regulations of
the blockade. Each morning above the cloudbank that hid the

long blue line of the Cordilleras the snowy cone of seventeen-thousand-foot Orizaba — the Mountain of the Star — turned rose-color in the sunrise; each evening the gigantic mass of the Cofre de Perote loomed against the sunset; and all night long the lighthouse on Sacrificios glowed and darkened and glowed again.

That lighthouse, perhaps on account of the visits of the British mailboat, was kept burning for months after the establishment of the blockade and was of enormous help to Conner's ships in keeping their nightly stations. Lieutenant Raphael Semmes, in command of the ill-fated brig *Somers*, learned a lesson from it that he applied to the advantage of the Confederacy fourteen years later by destroying the lighthouses at the mouths of the Mississippi and thereby hampering the Federal blockade. On board the *Raritan* Semmes, the "rebel pirate" to be, shared a cabin with John Ancrum Winslow, whose *Kearsarge* was to sink Semmes's *Alabama* off Cherbourg in 1864, and the fact that each of them had lost his ship on this blockade drew the two men together.

They were by no means the only officers in the squadron whose names were to become famous in the war to which this war was a kind of prelude. There was Josiah Tattnall, the Tattnall of the Pieho Forts and "Blood thicker than water" ten years later. To him was to fall the invidious task of destroying his own ship, the famous *Merrimac*, in 1862. There was David Dixon Porter, who was to be all but successful in stopping Semmes's depredations on Northern commerce at their very beginning. And soon to join the squadron were David Glasgow Farragut and Franklin Buchanan, who commanded the *Merrimac* in her two battles and gave Farragut the fight of his life in Mobile May. Among the ships, too, were names that would have looked ominous to a seer. Conner's flagship, the *Cumberland*, was to be Buchanan's first victim at Hampton Roads, and the *Mississippi* was to be lost under Confederate gunfire when Farragut passed the batteries at Port Hudson.

The performance of the squadron, however, had not

matched the potential ability of its personnel. David Conner, its commander, was, like Sloat, an officer of long and successful service and of a frail constitution: he suffered severely from neuralgia. But unlike Sloat, unfortunately, he clung to his command as long as he was permitted to do so, and contented himself with reducing blockade-running to a minimum and making a few half-hearted attacks on Mexican ports that would have been excellent sources of fresh provisions and water and in which the few and small vessels of the little Mexican navy had taken refuge.

It was to be said for him that he lacked the light-draft gunboats and small swift steamers that were needed to negotiate the shoal water on the harbor bars of these places. But the newspaper writers at home, whose nautical experience, Conner's officers suspected, did not go beyond a few rides on high-pressure steamboats on inland rivers, kept asking: "Why does not the Navy do Something?" The administration grew concerned about the "noise" they were making and sent Matthew Calbraith Perry, who would open that Box of Pandora, the Hermit Kingdom of Japan, in 1853, to assume command upon Conner's retirement.

In October, acting as vice commodore, Perry had taken the town of Frontera on the Tabasco River. It was he who had occupied Tampico, and by the capture of Laguna del Carmen off the coast of Yucatán in late December he had closed an important supply route to the Mexicans and given the American naval officers a place where they could get their linen washed in something less abrasive to their skins than sea water.

The necessary light-draft vessels and small steamers had arrived by this time. Others had been captured in their ports of refuge, and in the little steamer *Petrita*, late of the Mexican service, Scott, accompanied by his generals and those able young engineer officers of his, Lee, Joseph E. Johnston, Beauregard, and Meade, set out on March 7 to reconnoiter the landing-place that Conner had selected, the adjacent coast, and the fortress of San Juan de Ulloa.

To approach the fortress was a foolhardy proceeding in the opinion of the younger officers. Conner had been instructed to make no attempt against it, and even "Old Bruin," as Perry was called in the service, had no inclination to attack it, although certain newspapers at home, unmindful of the difference between Conner's frigates and the line-of-battle ships with which the French had reduced it eight years before, had urged that it be taken. It had, moreover, been greatly strengthened since the French attack, and a number of modern guns had been mounted in its water batteries. At a range of a mile and a half these opened fire on the *Petrita*. One shell went over her, one short. The next was fairly in the middle of the bracket, but by good luck burst high above the little vessel, or the expedition might have been brought to a sudden stop then and there by the loss of its commander and every one of its senior officers.

§4

The reconnaissance caused no change to be made in the choice of the landing-place. It was a stretch of open surf-beaten beach opposite the island of Sacrificios and about three miles to the southwest of Vera Cruz, beyond, or at, the extreme range of the most powerful guns of the fortress. High sandhills commanded it, and enemy troops were seen moving among the chaparral behind them. But there was no better place available, though its exposure to the prevailing storms of the season was demonstrated at once by a norther that made it necessary to postpone the landing for three days.

On the 9th, however, the large warships, to which the troops had been transferred for this operation, took up their assigned positions off the shore. The light-draft gunboats anchored in a line in front of them to cover the attack with their fire. From the ships the troops of the First Division, 4,500 in number, descended into sixty-five surfboats, each of which was manned by five or six sailors under a naval officer, and the *Princeton*, with the boats towed behind her in two long columns, headed for the shore.

Across the water, at Sacrificios, the rails and rigging of the British mail steamer and the foreign men-of-war were thick with spectators, for there had never before been a landing of such size under such conditions. The French had put nine thousand men on a beach in Algiers in 1830, but that had been in a sheltered bay with no enemy at hand, and they had lost between thirty and forty men in doing it.

As the water shoaled, the *Princeton* cast off her tows. The boats formed line and raced for the beach. When they grounded, the troops, with Worth and his staff at their head, leaped into the surf, formed line on the sand, charged the sandhills, and topped them with a cheer. There was no opposition save for a single futile shot from a gun that was found abandoned among the chaparral next day. Shells from the gunboats drove off a force of about three hundred cavalry that hovered in the distance. By sunset the Stars and Stripes were flying above the beachhead. The volunteers followed Worth's division, while the bands played *Yankee Doodle*, *Hail Columbia*, and *The Star-Spangled Banner*. Twiggs's division landed next, and at ten o'clock that night ten thousand troops had been put on shore, with two days' provisions, and without the loss of a man.

Next morning, in spite of ambuscades and the threat of a charge by enemy lancers, Pillow's brigade of volunteers seized the high hill of Malebrán behind the beachhead. Quitman, Shields, and Twiggs pushed in succession inland and northward. But the marching was hard, up, down, and between considerable hills of heavy sand, in stifling heat, and exposed to continual sniping from the dense undergrowth and desultory shelling from the castle and the bastions of the city. It was four days after the landing that Twiggs's division completed the investment by reaching the sea with the Mounted Rifles at the village of Vergara, two miles northwest of the Mexico Gate on the road to Jalapa, though the distance from the landing-place was only about five miles in an air line.

The army now held a line about seven miles in length on the summits of a chain of sandhills that faced the city at a distance varying from a mile to a mile and a half and provided the camps with excellent protection from the enemy's active and accurate artillery. The aqueduct, the city's principal source of water, was cut; trenches were dug; enemy outposts were driven in; and natty Lieutenant Beauregard tore his uniform to rags in the thorny scrub as he located advance positions suitable for siege batteries.

But now followed days of maddening delay. Northers slowed the debarkation, hurling huge waves up the beach to work havoc among the wagonloads of shells, the tentage, the mess-bags, and the barrels of bread that were stacked at the foot of the sandhills. Transports were driven ashore with crews and soldiers clinging to their shrouds. By the end of the siege the wrecks of thirty brigs and schooners lay amid the surf. In the wreck of one vessel between one and two hundred horses were drowned.

Short of the means of land transportation to begin with, the expedition could ill spare them. And still more of its precious animals were lost through the primitive method of unloading them, which was simply to drop them into the sea and trust to their instinct of self-preservation to bring them to land. Wagons were few in number. Men went hungry in consequence and waded into the surf to salvage such windfalls as a hogshead of wine, a keg of butter, or even a box of ground pepper. Tentage could not be distributed. The wet windy nights were so bitterly cold that even tough old Twiggs complained, and when the weather was fine, the blowing sand got into everything from eyes and ears to mess kettles. Jiggers attacked the feet, sand flies every exposed portion of the body. The fleas were so multitudinous that it was wise to rub oneself all over with pork fat if one wanted an uninterrupted night's sleep.

Mounted rancheros and guerrillas on foot kept pecking away at the lines. They accomplished nothing important, but they kept the sentinels in such a state of nervousness that when Lee returned one night from scouting close to the city walls, his coat was burned by the pistol flash of an excited lad who fired before he could establish his identity. Harney, however, who went scouting with his dragoons some ten miles to the southward, had a brush with the guerrillas at the Medellin bridge, so severe that Patterson and the Tennesseans went out to help him, and the Americans lost several killed and wounded.

Meanwhile work on the lines went on unceasingly, for Scott's standards were academic, and he insisted on the proper construction of entrenchments, batteries, and magazines. Since animals were lacking, manpower had to take its place. The volunteers, though their behavior at Tampico had been such that sentinels with fixed bayonets were necessary to preserve order in the dance halls, rose to the occasion nobly. Their brethren under Taylor back at Agua Nueva had refused to degrade themselves by loading supplies, which had, in consequence, to be destroyed to prevent their falling into the hands of Santa Anna. But these men toiled day and night, carrying provisions and ammunition, building batteries, and hauling on stout wagon frames through the ankle-deep sand the seven ten-inch mortars that were all Scott had with which to begin the bombardment.

Mentally conditioned perhaps by what they had read and heard of Taylor's campaigns, even the newest regiments appear to have suffered fewer growing-pains than those that landed on Brazos Island a year earlier. The Tennesseans, heavily bearded men in oilcloth hats and gay-colored serapes, armed with rifles that were — many of them — their personal property, had been seasoned by marching across Arkansas and Texas and on by way of Victoria to Tampico. In the 1st Pennsylvania, however, which had been organized only three months before, were boys who sent their home letters to such addresses as "Three Locks above Lewistown."

There had been free fights at the election of its field officers at Pittsburgh, and its D Company, "the Killers," had been a nuisance to the police of New Orleans while the regiment was waiting for its transports there. But here all did their part.

But as it became evident that the mortar fire was not damaging the fortifications, only wrecking the city, there were murmurings among those who had been with Taylor. Had not Monterrey been taken in three days, whereas Scott had lain before Vera Cruz for more than two weeks and accomplished nothing? Worth and Twiggs urged him to take the place by storm.

According to Scott's way of thinking, however, it was not good generalship to sacrifice men where brains and gunfire would accomplish the same result. He had before him a strong fortress and a walled town strengthened by massive forts and bastions, armed with a more than adequate artillery, and held by four thousand or five thousand troops who were supported by a population confident that they would soon be relieved by an army from Mexico City and animated by a valor that was as ardent as it was ignorant. Women of every class had turned out to work on the fortifications. Every preparation was made to defend the city street by street and house by house.

Scott saw that to take it by assault without first breaching the walls would cost him between two thousand and three thousand men, whereas he had none to spare if he were going to advance into the interior, as he soon must in order to escape the yellow fever. He shrank, moreover, from the indiscriminate slaughter that would necessarily ensue upon such an attack, delivered, as it must be, under cover of darkness. But since his siege train had not even yet arrived, he had to turn to the navy for the proper artillery. It touched his professional pride to do so. He had wished to keep the siege entirely an army affair, and Perry, who had by this time succeeded Conner in command of the squadron, took full advantage of his difficulty. "Certainly, general," Perry replied to his request for heavy guns. "But I must fight them."

Three long 32-pounders and three 8-inch shell guns were hoisted out of the warships and ferried to the beach, where pairs of huge timber wheels awaited them. They weighed more than three tons apiece, and it was more than three miles to the well-concealed battery that Lee had built for them within eight hundred yards of the city wall. But sailors and fifteen hundred volunteers hauled them into position. Worked by relays of sailors from the ships, they opened fire on the 24th. It was the heaviest battery, thought Raphael Semmes, who knew his military history, that had ever been mounted in a siege. And on the next day four 24-pounders and two 8-inch mortars were added to it.

Already the bombardment had been impressive enough. Now "awful" was the word that both Scott and Lee used for it. Hitchcock called it "horrible." In reply the Mexican guns worked fast and well, but with poor luck. They blew holes in the sand big enough to bury a horse. They riddled the stone wall of the cemetery that stood near the naval battery, smashed the mortuary chapel, dug up graves, and strewed the ground about it with bones and skulls. They ripped the sandbags and rawhide facings of the embrasures. But when their shells fell inside a battery, they either failed to burst or, bursting, killed and wounded few and did little damage.

Inside the city, on the other hand, the huge American projectiles plunged through supposedly bombproof roofs, burst, and gutted the interiors and set them blazing. One, smashing through the roof of a church, killed the women and children at prayer before the altar. The ground quaked. Bells rang without human hand to swing them. And sometimes, between the explosions, the American outposts near the walls could hear shrieks and wailing. Civilians took refuge in deep mercantile storage vaults or camped in the only safe area above ground, the mole between city and castle. Great smoke clouds arose above castle and city, merged, and hung there like a thundercloud, reddened by the bursting shells and the glare of the Congreve rockets. When the moon rose, it shed a ghastly radiance over the scene. A norther blew with such force that even the line-of-battle ship *Ohio*, which had arrived at last, had to send down her upper masts and yards; but the bombardment did not slacken.

On the night of the 25th, under a flag of truce, the foreign consuls came out to ask that it cease long enough for the women and children to be evacuated. Scott refused to see them but sent them a reply reminding them that he had given ample warning and opportunity for such an evacuation before he opened fire and stating that unless the city surrendered he would open with still more guns in the morning.

Actually only about eighty soldiers had been killed or wounded, and of the civilians a hundred had been killed and an unknown number wounded. There was still plenty of ammunition and sufficient food and water to sustain life. But the whole southwest quarter of the city had been destroyed, and the morale of both garrison and inhabitants had been ruined. The morning of the 26th saw another flag of truce issue from the lofty arched gateway of Fort Santiago, which formed the southern end of the fortifications. It came from the Mexican commander this time. At midnight on the 27th articles of capitulation were signed, and the American soldiers, who had been busily making fascines to fill the moat for an assault on the breach that had been made in the western wall of the city, were set to smartening their arms and accouterments for the ceremony of surrender.

Stained, dingy, and ragged, nevertheless, from their long days and nights of labor in trench and thicket, they presented a sorry contrast to the Mexicans in smart green or blue, or in white under red pompons, who marched out to the music of their bands on the fine morning of March 29 to pile their arms between the lines of American soldiers, sailors, and marines drawn up to receive them. They were released on parole, since Scott had neither the men to guard them nor the means to feed them or to send them to the United States. But there turned out to be more than five thousand of them, including five generals, eighteen colonels, and thirty-seven lieutenant colonels, who were thus put out of action — at least, theoretically — for the rest of the war. Some 350 or 400 guns were captured, among them — ironically enough — some pieces bearing the initials W. P. F., which stood for West Point Foundry, and sixteen long 32-pounders of English make, which were the finest the American artillery officers had ever seen.

But best of all was the surrender of the strong fortress of San Juan de Ulloa along with that of the city: Scott had feared that it would have to be reduced by starvation and bombardment in a separate operation. And, thanks to his stubborn adherence to the textbook principles of siegecraft, deep trenches, soundly constructed batteries, and buried magazines covered with timber and earth, all this had been won at a cost of only nineteen killed and sixty-three wounded.

Worth's division marched into the city to the customary tunes. The Stars and Stripes went up over the strong forts of Santiago and Concepción and the grim ramparts of San Juan de Ulloa while the guns of fleet and army roared in salute. A crowd of Mexicans was hired to clear the streets of the debris and rubbish of the siege. A landing party from the squadron took over the castle and set about the hopeless task of cleansing it of the accumulated filth of centuries as another American squadron was to do sixty-seven years later. And Colonel Bankhead was sent off to Washington with evidence of the triumph: the flags of city and fortress, a whole sheaf of captured regimental colors, and twelve handsome cannon.

§5

Believing strongly in a policy of conciliation, Scott released one of the generals and thirty-seven of the other captured officers to go to Mexico City, where he believed they would exert an influence for peace. He caused ten thousand rations of bread, meat, and rice to be distributed among the poor of Vera Cruz, where his troops had anticipated his liberality by sharing their rations with the hungry soldiers of the surrendered garrison. He issued a proclamation assuring the people of security in their lives, property, religion, and trade, and made good the promise by hanging an American civilian employee for rape and sending two of his soldiers to the dungeons of San Juan de Ulloa for stealing. Such treatment by the military authorities was a welcome innovation to Mexican civilians and augured well for the Military Department of Vera Cruz, which he proceeded to organize.

The customhouse was opened. The markets were soon filled with fruits and fresh vegetables. Enterprising American newspapermen who had accompanied the army brought out the *Vera Cruz Eagle* from a Mexican printing office, using coupled *v*'s for the *w* that the Mexican alphabet lacked. Upon Scott's request that American chaplains be allowed to use some of the churches, the customary religious services were resumed. Scott accepted an invitation to attend one of them and found himself, with a large lighted taper in his hand, being led about the consecrated edifice by a gorgeous procession of ecclesiastics while his staff followed him, struggling to suppress their smiles at the predicament of their general, who had once been a presidential candidate and was likely to be one again, and was now participating in rites that were anathema to the majority of his countrymen.

He was equally happy in the impression that he had made upon his troops. They had begun the campaign knowing little about him, those from Taylor's command resentful of him, and all prepared to find him an unreasonable and petulant martinet. Even among the officers there were few whose acquaintance with him was such as to nullify his reputation as "Old Fuss and Feathers." They had expected him to insist upon the very trimming of their beards according to regulations. At a regimental dinner at Tampico a toast to his name had been received with marked coldness. But his management of the siege had changed all that. The troops, and even the officers and sailors from the fleet, who had grumbled at what they regarded as unnecessary labor on the batteries, were now quick to appreciate the care he had taken of their lives and safety in circumstances in which a Taylor or a Twiggs would have gone in for quick results and the glory that springs from "a big butcher's bill." He had, moreover, the gift of saying the right word to them at the right time, of always seeming to expect their best of them, and to the end of the campaign they gave him of their best gladly.

Difficult and petulant he was and continued to be. He would rave for minutes together at a mistake in the copying of a letter and flare up at the teller of an unwelcome truth. But he was quick to make courteous amends for his ill temper, and in great matters he was magnanimous. He knew by this time that the report of Polk's intrigue to supersede him by Benton was only too true, and the first communication that he received from the administration after the capture of Vera Cruz was Marcy's letter reprimanding him for Harney's court-martial. He "felt" these things, Hitchcock observed, but they made not the slightest difference in the performance of his duty.

He had ignored Hitchcock's action in the conflict as to seniority between Worth and Twiggs the previous spring and had made that officer his inspector general. A lack of tact could not be charged against a general who managed to obtain mutual co-operation from such an ill-assorted group of division and brigade commanders as the meticulous Worth; "Old Davy Twiggs, the Bengal Tiger"; Patterson, the Pennsylvania militia general and wealthy Philadelphia merchant; Quitman, and the other "political generals." Of these, Shields, who, like Quitman, proved himself to be an able leader, was commissioner of the Land Office and Polk's intimate friend. Pillow, whose men hated him for his harshness and arrogance and who knew so little of warfare that he was said to have ordered the ditch to be dug on the inside of the fortifications at Camargo, was a congenital troublemaker and set himself up as the President's personal representative with the army.

From such, Scott could take refuge with what he called his "little cabinet," of which Totten, his chief engineer officer, was a member. Others were Lee and Hitchcock and Lieu-

tenant Benjamin Huger, whose tardiness and inactivity were
to be blamed for Lee's failure to destroy the Federal army in
the Seven Days' Battles. Hitchcock, still reading philosophy
in his spare time, kept up a correspondence with the Reverend Theodore Parker on that subject and achieved "some of
the clearest views of Spinoza's doctrines" that he had ever
had, but they did not prevent him from being a first-rate staff
officer.

There was opportunity now to put up tents and make
Camp Washington — the name given to the whole straggling range of bivouacs outside the city walls — into what a
proper camp should be. But there was little rest for anybody.
The first week in April, which was regarded as the deadline
for the beginning of the yellow-fever season, was only three
days off when Vera Cruz surrendered. To get the army out of
the sickly Tierra Caliente at once was essential to the success
of the campaign. Immediately the need of transport became
acute. Of wagons there were only 185, although, to be sure,
3,000 were on the way, and 1,100 draft animals must, somehow, be made to do the work of seven times that number.

In the hope of supplying this deficiency Quitman's brigade
was sent overland some fifty miles to the southward to co-
operate with the Navy in the capture of the town of Alvarado.
They found the place already in American hands. The Mexican garrison had evacuated it, and the civil authorities had
surrendered it to a naval lieutenant who had been blockading
it. "Old Bruin" Perry court-martialed the young man and
sent him home in disgrace for exceeding his orders — a sentence that Polk, with his usual sense of justice where politics
were not involved, disapproved. The New York *Sun* of May 7
broke into derisive verse:

> *But not a soul were there to whip,*
> *Unless they fought a shadow. . . .*
> *And there was spoiled the pretty sport*
> *Of taking Alvarado.*

But though Quitman returned with neither mules nor laurels, he brought back a herd of four hundred or five hundred fine horses, which were right welcome, since most of the cavalry still lacked their mounts.

There was good hope of getting draft animals at Jalapa, however, and Scott started Twiggs's division and a part of the volunteers marching for that place on April 8 and 9, to the annoyance of Worth, who maintained that his seniority gave him the right to be always in the lead. It had been known for some time at Vera Cruz that Santa Anna had returned to Mexico City, and there were persistent rumors that he was about to advance against Scott with a large army. The rumors were disbelieved at American headquarters, however. It was thought there that Santa Anna had been kept too busy in quelling a revolution at the capital to be able to organize a force of any importance, and American officers and men alike looked forward to the easy occupation of "summer quarters" at Jalapa, there to await either the arrival of reinforcements or the negotiation of a peace without further fighting. After Twiggs went the rest of the volunteers and a siege train composed of six guns, of which only four were heavy. Animals to draw more could not be spared, although tentage was reduced to three tents for each company and the trains doubled back for second and third loadings.

Across the thirty miles of coastal plain the heat was terrific, the road "sandier than in New Jersey" during the first day's march and, when it turned to good macadam on Santa Anna's estate, shut in by rock cuttings and forests of palms and limes. There were many blistered feet and much diarrhea among the new troops. All Pillow's severity could not stop them from throwing away their equipment and arms, and not even the sight of the mutilated bodies of strayed comrades who had been cut off and murdered by guerrillas could keep them from straggling. The magnificent National Bridge, whose stone arches, fifty feet in height, spanned the Antigua River where the hills began, brought to many of them homesick memories of the bridge over Conestoga Creek east of

Lancester in Pennsylvania. But when word came down the line that Santa Anna was actually holding the road up front with a strong army and many guns, they gave a "huzza for the fight ahead," their sickness, hardships, and fatigue forgotten. They took a swim in the river, obtained the materials for a chicken dinner from the local inhabitants on a promise to pay for them on their return, and smartened themselves up for a dress parade that their shabby uniforms and sketchy equipment made laughable even to themselves.

§6

Santa Anna had accomplished something like a miracle in order to stand as he did at Cerro Gordo early that April, barring Scott's way with an army of 12,000 men and more than forty guns. His retreat after Buena Vista had cost him not fewer than 3,000 men. He had reached San Luis Potosí with but a comparatively small part of his army in formation. The rest of the survivors straggled in behind him as best they could, and across the desert the road was strewn with the bodies of hundreds who had died of their wounds, of hunger, or of exhaustion. But on the evidence of three captured cannon and a single stand of American colors he had convinced his countrymen that he had won a great victory.

At San Luis Potosí he learned that confusion reigned in the capital. Vice President Ferías had aroused the resistance of the Church and of all people of property by attempting to enforce drastic laws for the raising of funds to carry on the war. Moderates, Centralists, and Federalists, Santanists and Clericals fought each other in the streets and were of one mind only in their hatred of Ferías.

With his two best brigades, Santa Anna marched promptly southward. Women strewed flowers in the path of "the Victor of Buena Vista." People of various factions went out from Mexico City in their carriages as far as Querétaro to enlist his support. At Guadalupe Hidalgo they sang a *Te Deum* in honor of his defeat of Taylor on the day that Scott's mortars began to smash the houses of Vera Cruz. There were no *vivas* for him in the capital, but it was evident there that nobody else could repel the invader. He was elected President. To get rid of Ferías the office of vice president was abolished. A "substitute president" was elected to function while Santa Anna was in the field, and the clergy tendered two millions of actual money for the prosecution of the war.

Working with his usual energy to organize a new army, Santa Anna heard with fury of the fall of Vera Cruz. He had expected the place to hold out much longer, and he called the surrender disgraceful. He issued a proclamation tinged with a poetic melancholy rather than confidence: "Mexicans, do not hesitate between death and slavery. . . . Awake! A sepulcher opens at your feet. Let it at least be covered with laurels!" And on April 2, in his well-equipped campaign carriage, he set out for the new seat of war.

He had already given orders for the defense of the road to the capital, but he now discovered that little had been done to fortify the several places where it could be easily defended. From the National Bridge, where fortifications had been begun, the troops had fled on hearing that Vera Cruz had fallen. But there was an excellent position about a day's march to the westward at the ranch of Cerro Gordo. There the road, after crossing the little Río del Plan, wound upward for six or seven miles through a rocky defile and emerged on a narrow plateau only after passing between high hills from which batteries could sweep it with direct and cross fire.

At this point Santa Anna placed his army in position, certain that he had only to win a defensive battle and yellow fever would do the rest. The five-hundred-foot-deep and all but impassable ravine of the river's course secured his right. To defend his right front he built batteries on three projecting tongues of the plateau. A battery on the road itself covered the exit from the defile, and on its left the conical hill of El Telégrafo, with stone fortifications and a stone tower on its summit, presented a steep slope more than five hundred feet high to the enemy's advance. Behind this he fixed his headquarters at the Cerro Gordo ranch, established his camp, and stationed his reserves. To the left of the ranch the country was so rough that, although his chief engineer told him otherwise, he did not believe that a rabbit could get through.

Previous defeats, the fall of Vera Cruz, and some sickness had impaired the morale of the Mexican troops, though an effort had been made to whip up their fighting spirit by telling them that the Americans had sold some of the churches in Vera Cruz to Protestants, Mohammedans, and worshippers of Venus. A little more than half of them were National Guards from the capital, but 5,600 were regulars of the old army; thirty-five of their guns bore directly on the highway, which appeared to be the enemy's only avenue of approach; palisades, parapets, and abatis covered the whole front; and the ground had been cleared to afford an excellent field of fire.

It was, indeed, a position that might have been a death-trap to an army under such a general as Taylor. Twiggs was leading his division straight into it on the morning of April 12 when the Mexicans, opening fire too soon, warned him of his danger. Even so, only the opposition of Patterson prevented him from launching a headlong attack next day, although the project looked hopeless to Lieutenant U. S. Grant, and Lee called the cliff on one side "unscalable" and the ravine on the other "impassable."

Back at Vera Cruz, Scott heard with astonishment that Twiggs had encountered serious opposition. He dropped the work he was doing, and by the afternoon of Wednesday, the 14th, was at Plan del Río, the little village at the crossing of the Río del Plan, raising an old straw hat in acknowledgment of the cheers of the soldiers, who had been in more than a little fear of what Twiggs's impetuosity might lead them into.

Worth came up with a picked force of 1,600, which gave Scott a strength of 8,500 all told. But Scott devoted the next two days to a careful reconnaissance, in which Joseph Johnston was severely wounded. Lee, who had begun his scouting at the head of Wool's march and had continued it under Taylor, saved himself from capture or, more probably, death by lying motionless for hours behind a log in the rear of the Mexican position while enemy soldiers kept passing within reach of his arm to visit a near-by spring. He returned to report that he had found a way across Santa Anna's front by which the enemy's left flank could be turned and, in all probability, his retreat cut off, and on the morning of Saturday, the 17th, he began to guide Twiggs's division along it.

The going was terrible, much of the route overgrown with oak, chaparral, and cactus that had to be cleared from it, and it ran up and down over declivities so steep that the guns had to be hauled up and lowered by manpower. Twiggs, moreover, disdainful as ever of all finesse, threw away the advantage of surprise by refusing to halt the column long enough for Lee's engineers to screen with brush a short space where its march was exposed to enemy observation. Santa Anna promptly occupied in force the hill of Atalaya, which stood about five hundred yards in front of El Telégrafo and was Twiggs's first objective. Twiggs stormed it, although his orders were to wait and co-operate in the general attack that Scott had planned with meticulous care for the following morning, and he then proceeded to sacrifice ninety men in killed and wounded in an impulsive and necessarily unsupported attack on El Telégrafo.

Santa Anna, now forewarned, planted guns to protect his camp from a turning movement and strengthened and reinforced his position on El Telégrafo during the night. By the rays of a clear sunrise the Americans could see him, dressed in civilian clothes, galloping on a gray horse from point to point along his lines. The Mexican trumpets blared a challenge, and the American guns and the rocket battery, which had been sweated up to the summit of Atalaya in rainy darkness, answered them.

Again, and this time in spite of Lee's earnest remonstrance, Twiggs refused to wait for the consummation of the general plan. He knew that Shields was swinging wide to his right to come down on the Jalapa road in the rear of the whole Mexican army; one of his own brigades was advancing upon the

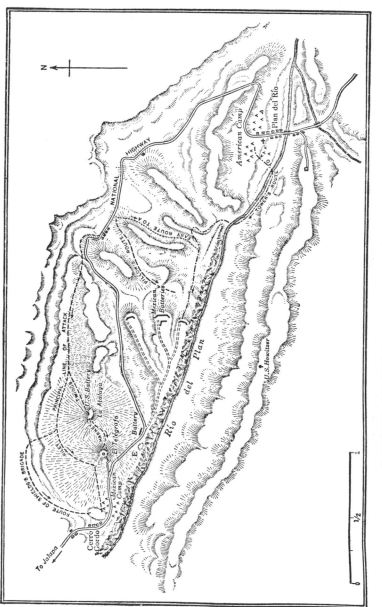

BATTLE OF CERRO GORDO, GENERAL PLAN

ranch of Cerro Gordo itself; but he deflected this to attack the left of the position on El Telégrafo and sent the 3rd and 7th Infantry and the 1st Artillery against its steep and lofty front. The Mexicans held on with tenacity. It was bayonet against bayonet at a breast work of palisades at the foot of the slope. Then the blue line moved slowly up amid brush and cactus, burst through the abatis, crossed the fire-swept cleared ground, yelling and cheering, though motionless or writhing figures marked its course, and, with the saber of the tall and reckless Harney at their head, swept over the stone wall on the crest in a welter of pistol shots, bayonet thrusts, and the blows of clubbed muskets.

Down came the red, white, and green flag from the staff on top of the stone tower. Up went the Red, White, and Blue in its place. Around swung the captured guns, with Americans at their trails, to speed the fleeing enemy with their fire. The fugitives simply overwhelmed the crack 11th Infantry and the Grenadiers whom Santa Anna hurried forward to restore the action. Riley's men plunged downhill toward the Mexican camp. And now Shields's brigade, on whose appearance the whole action was to have depended, burst up from the chaparral of the ravine beyond the camp. The enemy cannon posted there routed the leading companies and gave Shields a wound that was thought to be mortal. But the rest of his command made for the highway, and a part of Riley's captured the cannon.

Two thousand Mexican cavalry, who had been stationed on the road to deal with just such an eventuality, wheeled about and galloped for Jalapa and safety. A shout that the Yankees had seized the road swept along the Mexican lines, and after it rose the cry of "Save himself who can!" Those who could still do so followed the cavalry. Many — Santa Anna among them — went over the rim of the canyon, plunging down the two steep paths that led to the Río del Plan. Cut off from road and canyon alike, the troops at the three batteries on the Mexican right surrendered.

It was well for the American volunteers who had been sent

against that part of the Mexican line that their work was thus done for them. For Pillow, who was supposed to lead them, botched his job. He got one of his regiments badly cut up by sending it in where the enemy were strongest instead of where they were weakest. He confused his green troops by reversing their order of march, and finally — "Shot to pieces," he said — left them without a leader when a stray grapeshot found him behind a rock too far to the rear to suit his fiery Tennesseans, and wounded him in the arm.

Scott, who could expose himself to fire with a nonchalance equal to Taylor's, had sat his horse, watching the battle, under what an observer described as "a canopy of balls." He might have complained that he would have captured Santa Anna's entire army if Twiggs's charge had been held back until Shields's men had reached the highway. But, with characteristic generosity, he praised it, bubbling over to a mere lieutenant that it was "the most beautiful sight he had ever witnessed." He rode among his victorious soldiers with tears of pride and joy running down his cheeks, congratulating them on their performance more as if he had been their elder comrade than their general, and he greeted his old enemy Harney with warm friendliness.

He had good cause to rejoice. In spite of Twigg's impetuosity, few battles have worked out more nearly according to plan than Cerro Gordo. In orders issued the previous day he had stated that the enemy position would be turned "probably before 10 a.m.," and it was but a little after that hour when the dragoons and light artillery that had been held in the defile for the proper moment went thundering up the Jalapa highway in pursuit.

They chased the fleeing foe to within four miles of Jalapa, and troops who marched along that road next day found it strewn with the bodies of men and horses cut down in flight. Some of the infantry and some other guns were pushed forward a little way, but there was no sign of organized resistance, only fugitives in huddled flocks, whose rout was quickened by long-range shell fire; the day was hot, our soldiers exhausted by marching and fighting. On the field they shared their rations and the water in their canteens with the Mexican wounded, winning thereby the praise of the captured Mexican surgeons, who noted that they brought in wounded enemies with the same care that they gave to their comrades.

The American losses amounted to 30 officers and 387 men — only 64 were killed — and Robert Anderson of the artillery, with the losses at Monterrey in mind, was moved to note that "matters are managed here differently." The Mexican casualties were estimated at between 1,000 and 1,200. The prisoners numbered 3,000. Again, as at Vera Cruz, these had to be paroled. But some of the officers refused parole, among them General de la Vega, who had been captured at Resaca and exchanged, and who preferred to be sent to the United States rather than return to his own country while he could not fight for it. The wily Ampudia narrowly escaped capture, his good horse, which he had named General Taylor, carrying him over a high stone wall when the dragoons thought they had him cornered.

Forty-three cannon and some four thousand small arms were taken and destroyed, since Scott lacked the means to move the former, and the latter were too old to be worth keeping. Large stores of ammunition were found in caverns near the batteries. Quantities of clothing and provisions were captured and the Mexican military chest, containing eleven thousand dollars in specie, of which one broken bag supplied some vigilant volunteers with the first money they had seen since they had been paid at Tampico. Among the booty were Santa Anna's campaign carriage, which contained his official and private papers, and three of its team of fine black mules. He was said to have fled on the fourth, and a wooden leg that was advertised as his became an attraction at Barnum's Museum in New York the following winter.

About nine o'clock on the morning after the battle the vanguard of the victorious army marched into Jalapa to the music of its bands, with ranks carefully dressed, bayonets fixed, and flags flying. Crowds of people who appeared to be neither unfriendly nor afraid lined the streets. High in the steeples above them the church bells rang peals of welcome, and if some groups of handsome girls laughed at the motley clothing of certain volunteer regiments, it was good-natured laughter. Santa Anna was finished so far as Jalapa was concerned. The city, its authorities and people alike, was eager to be on good terms with a conqueror as liberal and enlightened as Scott showed himself to be.

CHAPTER VIII

Marking Time

§1

Oh, de telimagraph's good for to transport de lightning,
Or to get de news from Mexico when de Yankees is
afighting.

So SANG Christy's Minstrels in *The Trabbler's Song.* For
this spring, like the last, was filled with news that was made
the more glorious by rumors flying before it to the effect that
Taylor had been defeated and was retreating after the loss
of six guns and two thousand men. On March 31 the country
had word of Buena Vista and of Scott's successful landing
at Vera Cruz. Eleven days later it heard of the surrender of
the city and of the castle of San Juan de Ulloa.

On April 30 came the story that Santa Anna, with fifteen
thousand men, was confronting Scott on his march inland,
but the seven days of suspense that followed were lightened
by the report of Doniphan's victories at El Paso on Christmas Day and at the Sacramento on February 28 and of his
occupation of Chihuahua on March 1. The news of Cerro
Gordo followed, with a glory that eclipsed the navy's capture
of Tuxpán and Tabasco.

On May 7 New York staged a magnificent celebration. It
began with a salute of cannon at the Battery at daybreak.
At noon salutes of a hundred guns roared out at the Battery,
in Washington Square, and at Harlem. Flags flew everywhere; one hundred and fourteen of them draped the Herald
Building. There was a great parade of the militia in the
afternoon, and that night Castle Garden, all the hotels, and
many other buildings were illuminated. The City Hall shone

with 3,600 sperm candles and 700 lamps of various colors. Rockets soared and burst overhead. Four hundred thousand people packed Broadway and City Hall Park with a solid mass of humanity.

Even such haters of the war as Mr. Hone turned out with his wife to see the show, moving with the tide — for it was "impracticable" to do anything else — as far as St. Paul's Church, thence up Chatham Street, and home by way of the Bowery, where there were transparencies of Scott in uniform and Taylor in a frock coat and broad-brimmed beaver hat as he was supposed to have appeared at Buena Vista. There was some swearing and a little screaming, but the crowd was generally good-natured, Mr. Hone noted tolerantly.

Indeed, Taylor's successes and the mounting wave of his popularity as a candidate for the Presidency had begun to make the war almost respectable in Mr. Hone's opinion. No more did he write, as he had done in November, that the decline of the glory of ancient Rome commenced with the conquests of Julius Cæsar. All classes, even the Quakers, he believed, were for Taylor for president. The so-called "Mexican Whigs," who called it "a war against God" and were demanding the withdrawal of American troops from all Mexican territory and an immediate peace, saw in him an unbeatable candidate. Had not the administration, in its effort to discredit and ruin him, stripped him of his best troops and abandoned him — "deserted" was their word for it — in the face of overwhelming numbers?

Washington had its victory celebration on the 8th, the anniversary of Palo Alto. Its brilliancy was somewhat dimmed by the President's forbidding the illumination of the Treasury and the State Department buildings : he considered them "very combustible" and feared for the invaluable public records and documents contained in them. He caused the White House to be illuminated, however. Many other buildings were bright with lamps and candles, and between the Capitol and the Navy Yard a hundred tar and turpentine barrels, piled in a pillar forty feet high, blazed skyward in the night. A week later Colonel Bankhead arrived with the trophies of Vera Cruz. They were placed on exhibition in the War Department, and the city had another day of triumph.

But military glory had little appeal for Polk, and he saw none in Buena Vista, a battle that, he maintained, ought never to have been fought, and would never have been fought if Taylor had not flagrantly disobeyed his orders. He forbade the army to honor it with salutes. He deplored its losses as unnecessary. Among the many officers who had been killed that day were several men of distinction and the sons of distinguished fathers: Henry Clay, Junior, and George Lincoln, son of Levi Lincoln, a former Governor of Massachusetts; Colonel John J. Hardin of Illinois, of whom Abraham Lincoln said: "We lost our best Whig man"; and Colonel Archibald Yell of the Arkansas Cavalry, who had been Governor of his state and left Congress to take part in the war. The President felt his death as a personal loss, feared that he had died poor, and resolved to educate his son if that proved to be true.

The general adulation of Taylor and Scott seemed to Polk absurd. All winter the street boys in Philadelphia had been singing:

> *Old Zac's at Monterey,*
> *Bring out your Santa Anner;*
> *For every time we raise a gun,*
> *Down goes a Mexicaner.*

But Taylor had blundered in every one of his battles and owed his victories to the fighting of his men. "The truth is," Polk wrote in his diary, "our troops, regulars and volunteers, will obtain victories wherever they meet the enemy. This they would do if they were without officers to command them higher in rank than lieutenants. It is injustice, therefore, to award the generals all the credit." He determined to make officers of a number of privates who had distinguished themselves, though this should be at the expense of an equal number of graduates of West Point, and when the Adjutant General was dilatory in presenting him with a list of deserving candidates, he let it be understood that he would put up with no nonsense about it.

He made Jefferson Davis a brigadier. After the performance of the Mississippi Rifles and their colonel at Buena Vista he could hardly have done otherwise. Pillow turned up in Washington with that wounded arm of his still in a sling, while down at Jalapa the officers of the 2nd Tennessee were preparing a scathing statement of his conduct at Cerro Gordo and an Ohio boy, writing about Pillow's going home on a short leave, added: "if the Tennesseans don't shoot him." The statement was published in the *Picayune* but did not prevent the President from sending him back to Mexico a major general.

At least, generalships had their use as a means of distinguishing reliable Democrats, and Democrats as reliable as Pillow were few and seemed to be growing fewer from day to day, outside the army as well as in it. The party was split, both factions, as Polk saw them, lacking in patriotism, making a hobbyhorse of slavery, and forgetting that the Constitution had settled that issue, as Polk earnestly believed it had done. In April Calhoun had come out with an address to the American people in which he put slavery forward as a test in the next Presidential election, and the anti-Calhoun crowd in the North had welcomed it.

In the House the Southern members had voted against the antislavery provision in the Oregon bill. As to any territory to be acquired from Mexico by purchase, it was argued in the South that it was the slaveholding states that would pay for it. For the revenues of the Federal government were derived mostly from duties on imports, imports were paid for by exports, and one half of the exports of the country was made up of Southern cotton. Q.E.D. Virginia resolved not to recognize any act to keep slavery out of acquired territory — a sentiment that was promptly concurred in by the Governor of Mississippi and a Democratic convention in Alabama.

On the other side, although the $3,000,000 bill had been passed without the Wilmot Proviso, half of the non-slaveholding states had sent in resolutions demanding that no more slave states should be admitted to the Union and that hereafter there should be no more slavery in the territories. And an attempt to get an endorsement of the Wilmot Proviso through the Democratic Convention in New York caused an uproar.

The *Richmond Whig* came out against the acquisition of any territory, prophesying that it would prove to be a "fatal gift." The *National Intelligencer* and other opposition newspapers were doing all they could to hinder the prosecution of the war: not because they felt any sympathy for the Mexicans, but in order to keep the administration from gaining credit by making a successful peace. The administration newspapers were divided on the issue, North against South.

Even more disquieting than all this — if it be true that the makers of a people's songs wield more influence than its rulers — was the recent verse of the allegedly gentle Quaker poet Whittier. His Ellen paused in singing at her wheel at her low cottage door hardly long enough to listen to her "Haughty Southron" suitor, who urged her to "let those Yankee fools spin." She sent him to the right about with:

> *Thy home may be lovely, but round it I hear*
> *The crack of the whip and the footsteps of fear,*

and added that the Yankee girl would sooner be in fetters with his slaves than share her freedom with him.

With the true pacifist's predilection for celebrating the virtues of his country's enemies at the expense of those of its champions, he wrote in "The Angels of Buena Vista" of "the noble Mexic women" succoring the wounded of both sides after the battle and calling down, over the body of a dead American:

> *A bitter curse on them, poor boy, that led thee forth.*

In a poem on Yorktown and its memories of the Revolution he exclaimed:

> *Bear witness, Palo Alto's day,*
> *Dark Vale of Palms, red Monterey,*
> *When Mexic Freedom, young and weak,*
> *Fleshes the Northern eagle's beak.*

And he bade Prussia and Russia laugh at

> *Brave sport to see the fledgling born*
> *Of freedom by its parent torn,*

with the assurance that "Spielberg's cell" and "Siberia's frozen hell" were quite safe. For:

> *With Slavery's flag o'er both unrolled,*
> *What of the New World fears the Old?*

An English correspondent of Mr. William W. Seaton of the *National Intelligencer* wrote to him: "That 'repudiating' America should have invaded a younger and neighboring republic because it had not and could not pay its debts shocks serious English society." Had Mr. Polk known of this he might have given one of his wry smiles at its unconscious hypocrisy in a decade that had seen Great Britain involved in the Opium War and the acquisition of Hong Kong and Sind. And few Englishmen of the time could have been made to understand that repudiation had been the concern of the several states, not of the Federal government. The finances of the latter, thanks to the repeal of the Corn Laws, the famine in Ireland and Germany, and the victories of the armies in Mexico, were now such that the banking firm of Corcoran and Riggs had — as Mr. Hone noted with satisfaction that May — made a fortune out of underwriting the whole of the latest issue of United States six-per-cent bonds.
More exasperating than the transatlantic pharisee and the

Quaker fanatic were certain professional firebrands of South
Carolina and other parts of the South. Among the urbane
and cultivated Southern visitors at Saratoga and Newport
each summer there appeared occasional planters whose speech
and bearing seemed to justify what the abolitionists charged
against all slaveowners. Said one of these objectionable characters when a New York businessman expressed admiration
for the tough and limber walking-stick his caller sported: "I
carry that, sir, to chastise insolent Yankees with."

§2

Mr. Secretary Mason called one afternoon in mid-April
and persuaded the harassed President to go for a buggy ride
with him. But he half spoiled it by telling him that Calhoun
had come out for Taylor for president. It turned out not to
be true, but Polk, who had heard rumors to the same effect,
believed it for the time being. He well knew that Taylor was
in a receptive state of mind. At the end of May *Niles' National Register* quoted from a letter that the Hero of Buena
Vista had written to a citizen of Louisiana: "In regard to
the presidency, I will not say that I would not run, if the
good people of the country require me to do so, however much
it is opposed to my wishes."

The presidential diversions continued to be as few, and
the distractions as many, as they had always been. Mrs. Polk
came home from church with a chill that developed into a
persistent case of the ague common in Washington when the
warm weather brought the mosquitoes in from the garbage-
strewn tidal flats along the river. A daughter of Mr. John
Quincy Adams came to a presidential reception and had to be
treated with marked civility, since she was the first member
of that family to darken the doors of the White House since
the Polks had moved into it.

The President had, naturally, to attend the elaborate cere-
mony of the laying of the cornerstone of the new Smithsonian
Institution building, with the military, Odd Fellows, and
Masons parading in full regalia. And he now had to spend

some hours each day "in the red parlor above stairs," sitting
to Thomas Sully, the painter of Queen Victoria, Jefferson,
and Lafayette, who had been commissioned by the Dialectic
Society of the University of North Carolina to paint them a
portrait of their distinguished former member.

It seems to have been a relief, however, to take a recess in
the midst of one Cabinet meeting and go downstairs with his
advisers to receive the celebrated dwarf General Tom Thumb,
who had lately returned from a European tour of which the
profits were reported to amount to £150,000.

What chiefly concerned Polk and his Cabinet at this time
were efforts for a negotiated peace, for the election was now
only eighteen months away. News of Cerro Gordo had not
yet been received, but that of Vera Cruz and Buena Vista
caused the moment to appear propitious. Polk, indeed, with
his indomitable persistence, had never ceased to work secretly
for that end. In January he had sent Atocha on a second
mission to Mexico and, undiscouraged when that dubious
agent returned with word that the Mexican government demanded the raising of the blockade and the withdrawal of
American troops from Mexican territory as a preliminary to
any negotiations whatever, had allowed Buchanan to appoint
Moses Y. Beach as a secret agent in the Mexican capital.

Beach, who was the proprietor and editor of the *New York
Sun,* had gone to Mexico from Havana with a British passport and letters of introduction from Roman Catholic prelates in the United States to further a project of his for a
canal across the Isthmus of Tehuantepec. He made influential friends, but became involved with the Clericals in the
chaotic intrigues and disorders that ended in the overthrow
of Ferías and had to flee for his life.

Polk's present plan was to send to Mexico a regular ac-
credited peace commissioner who should join Scott's army
and move with it, ready to seize the first opportunity to open
negotiations. The question in the Cabinet was whom to send.
The appointment of any prominent Democrat would offend
all who did not belong to his particular faction of the party,

yet the commissioner must be a man of sufficient importance
to command the respect and confidence of the Mexican government. Scott, of course, had repeatedly proved himself to
be a negotiator of the first order. But if anybody in the
Cabinet remembered that, he doubtless remembered also that
Scott was already by way of winning only too much glory for
a Whig.

The choice fell upon Nicholas P. Trist, whose position as
Chief Clerk in the State Department ranked him second to
Buchanan himself in that hierarchy and gave him sufficient
eminence for the mission. A Virginian by birth and forty-six
years of age, Trist had at one time been a cadet at West
Point, had studied law in the office of Thomas Jefferson, and
had married Jefferson's granddaughter Virginia Randolph.
Henry Clay had found him a clerkship in the State Department. He had served President Jackson as private secretary,
and for eight years he had been consul at Havana, where he
had learned Spanish thoroughly and gained an understanding of the Latin character and temperament.

He was summoned to the White House and there, in the
presence of Secretary Buchanan alone, was impressed by the
President himself with the absolute secrecy of his mission. A
single clerk in the State Department was entrusted with
copying the necessary papers, which set forth the terms that
the commissioner was empowered to offer to the Mexican government. The boundary they proposed was the Rio Grande
as far as the 32nd parallel, thence along that parallel to the
middle of the Gulf of California, and thence southward down
the middle of the Gulf to the Pacific, the provinces of Upper and Lower California and New Mexico thus going to
the United States. The treaty, moreover, was to secure to the
United States the right of passage and transit across the
Isthmus of Tehuantepec. For all this Trist was authorized to
offer, in addition to the assumption by the United States of
the unpaid balance of the claims of United States citizens
against the Mexican government, $30,000,000, or $20,000,-
000 for New Mexico and Upper California alone, or $25,-

000,000 for the two if transit across the isthmus was included with them. But he must obtain New Mexico and Upper California or there would be no treaty at all.

Trist, traveling incognito, set out for Mexico and Scott's headquarters on April 16. His mission, the President thought with satisfaction, was a profound secret, especially from the editors of the opposition newspapers, who, if they knew of it, would do all in their power, Polk felt sure, to cause it to fail. Great was his anger and mortification, therefore, when five days later he read in the *New York Herald* a remarkably accurate and detailed account of his agent's departure and the purpose of his journey. Undoubtedly there had been treachery somewhere. But where? He wrote in his diary that he had not been "more vexed and excited" since he became President. He could not doubt the loyalty and discretion of his Cabinet, and although Buchanan had vouched for the man, his suspicions centered on the clerk who had copied the papers. For there were Whigs, he believed, who would send a courier to Mexico or go to any other expense to discourage the Mexican government from making peace before the next election.

Meanwhile he had not ceased to busy himself with details on the purely military side of the war. For Marcy, now fairly submerged in them, was showing the strain of his work. Recruiting had not been going well since enlistments had been required "for the duration." In Virginia, for instance, though they sang:

> *I'll sling my knapsack on my back, my rifle on my*
>   *shoulder,*
> *And to Mexico I'll proudly go to be a gallant soldier,*

the recruiting officers finally turned to Maryland to fill their quotas. The army at Cerro Gordo was the most representative of the whole country of any that had fought in the war so far. But the popularity of the war had waned, and it continued to wane as Taylor stood still in the Saltillo country, and Scott, who had pushed forward to Puebla, halted there because many of his regiments were entitled to be discharged and the men were not re-enlisting. Lew Wallace, who returned with his regiment of time-expired men from the Rio Grande country that summer, was disgusted by what he remembered years later as the "poor, cheap" reception they were given at New Orleans.

When the newly raised regiments were apportioned, however, there were enough men — according to the War Department's figures — to give Scott a total force of 20,000 and Taylor 12,000. The President directed that Scott should have first call on reinforcements, since Taylor stated that he himself could not advance farther without more troops than the government was able to send him. This arrangement was a wise correction of orders that had been deflecting troops from Scott to Taylor on account of the anxiety for the latter that had been felt in Washington before the victory of Buena Vista. But what was not understood at either the White House or the War Department was that, owing to the ravages of disease, regiments that left home a thousand strong arrived at the front with only 300 or 400 effectives.

Polk also gave orders that Mexican officers, instead of being paroled, should be sent to the United States, whence they might be exchanged for American officers who were prisoners in Mexico. He planned a government courier service across Alabama so that he might receive news of the war as promptly as the *Baltimore Sun* received it, and on May 28 he set out to attend the commencement exercises of his alma mater at Chapel Hill.

The trip turned out to be balm to his weary spirit. Richmond, Petersburg, and Raleigh received him with processions, illuminations, fireworks, and salutes of cannon, with banquets and speeches. Governors and political leaders hastened to join his special train. His progress he described, with an engaging naïveté, as "a continued triumphal procession." It seemed as if all North Carolina came flocking to do honor to their university's two distinguished alumni, the other being Secretary Mason, who accompanied the President.

Polk visited his old room, which he had left for the last time twenty-nine years before, and attended the examination of the senior class in international and constitutional law and an oratorical exhibition by sophomores and freshmen. He sat through the interminable commencement exercises of that day: from ten in the morning until half past five in the afternoon, with a recess of an hour and a half for dinner at one. Betweenwhiles he "was introduced to hundreds, male and female." Or so he wrote where a man less naturally unassuming might have written that they were introduced to him. It was Saturday, June 5, before he returned to Washington, and he arrived there with the feeling that the attention paid him throughout his trip was all that he could have desired.

Among his callers the following Monday was enterprising young Mrs. Frémont, who tried in vain to wangle from him an expression of approval of her husband's conduct in his clash with Kearny in California. With her came Kit Carson, who had lately arrived in Washington, bringing her letters from her husband and dispatches from him to his father-in-law the Senator, and to the War Department. That evening Polk had a long talk with Carson about California affairs and especially about the conflict of authority between the military and naval commanders. He decided that Kearny was in the right, but hoped that, since the matter was settled, there need be neither a court-martial nor the court of inquiry that Senator Benton was soon demanding for his son-in-law.

More serious trouble came on Saturday of that week in the form of dispatches from Mexico. Trist had arrived at Vera Cruz, it appeared, and had informed Scott of his mission in a communication so pompous and tactless as to drive the general to one of his most furious epistolary outbursts. Negotiation with the enemy, Scott asserted, was his prerogative as Commander-in-Chief, and his alone, nor would he take orders from a mere clerk, though that clerk did represent himself to be the personal representative of the President of the United States. When the dispatches left Jalapa, Trist had been at army headquarters six days, but Scott was still refusing to see him.

The tone of the general's dispatches was such that Polk considered them not only insubordinate but insulting to both Mr. Trist and the government. And as if this were not enough, a dispatch from Commodore Perry stated that Scott had rejected the Secretary of the Navy's request for co-operation in an effort for the release of a young midshipman, a prisoner in Mexico City, who was threatened, on the flimsiest evidence, with being hanged as a spy.

Polk would dearly have loved to punish the arrogant officer by removing him from command. He decided that if Scott continued to maintain that he was the only channel through which communication could be held with the Mexican government he would have him arrested and tried by court-martial. For the present, however, he contented himself with directing the Secretary of War to rebuke him and to repeat in a peremptory manner the order to forward to the Mexican government at once the dispatch of which Mr. Trist was the bearer.

He was still irritable some days later when word that he was about to leave for a trip in the North caused his office to fill with place-hunters as if, he wrote, "the Government was about to come to an end." He gave none of this "herd of loafers" offices and treated them "almost harshly." The legislatures of Maine and New Hampshire and many other bodies in the North had invited him to visit them. He stopped in Baltimore, Philadelphia, New York, Boston, Portland, and elsewhere. He had never been in New England before, and he liked it. He enjoyed the trip greatly — not least, apparently, for the opportunity it gave him to decline an invitation from ex-President Van Buren, which he took to be no more than a gesture of formal courtesy. The warm and respectful reception that was given him he was pleased to accept, as he had accepted the demonstrations in the South, as a tribute paid not to his personal popularity or to the leader of the Democratic Party but to the President of the United States.

On his return to the capital he found still more annoying dispatches awaiting him. Scott, it appeared, had written foolish and bitter letters to Trist; Trist had replied in a letter equally foolish; and Scott's latest dispatch to the Secretary of War was filled with passion and vanity and seemed to the President to be highly insubordinate. Worse yet, Scott appeared to have committed a grave military error. He had given up his post at Jalapa and concentrated his forces at Puebla and Perote, thus leaving his whole rear exposed to the enemy. Two strong bodies of reinforcements marching inland from Vera Cruz had been compelled to fight their way through large bands of guerrillas.

It was with a sour smile that the President received from Count Bodisco the glad tidings that the Czar was again a grandfather. He replied that he was sorry he could not reciprocate the civility by making a similar announcement on his part.

§3

"Mexico has no longer an army," Scott wrote enthusiastically to Taylor in the first days after Cerro Gordo. It seemed so indeed. Worth, whom he pushed forward from Jalapa, found the naturally strong and heavily fortified position at the pass of La Hoya undefended, trenches empty, and guns abandoned in their emplacements. The strong brown walls of the castle of Perote were yielded without a shot. Eight miles out of Puebla he met and drove off with a few salvos of his light batteries a strong body of Mexican cavalry, and the city, with its 75,000 inhabitants, capitulated without delay when he arrived before it on May 15, although his force numbered only 4,000 men. It was a stronghold of the Clericals, and Santa Anna had been there on the 11th, increasing his local unpopularity by severe requisitions. After Cerro Gordo the Mexican commander had made good his escape southward across the mountains to the city of Orizaba and had managed to rally there both his badly shaken self-confidence and some four thousand men from the remnants of his shattered army. "What has been lost except a position and some cannon?" he asked rhetorically. Summoning to the colors every citizen between the ages of fifteen and forty, he set out with his troops for the city of Mexico. Had he remained on Scott's flank at Orizaba, as Washington remained on the British flank at Morristown in 1777, he might have forced Scott into the highly inconvenient maneuver of attacking him. But he had to consider what might happen to him politically if he remained away from the capital. The cold reception that was given him at Puebla showed him clearly how uncertain was his hold upon the country.

Puebla made a holiday of Worth's arrival. Vera Cruz, Cerro Gordo, and Buena Vista — of which the people had learned the sorry truth by this time — had made them hopeless of winning the war. The *Monitor del Puebla* advised them "to await with resignation the terrible blow with which Providence chooses to afflict us." They hated the Americans, but they hated Santa Anna more, and the terms of surrender that Worth granted them were fantastically liberal, going so far, indeed, as to give the Mexican courts the right to try Mexicans who were accused of the murder of American soldiers. This concession he balanced with a circular warning his troops against a purely imaginary plot to poison them. He seems to have been in a sad state of nerves about his position. He acted, without investigation, on every vague report — of which there were many — that the enemy was approaching in force. His drums beat to arms so frequently that these alarms got the name of "Worth's scarecrows" among his men, and it took Scott's arrival late in May to put a stop to them, though Scott himself had plenty of cause for anxiety.

For not long after boasting that Mexico no longer had an army, Scott might have written the same thing about himself with almost equal truth. Seven of his regiments were composed of volunteers whose time was almost out, and out of thirty-seven hundred of them only enough to make up one company were willing to re-enlist. Incompletely equipped to begin with, only partially disciplined, and lacking transportation to repair the losses incident to march and battle, most of them were in a wretched condition.

Jalapa was a very fine place if one was quartered in the city, which Lieutenant Semmes described as "a delicate mosaic set in a massive frame of emerald." The inhabitants were the first recognizably white people that the soldiers had seen in Mexico. The shops were soon filled with American goods. The *American Star,* by the publishers of the *Vera Cruz Eagle,* appeared on streets redolent of American cigar smoke and tobacco juice. One could see *The Bombardment of Vera Cruz* and *The Battle of Cerro Gordo* presented by an American company at the American Theater and practice soldier Spanish on the laughing, handsome, half-clad girls who rubbed and pounded the officers' linen at the public *lavaderos* and who seemed to find in the husky North Americans a pleasant change from the less virile males of their own race. For the officers there were ladies at grated windows and on flower-hung balconies, there were dances, and at night the low flat house-fronts echoed sweetly to the notes of the serenading harp and guitar. But the troops who were bivouacked outside the city — and these were the greater number — called it "Camp Misery."

The approach to it was misleading. Not many miles from it one passed the truly palatial mansion on Santa Anna's estate of Encero. Scott had stationed a guard there to prevent pillage, and the grateful custodians took pride in displaying the lordly gardens, the stores of fine china and glass, and the paintings representing the campaigns of Hannibal and Napoleon to goggle-eyed youths from the backwoods of Illinois and Georgia. Thence the road led on between fine two-storied haciendas that stood among sunny orange groves and had fountains playing in their courtyards. But Camp Misery was on a desert waste where the rain seemed to pour down continually and the icy wind from the surrounding snow peaks froze water at night.

There were no tents, owing to the lack of wagons to move them forward, and finding or stealing material for shanties was difficult. There were no clothes to replace the ones that siege, march, and combat had worn threadbare and ragged. Food grew so scarce that the volunteers, who had been paid only two months' wages in eight months of service, rushed and plundered the wretched huckster women's stalls on the fringes of the camp, and the New Yorkers took to robbing houses when they were not fighting among themselves. Foraging parties were ambushed by mounted guerrillas, who had put a death's-head and the motto "War without pity" on the pennons of their lances. From little groups of stragglers who went out into the brush in search of *"carne,"* the silent lasso snatched more than one, and their bodies would be found later, stabbed and mutilated. Cold and exposure, the reckless eating of guavas, mangoes, and avocados, and the swilling of cheap brandy brought on ague and diarrhea. The sick list grew from day to day, and many died.

So it was little wonder that almost all who could went home. In the slang of the day, these men from Georgia, Alabama, Tennessee, and Illinois "had seen the elephant." They took pains, however, to explain that it was not Scott but the government that they blamed for the mismanagement that had disgusted them with the war. They knew it was not his fault that he lacked the money with which to pay them; that wagons, worn out by doubling back and forth on the mountain roads in the effort to bring up tentage, provisions, and supplies, broke down and the mules died in their harness; and that there were not enough horses to enable the cavalry to deal with the ubiquitous guerrillas.

They offered to remain with the general for their full time, if he would permit them to do so. But Scott, who had Marcy's order to make their health his first consideration and was painfully aware that every day now made the *vómito* more deadly in the *tierra caliente,* through which they must pass in order to embark, sent them off early in May. In June six hundred men, guarding a convoy that contained between $2,000 and $3,000 in specie, fought their way up from Vera Cruz and, with the aid of the Jalapa garrison, reached Puebla on the 3rd of July. But Scott saw his army shrink to 5,820 men before any considerable reinforcements reached him, and by the end of May he had reason to believe that Santa Anna had created an army of 7,000 regulars and 15,000 National Guards.

Through the interminable weeks of waiting, however, he maintained an appearance of complete confidence. Hardly recovered from an attack of the prevalent ague when he took horse for Puebla, he cheered the bored and diarrhea-ridden troops at Perote with the assurance that there would soon be "fighting enough for all." With a sympathetic understanding of the Latin enjoyment of display, he rode into Puebla in a glittering cavalcade, the Mounted Rifles heading the column, and behind them a crack squadron of dragoons under the command of Philip Kearny, who had spent his own money to mount his men on horses of a uniform shade of gray, and who was to die fighting for the Union at Chantilly in 1862. Puebla gave Scott a welcome that reminded one observer of a New York crowd on a holiday.

Since he had left the infantry of his escort at Perote and had pushed on with the cavalry without seeing a single enemy except some squadrons of lancers that kept well ahead of him, he put a quick stop to the fears that had on one occasion kept Worth's whole division under arms for an entire day. To settle the difficulties caused by Worth's permitting the local courts to try Mexican offenders against American soldiers, he simply republished his Order No. 20, establishing martial law. That seemed to be the best way to spare Worth's feelings. And he requested Worth to withdraw his circular of warning against the poison plot.

At Jalapa he had issued a proclamation to the Mexican people, in which he praised the valor of their soldiers and blamed for their defeats the generals whom they had "long supported in idleness." He dwelt upon the high taxes that had been levied upon the clergy and peaceable citizens by those ambitious men. He called attention to the fair treatment given to the Church by his troops — many of whom were Roman Catholics — and urged the Mexicans to rid themselves of their unscrupulous masters. The United States, he concluded, would send a hundred thousand men to win the war if so many were necessary, but what the Americans desired was peace. And Colonel Hitchcock followed his commander with an address to the Mexican people in which he told them, among other things, of the death of Scott's daughter as a nun in an American convent.

At Puebla the clergy gave Scott great hopes of peace through a revolution to be engineered by the Clerical Party in the capital, and he did everything in his power to conciliate them. Undeterred by his experience in the church at Vera Cruz, he took his generals and his entire staff to High Mass in full-dress uniform on Trinity Sunday, when they found the music sublime and the pillars of the Cathedral gorgeous in swathings of rich damask velvet. He issued a general order to prevent any insult to the ceremonies of Corpus Christi Day. But this came out so late that the services were held inside the churches: so great were the ecclesiastics' fears of Protestant bigotry.

The wisdom of the proclamation in pointing out to the Mexicans their political shortcomings was much doubted in some quarters. But the proclamation was effective enough to make Santa Anna, who read it in his capital, furious. Mexico City newspapers published a warning against the American blandishments: "Mexicans, beware! These Yankees, when in Jalapa, where there were plenty of pretty women, and where gallantry was the order of the day, were obsequious and attentive beaux; but now that they have arrived in Puebla of the Angels, where religion is in vogue, they have suddenly become saints."

But it was not for nothing that the American commander bowed down in what the more Protestant of his followers

doubtless regarded as the House of Rimmon. Before long
he had local agents who provisioned his troops from the surrounding country, where the abundant crops — the altitude
was 7,000 feet — reminded him of those about Frederick in
Maryland, and he was able to make arrangements by which
he supplied his men with clothing and shoes of local manufacture. Hitchcock made contact with a bandit chief who was
disgusted with Santa Anna, and through his good offices
mustered into the service of the United States a spy company of some two hundred former highwaymen. The army
promptly named them the Forty Thieves, but they proved
to be highly useful in gathering information and in other
ways.

Although the atmosphere of La Puebla de los Angeles was
predominantly ecclesiastical, the city had its charming secu-
lar side. Volunteers from rural Ohio might wonder how the
many priests and nuns whom they saw on the streets "could
make a living"; the five hundred bells of the numerous
churches might remind even Catholic Raphael Semmes of
Bernal Díaz's description of the gongs in the Aztec temples;
but it was a gay crowd that thronged the handsome *portales*
surrounding the Grand Plaza. The Bishop's Palace contained a gallery of fine paintings, some of which were the reverse of religious. At the Tivoli and the Paseo every afternoon sherbets were drunk, there was dancing on the lawns to
the music of the American regimental bands, and the American officers vied with the native cavaliers in displaying their
horsemanship before the assembled carriages.

Evenings one could attend performances by the American
theatrical company, which had followed headquarters from
Jalapa, or cultivate one's ear for Spanish by listening to a
play by Mexican actors. Dances were numerous, and some
Puebla ladies of good position attended them. Young married officers continued to write home, as they had been doing
since the beginning of the war, that they had not seen a single pretty Mexican woman. But others appear to have been
less hard to please. On Sundays there were Protestant serv-

ices at headquarters, a recent law having provided chaplains for the army. The Commander-in-Chief held frequent levees in his quarters in the Governor's Palace, which fronted on the Grand Plaza. He was a delightful host, although that egotism of his did sometimes betray him into monopolizing the conversation.

A kind of vigilant tranquillity brooded over the place throughout June and July. Officers carried their sabers and went wide at corners when they were out of doors after dark. Enlisted men were not allowed on the streets except in groups of six accompanied by a noncommissioned officer. Some troops were quartered in the Mexican barracks, and one fourth of them were kept always under arms. An occasional soldier who had run the guard was murdered. But there was little crime or lawlessness, and that little was confined to the lower orders. Scott managed to give the soldiers two and a half months' pay, which amounted to $17.50 for a private, and even the volunteers were guilty of only a few depredations. The administration of military justice to civilian offenders appears to have been singularly lenient. At Perote the murderer of an American soldier was let off with a flogging when it was proved that he had been drunk at the time of committing the crime.

Scott kept the troops around Puebla busy with continual regimental drills and weekly brigade and divisional exercises; there was much reconnoitering and mapping of the roads that led to the enemy's capital; and he gave each corps in turn the variety of an excursion to the near-by ruins of the ancient city and pyramid of Cholula. The Fourth of July was celebrated with a national salute at noon, and a rocket for each state was fired that evening. Eggs were to be had for twenty-five cents a dozen, butter for a dollar a pound, and a pound of Bologna sausage for fifty cents. Claret and sherry were served at the headquarters messes of the brigades, and a "plain dinner" given by Colonel Butler of South Carolina included turkey and ham, chicken salad and sardines, pie, wines, and brandy, and kept his guests five hours at the table.

Some officers had sufficient leisure to start a squabble over the apportionment of credit for various feats of arms at Cerro Gordo. Scott, who had evidently felt that there was more than enough glory to go around, had praised everybody — even Pillow — so indiscriminately that Worth had called his report of the battle "a lie from beginning to end," and now Scott found it necessary to institute a court of inquiry to settle these differences. Worth, who was suffering from a persistent illness, demanded a court to investigate the propriety of his poison-plot circular and the terms of capitulation he had granted to the city of Puebla. Reluctantly Scott appointed three generals to review these matters: Quitman, Twiggs, and Persifor Smith. They found the capitulation terms to have been "improvident and detrimental to the public service," the circular "highly improper and objectionable." Scott could not do otherwise than approve their verdict, but it marked the ending of a lifelong friendship between him and Worth and the beginning of the bitter feud from which — thanks to the intriguing Pillow and Polk's devotion to party — all concerned were to emerge less than a year later with glory tarnished and wilted laurels.

Back at Perote during these weeks of waiting, the garrison was kept busy by continual alarms and incursions of guerrillas. This was perhaps as well, for in spite of their experience in battle one company elected a popular private to a vacant lieutenancy instead of their efficient orderly sergeant, who was the other candidate for the office. Mexican life thereabouts seemed to fall rather depressingly into its old ways. The stage coach ran regularly from Puebla to Vera Cruz and was robbed as regularly as ever. The courier from the British legation at Mexico City came through as usual, mysteriously unscathed. But the army's mails were infrequent and irregular. Messengers with the outgoing bags would be found hanged or with their throats cut, and intimate family letters appeared in translation from time to time in the Mexico City papers, especially if their contents reflected in any way on American manners or morals.

The "diarrhea blues" were endemic at Perote, the daily rains and the cold winds from the snow-clad summits of Orizaba and Popocatepetl made recovery slow and difficult, and the line of shallow graves behind the castle grew steadily longer. In general, however, the health of the troops improved greatly after the early days of June, when a thousand of them were down with dysentery and ague. Some deserted — between two hundred and three hundred, it was said — and a Belgian and a German were tried for inciting them to do so. But the fighting spirit of the rest was undiminished.

Like the enlisted personnel of all United States armies in wartime, they presented a fair cross-section of the country's population. They ranged from the bad and the worthless to cultivated young men who had enlisted for the love of adventure, and included mechanics and farm hands, and doctors, lawyers, and merchants who had made a failure of life. But they were unanimous in hating most to hear a rumor of peace: they wanted no peace short of the Halls of Montezuma. And in that small army little happened, even at headquarters, that the humblest rear-rank private did not hear about through the gossip at the latrines or did not read about as soon as his home newspaper arrived with the communications that the numerous correspondents with the army had sent to the United States. Late in June a captain of artillery knew that Scott had asked to be relieved and felt that the general had "good cause for complaint." On July 2 a report from New Orleans stated that Scott had been ordered to suspend operations until the arrival of his successor, who was believed to be the incapable and hated Pillow. And upon Trist's appearance on the scene the gentlemen of the press spread the news that he had been sent as a sort of "generalissimo."

Officers and men alike resented Trist's presence, the soldiers believing, as they hoped, that he had come on "a fool's errand." "How are you, Peace?" wrote one of them in his diary: "Peace in a pig's eye!" All were heartily on their commander's side in the ensuing quarrel and, borrowing his phrase of the previous May, talked about "a fire in their rear." The officials at Washington, they thought, "must be crazy or don't know what they are doing." And when Captain Robert Anderson heard that the general had expressed his "just indignation" at the government's negligence and mismanagement in "another bitter truth-telling letter to the Secretary of War," he wrote his wife with evident satisfaction at its probable effect upon "the little men at Washington."

Anderson and his kind had, to be sure, a special grievance in Polk's policy of appointing officers at the expense of those who, as Anderson put it, had been "fool enough" to stay at West Point until they were graduated. One of these appointees from civil life was now a colonel commanding second lieutenants who had been his classmates at the Military Academy. The West Pointers lacked the experience that the next war was to give them in the endurance of that kind of injustice.

§4

Mr. Trist appears to have discarded his futile incognito as soon as his ship, the revenue cutter *Ewing*, dropped the pilot off the mouths of the Mississippi. He arrived at Vera Cruz on May 6 in an aura of such self-importance that a correspondent from New Orleans reported to his paper that "Mr. Trist is *the government* in Mexico." Delayed at Vera Cruz by a brief illness, he wrote to Scott in terms that matched his bearing, sent him in a sealed packet Buchanan's projected treaty for transmission to the Mexican Minister of Foreign Affairs, but did not favor the general with either a copy of his own instructions or a copy of the treaty, as he was supposed to do.

Marcy had not neglected to write to Scott about Trist's mission but, not anticipating the commissioner's lofty behavior, had dealt with it only in general terms. Scott, who was already resentful of the deflection of his reinforcements to Taylor and had become suspicious of the administration because of its failure to give his expedition adequate support, replied to Trist's letter with all the unfortunate facility that was customary with him when he felt himself affronted. He wrote that he realized that the Secretary of War proposed to "degrade" him by requiring him, the commander of the army, to defer to the Chief Clerk of the Department of State the question of continuing or discontinuing hostilities. Nevertheless he demanded that if the enemy should entertain Trist's overtures, any proposal for an armistice should be referred to him. For an armistice, he pointed out, would involve the safety of the army, and for that he was responsible.

Unfortunately Trist also was gifted with the pen of a ready writer. He was on the road to Jalapa, where Scott still had his headquarters, when he received the general's letter, but he sat down at the first halt for the night and tore off page after page of angry and sarcastic rebuttal, which he put in his pocket for use later.

At Jalapa Scott caused him to be received with scrupulous courtesy and assigned to comfortable quarters. But the dispatch to the Mexican Minister of Foreign Affairs, its great red seals unbroken, was returned to him by the general's military secretary with no more than the intimation that at some future date he might be provided with an escort to enable him to open communication with the enemy, and by the General himself his presence was ignored.

After six days of this behavior, since Scott was about to go on to Puebla, Trist sent him a second letter: for the purpose, he wrote, of bringing down the general's thoughts from the "lofty regions" they dwelt in to the plain business of his mission. In terms of studied discourtesy he demanded that Scott forward Buchanan's dispatch without further delay, and with this letter he sent the one he had written on the road. Together the two amounted to thirty large pages.

Nine days later, at Puebla, whither Trist had followed the general as a member of the mess of Brigadier General Persifor Smith, Scott replied in kind. He had not read Mr. Trist's "farrago of insolence, conceit and arrogance," he wrote, but had been informed of its contents by the member of his staff to whom he had assigned that task. "The Jacobin convention of France," he continued, " had never sent to one of its armies in the field a more amiable and accomplished instrument. If you were but armed with an ambulatory guillotine, you would be the personification of Danton, Marat and St. Just, all in one."

He was thankful to the President, he informed Trist, "for not degrading me by placing me in any joint commission with you." He admitted that he had misunderstood Trist's mission at first: he had inferred that the commissioner was empowered to grant an armistice as a preliminary to negotiations. If Trist's negotiations should lead to an armistice, he would ask nothing more than the opportunity to pass upon its terms as they might affect the safety of his army. But he balanced this concession by concluding with the promise that any repetition of "orders or instructions" from Trist, or "a single discourteous phrase," would cause him "to throw back" the communication "with the contempt and scorn you merit at my hands."

Six days later (June 4), he wrote to Marcy asking to be recalled as soon as the cold weather — probably in November — should render Vera Cruz sufficiently free from the *vómito* to be safe for him to embark there "Cruel disappointments and mortifications," he told the Secretary, and "a total want of support and sympathy on the part of the War Department" caused him to take this step.

He had good cause for anger and chagrin without the seeming affront of Trist's mission. After Cerro Gordo he could have advanced and taken Mexico City and probably brought the war to a swift and victorious conclusion if he had been given the forces that had been promised to him. There were some in the army and many at home who criticized him for not having pushed on promptly with the troops he had. Chaos had reigned in the enemy capital in those first days after the destruction of Santa Anna's army. Pending the result of an election, Santa Anna had resigned the Presidency. But Scott had seen clearly what his critics either could not or would not see: that the occupation of the capital with a force of five thousand men, which was all that he would have been able to keep with him, would not have ended the war. Surrounded by a swarming hostile population, he would probably have been besieged in the city and would have had to be extricated, if at all, by a fresh expeditionary force.

He learned too late that in the opinion of Mr. Bankhead, the British Minister to Mexico, Buchanan's peace proposals would have been accepted if they had been forwarded immediately upon Trist's arrival in the country. Time dragged on, and the Clerical revolution so invitingly prognosticated by the clergy at Puebla did not materialize. By early June Santa Anna was again in power about as firmly as he had been before his defeat at Cerro Gordo. Upon the decision of the Mexican Congress to defer the counting of the election votes until September, he had withdrawn his resignation. With his ability to galvanize his countrymen into action, which amounted almost to genius, he was swiftly increasing the army, casting cannon, making powder, and fortifying every approach to the city. Throughout June and the early days of July the spies' reports of his numbers steadily mounted until, on the 16th of the latter month, Colonel Hitchcock, who managed the American secret service, had reason to believe that there were 30,000 men, paid and well fed — 15,000 of them well drilled — and sixty cannon ready to defend the capital.

But although Scott talked openly of "working with Polk's halter round my neck," he was no Achilles to sulk in his tent. On some of the nights when he was not receiving guests he might send a note over to that congenial Northern-born Mississippian, Quitman, to propose a quiet game of chess with hot toddy to follow. More often, however, he would assemble his staff officers at a late supper and keep them till past midnight in discussion of the military problems he laid before them.

His situation, moreover, became gradually less discouraging. Late in June, General George Cadwalader brought up from Vera Cruz three of the temporary regiments of regulars: the 11th and 14th Infantry and the Voltiguer Regiment, together with a large convoy of supplies and $250,000 in specie, which was almost as welcome as the troops. Pillow followed a few days later with about 2,000 men, although he had killed six and laid up a hundred and fifty more with sunstroke by marching them mercilessly across the hot coastal plain. And with him came Shields, who had made an almost miraculous recovery from the wound he had received at Cerro Gordo.

Both forces — as Polk heard with such sharp anxiety — had fought their way through the mountains below Jalapa with great difficulty. By this time the Mexicans had destroyed the bridges, which Scott's advance had found intact; river banks had to be cut down and fords discovered for the wagons and the trains of pack mules; and the numerous guerrilla bands united to assail the troops, who were thus almost disastrously impeded. Even west of Jalapa, where the resistance was generally less active, the garrison of Perote had to turn out to extricate Cadwalader from a serious situation at the pass of La Hoya.

The Perote troops, bored and disgusted by continual scrimmages in which they generally had several killed and wounded and frequently came off second best, had reached a state of mind in which they noted with satisfaction that Captain Walker of the Texans seldom brought in any prisoners. In the La Hoya combat they burned the near-by town of Las Vegas, which they knew to be a veritable nest of guerrillas. They became indignant when General Cadwalader, who was new to the war and all for waging it according to civilized standards, made the time-honored army reflection on their maternity in rebuking them for this misconduct.

Pillow found the opposition to his progress so strong and determined that he sent orders ahead for Cadwalader to wait for him at Perote. At Jalapa he incorporated with his command the little garrison, half of it convalescents, that Scott had left there, and on July 8 marched into Puebla at the head of these united forces, a train of five hundred wagons, and long strings of pack mules.

Nearly a month had now gone by since Scott's last letter to Mr. Trist, and there had been no change in the situation between the two. Trist continued to remain at Puebla, a member of General Quitman's mess; Scott continued to ignore his presence. But the commissioner had not been idle. He had got into communication with the British Minister at Mexico City, where the British colony was greatly disturbed by the prospect of a siege, with the possibility of sack and pillage to follow. Mr. Bankhead promptly sent the secretary of his legation to the American headquarters. A few days later Secretary Buchanan's projected treaty was in the hands of Señor Ibarra, the Minister of Foreign Affairs, and word came back that it would be considered at a session of the Mexican Congress to be called specially for that purpose. Santa Anna, the British secretary of legation reported, was in favor of negotiation.

Since Trist could not well go further without Scott's cooperation, any advance by the army being regarded as likely to cause the Mexican government to refuse to negotiate, he proceeded, near the end of June, to do as he should have done in the beginning: wrote to Scott civilly, telling him of the apparently receptive Mexican attitude, and submitted to him a copy of his authority to act as commissioner. Scott's reply established amicable, if purely official relations between them, and when Trist fell ill a few days later, Scott sent to General Smith, who had all along been trying to patch up the quarrel, a box of guava marmalade, "which, perhaps," he wrote in the note he sent with it, "the physician may not consider improper to make part of the diet of your sick companion." A personal meeting followed upon Trist's quick recovery, and acquaintance grew rapidly into a warm friendship.

Again the secretary of the British legation appeared at Puebla, this time with a hint that if Santa Anna were to receive ten thousand dollars in advance and the promise of a million to be paid when the treaty had been ratified, further military operations might become unnecessary. Trist took the suggestion to Scott: it involved a nice point of honor. Scott held that Trist would be corrupting nobody by making the payment, since the suggestion came, however indirectly, from Santa Anna himself, and might therefore act on it with a clear conscience. "Such transactions," he told Trist, "have always been allowable in war," and this one would undoubtedly save several thousand American lives.

Only after the ten thousand dollars had been sent to a certain English agent in Mexico City who knew what he was to do with it, and a million dollars of the secret service fund had been earmarked for the same purpose, did Scott call in his generals, whose approval, especially that of the influential Democrats among them, he desired. Pillow, who was fond of posing as the President's alter ego, favored the proceeding. So did Twiggs, who thereupon picked up his hat and went to his quarters, for the hour was growing late. Quitman disliked the idea of a bribe and thought that the people at home would fail to understand what would be gained by it and would disapprove of it accordingly. Cadwalader declined to give an opinion, and Shields, who had been a justice of the Supreme Court of Illinois, avoided committing himself. A warm friend of Scott, he wished the general to have no part in the transaction. Worth and Persifor Smith were absent, the former ill.

Scott explained that it was entirely Trist's affair and that he had placed the money at Trist's disposal only because the commissioner had under his control no funds for such a purpose. But he added, according to Colonel Hitchcock, who was present at the meeting, that although he would not tempt the fidelity or patriotism of any Mexican, "he knew of no code of morals which forbade profiting by a professed willingness to be bribed." Perhaps the thought of the many American lives that might be saved in this way influenced him. And, after all, there were many precedents for it in the presents of money that had been made by the government to piratical North African potentates and Indian chiefs to smooth the negotiation of treaties.

The meeting broke up with the understanding that the whole matter was to be kept a profound secret. But something of it leaked out, as something of most secrets did in that army. Two weeks before the meeting of the generals Captain Lee wrote home that Scott had offered to place $225,000 to Trist's order in Mexico City. The newspapermen got wind of the business, and in due time a garbled account of it appeared in the *St. Louis Republican*. And four days after the meeting Captain Lee and others spoke confidently of their expectation of an early peace.

But if the commissioner and the general had, as has been asserted, sold their souls to the Devil, they got the usual bad bargain. Word came back from Mexico City that Santa Anna, with the ten thousand dollars in his pocket, was convinced that the Mexican Congress would not alter the law passed immediately after Cerro Gordo, according to which any government official who negotiated with the enemy was to be held guilty of high treason. In fact, though the Americans did not know it until some weeks later, Santa Anna was convinced that with the army he now had under his command he could not only defend the capital against the invaders but also cut them off from the coast. On July 26 Colonel Hitchcock noted in his diary that hopes of peace had been "knocked into a cocked hat." The only optimistic note was to be found in Mr. Bankhead's opinion that if the Americans advanced into the Valley of Mexico as far as Chalco, peace would follow.

§5

The intrigue, however, had cost nothing but the ten thousand dollars and, in the opinion of the stricter moralists, an abrasion of the integrity of the Americans who engaged in it. The time that it gave to Santa Anna to increase his preparations for defense he would have had in any event. For Scott had still to await the arrival of the final reinforcement that would make it possible for him to advance, and three more weeks were to elapse before these troops reached Puebla.

They numbered 2,500 and were commanded by Franklin Pierce, who, sound Democrat that he was, had risen meteorlike to the rank of brigadier general in the six months since he had preferred enlistment as a private in the volunteers to the attorney-generalship of the United States, which Polk had offered him. Excepting a detachment of marines, the force he led out of Vera Cruz that July was composed of new raw troops, not yet half-disciplined and entirely unused to the hardships of a campaign.

By this time Congress had provided the army with ambulances, excellent vehicles of the type invented by Baron Larrey for Napoleon's *Grande Armée,* drawn by four horses and mounted on springs. Pierce's soldiers, with the American enlisted man's genius for misnaming any article that is new to him, called them "avalanches" and promptly filled them with the many who dropped, sick or exhausted, along the scorching road across the *tierra caliente.* Among the 2,500 in the brigade, there were 1,500 cases of dysentery, and the infusion of the prickly pear that they made and drank as a remedy was of little use. Of their nightly bivouacs a surgeon with the marines wrote with a curiously forceful delicacy: "the army was infected with an infirmity that made beds, taken in the dark, apt to be as uncomfortable as they were unsavory."

As the mule teams gave out, tents, tent poles, and baggage were tossed out of the wagons and left on the roadside. The men, even the marines, threw away everything they carried excepting their arms and accouterments. The stragglers formed a trail miles long behind the convoy, and the wolves and the lurking guerrillas with their lassos took a grim toll of them. Fresh mules were purchased at Jalapa. But such rumors of the column's distress filtered into Puebla that Scott sent Smith's brigade to succor it.

The castle of Perote looked like a great hospital, and a filthy one, to the newcomers. There was a double line of graves behind it by this time. Puebla, which they finally entered on August 6, seemed more cheerful, with shopkeepers speaking all the tongues of Babel, the signs of "The New York Eating House" and "The Soldier's Home" swinging before stately palaces, and even an American circus. Pierce made a ceremony of presenting the officers of the 9th New England Regiment to the commanding general. It was admitted by everybody that he had brought his command through its many difficulties with remarkable success.

With him came a battery of siege guns, but no funds in the form of specie, only $85,000 in drafts, which were unsalable at Puebla. This, wrote Hitchcock, was the severest blow Scott had yet received. The administration and others at home had long been impatient of Scott's policy of paying the army's way in Mexico instead of subsisting his troops at the enemy's expense. But sound policy had dictated his course. Forced levies on the country would have aroused the entire population against the Americans. But since they paid fair prices for all they took, they were preferable, invaders though they were, to Santa Anna's troops, who were apt to live at free quarters.

Pierce's arrival at Puebla brought Scott's numbers up to some 14,000. But of these, 2,500 were sick, and 600 were convalescents too weak to march. To guard the sick, whom he was compelled to leave behind him, he assigned the convalescents and a like number of effectives under the command of Colonel Thomas Childs, a veteran from Palo Alto days. For his advance, after reserving to himself the control of the dragoons, engineers, siege train, and howitzer and rocket battery, he organized the rest in four divisions.

The first two of these were composed of regulars of the old establishment: four regiments of artillery acting as infantry, seven of infantry, the Mounted Rifles, and three of his field batteries. Worth led the First Division, with Colonel Garland and Colonel Clark as brigade commanders; Twiggs the Second, with Persifor Smith and Colonel Riley at the heads of his brigades.

The Third Division Pillow commanded, Cadwalader and Pierce being the brigadiers. Technically it was composed of regulars: the Voltiguers and five of the new infantry regiments. But since they were authorized for this war only, they were more like the United States volunteer regiments of a half-century later. Four of them were loosely territorial in their make-up: the 9th New England; the 12th, whose men came from the two Carolinas, Missouri, Arkansas, and Texas; the 11th, which was made up of Pennsylvania, Delaware, and Maryland men; and the 15th, which had been recruited in Ohio and the newer Northwestern states of Michigan, Wisconsin, and Iowa. Illinois, Tennessee, and Louisiana had furnished the 14th. The Voltiguers came from Maryland, Virginia, Pennsylvania, Georgia, Kentucky, and Mississippi. A battery of regular field artillery stiffened this aggregation.

Quitman commanded the Fourth Division, with the brigades under Shields and Lieutenant Colonel Watson of the marines. It was composed of the marine battalion, the New York and South Carolina regiments of volunteers, and a detachment of the 2nd Pennsylvania. At home the country might be turning against the war, but every part of it seems to have been represented in this army.

The cavalry, which was commanded by Harney, was made up of parts of the 1st, 2nd, and 3rd Dragoon regiments, with Kearny, Sumner, and McReynolds heading the squadrons. Captain Benjamin Huger, Chief of the Ordnance Department, marched with the siege train.

On August 7, the very next day after Pierce's arrival, all preparations having been made, or as nearly made as circumstances and resources would permit, the advance began. Twiggs's division, with Harney's dragoons in front of it and the siege train following, led the way up the long road around the base of snow-capped Ixtacihuatl, which — as many an American officer that day remembered — the army of Cortes had taken more than three hundred years before. And they had good cause to remember. For, figuratively speaking, Scott had burned his ships as completely as Cortes had actually done. He had, as he wrote afterwards, "thrown away the scabbard" in abandoning his line of communications. He had to abandon them in order to advance: with five times the troops he had at his disposal he would not have had enough to hold them. But now let him lose one battle and he and his army were lost.

The London *Morning Chronicle* mocked at his movement as being "about as visionary as that of Napoleon on Moscow," and prophesied that the one thing more difficult than for his army to get to Mexico City would be for it to get back to Vera Cruz. The Duke of Wellington, whom he had known slightly in England years before, exclaimed: "Scott is lost! He has been carried away by successes. He can't take the city, and he can't fall back upon his base."

The divisions of Quitman, Worth, and Pillow, in that order, followed Twiggs, one day apart, but with only a half-day's march between any of them, so that they could quickly support each other. And a long train of wagons and camp-followers — sutlers, printers with their presses, editors and reporters, actors and circus riders, gamblers, jobbers, "certain frail but daring fair ones," *damas cortesanas*, sailors turned teamsters, and discharged soldiers — trailed after them in a rabble rout inconceivable according to modern ideas of war.

The troops marched out of Puebla with all possible martial pomp: bands playing, colors uncased, and bayonets flashing in the brilliant sun. A flag of smoke flew from the volcanic cone of Popocatepetl, which for the past three weeks had been showing signs of activity by the disappearance of the snow on its summit. Scott came galloping up the column, followed by the ringing cheers of his men, and each regimental band in turn greeted his passing with the strains of *Hail to the Chief*. The old man loved it, as he loved everything connected with his profession, and the troops swore by him.

Had he not told their officers in their hearing: "My greatest delight is in this fine body of troops, without whom we can never sleep in the Halls of the Montezumas, or in our own homes." What did thirty thousand Mexicans in a walled city and its surrounding forts amount to against ten thousand Americans such as they, with such a leader?

CHAPTER IX

Battle, Humbug, and Victory

§1

"THAT SPLENDID CITY soon shall be ours." So, Scott believed, must have run the thought of every soldier as he stood at last on the western slope of the mountains and gazed across the Valley of Mexico to the twin towers of the Cathedral, which marked the destination of his efforts. Below him white towns shone in the brilliant sunshine, broad lakes sparkled, and long straight highways ran between rich fields that filled a frame of snow-clad peaks, with the cone of Popocatepetl dominating the whole.

After what the troops had experienced on their way up to Puebla, they did not find these marches difficult, although for the first thirty-six miles the fields of tall corn that walled the road smothered the columns in their own dust. After that came the climb over the mountains: the Anahuac Ridge, 10,400 feet above the sea, where the bitter winds made the mounted men and officers shiver in their overcoats and scrapes. And presently came the thrilling sight of a swift little river whose waters flowed to the Pacific.

The road, for a mountain road, was fair though slippery enough to give some trouble with the artillery and the wagons on the steeper grades and the elbow turnings. But there was no other danger, no sign of opposition by the enemy. Pass after narrow pass where resistance could have been stubborn had been left unguarded. At one of these, entrenchments had been begun, but work on them had been abandoned. Santa Anna had decided to concentrate all serious resistance in the neighborhood of the capital and had given orders for no more than the harassment of the invaders on their march by guerrillas and certain regular troops.

But between jealousy of his power and suspicion of his motives, the local governor, the commanding general in the district, and the principal leader of the irregulars had failed to obey his orders, except the one enjoining them to avoid combat on unfavorable conditions. This they made sure of doing by avoiding it altogether, and many of the regulars deserted. The inhabitants, disgusted by the depredations of the guerrillas, met the Americans with friendliness and help.

Beyond the summit of the divide the road wound down the mountain in great loops, on which the white tops of the three-mile-long wagon train — there were nearly a thousand wagons in all — shone between oaks and tall pines three feet thick, and magnificent views presented themselves at every turning. Some thirteen thousand trees had been felled to bar the road, but only comparatively few of them had been hauled into position.

At the bottom of the descent the army came through immense olive groves and wide market gardens to the town of Ayolta, whence the shallow waters of Lake Chalco spread southward. Market canoes with bright cargoes of flowers, fruits, and vegetables clustered at the reedy margin, and lovely floating islets, like the floating gardens of Montezuma's day, dotted its smooth surface. The inhabitants were less forthcoming than those behind the mountains, locked their doors against the invaders, and shouted through the keyhole that they had lost the key. But to a threat of the *llave grande Americana*, which meant the ax of a pioneer, the reply was invariably prompt and compliant: *"Espera un momento, señores, que se abrá la puerta muy pronto."*

It was August 10, the fifth day after leaving Puebla, that Twiggs's division, with Scott and the headquarters staff accompanying it, arrived at Ayolta. It halted there, with Harney and his dragoons pushed out a mile and a half in front of it at the village of San Isidro. As the other divisions ar-

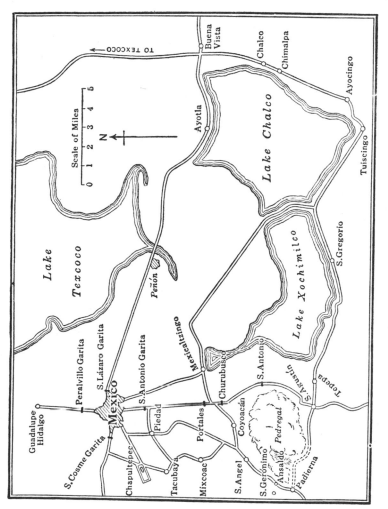

Scale of Miles
0 1 2 3 4 5

N

TO TEXCOCO →

Buena Vista

Chalco

Chimalpa

Ayocingo

Ayotla

Tuiscingo

Lake Chalco

Lake Texcoco

Peñon

S.Gregorio

Lake Xochimilco

Mexicaltzingo

Peralvillo Garita

S.Lázaro Garita

S.Antonio Garita

Churubusco

S.Antonio

Guadalupe Hidalgo

Mexico

Piedad

Portales

Coyoacán

Teepa

S.Agustin

S.Cosme Garita

Chapultepec

Tacubaya

Mixcoac

S.Angel

S.Gerónimo

Ansaldo

Pedregal

Padierna

VALLEY OF MEXICO

rived, closing the intervals between them as they neared their destination, they took up positions within easy supporting distance of one another: Worth to Twiggs's left rear at Chalco on the eastern shore of the lake; Pillow a little to the south of Worth; and Quitman at a crossroads called Buena Vista, where the road northward from Chalco intersected the Ayolta road.

At Ayolta the army was only fourteen miles from Mexico City, but all approaches to the capital were beset with difficulties and formidable obstacles. Seven miles to the front, where the direct road crossed an arm of extensive Lake Texcoco, it was barred by the isolated conical hill, between four hundred and four hundred and fifty feet high, named El Peñon Viejo. From the red ledges of this eminence three tiers of great guns frowned upon the watery plain. Troops swarmed on its ramparts and shouted down to the reconnoitering American officers that everything was ready to receive them.

The road that ran northward from the Buena Vista crossroads reached the city only after swinging round the northern end of Lake Texcoco and passing through Guadalupe Hidalgo, whence it entered the city from the north. It was lacking in forage and water, and the intelligence service reported that it was held by General Gabriel Valencia with reliable troops and, owing to his refusal to contribute his artillery to the defense of the fortifications of the city, a train of heavy guns.

To the west of El Peñon several highways approached the capital from the south. But the nearest of these could be reached by the army only by marching round Lake Chalco, threading the narrow isthmus between that lake and its western neighbor, Lake Xochimilco, and proceeding thence northwesterly to the town of Mexicalcingo. Mexicalcingo was only five miles from Mexico City, but it was strongly fortified; one side of it was protected by an arm of Xochimilco; and it was held by a numerous garrison. All of these roads, moreover, were built upon causeways, and between them recent heavy rains had turned into something like swamps the fields that had not been flooded by man-made inundations.

The results of several days of careful and daring reconnaissance were collated with the reports of spies and intelligence obtained through foreign residents in the city. The general's young aide-de-camp, Schuyler Hamilton, whose name indicates his distinguished descent from two of the worthies of his country's earliest days, was brought in severely wounded. Scott had sent him out with an escort of seventy dragoons to arrange, if possible, for the casting of cannon balls at a local foundry, and two hundred enemy lancers had routed and scattered his party.

Persifor Smith, with the Rifles, felt out the defenses of Mexicalcingo and penetrated far beyond El Peñon in a reconnaissance that Scott wrote of as "the boldest and most daring" of the war. Scott himself, accompanied by Trist, who was now his devoted friend, examined both positions personally and came near deciding to assail El Peñon by direct attack with three of his divisions, while Worth marched round Lake Chalco and supported the movement by a simultaneous assault on Mexicalcingo.

But Worth made strong and well-founded objections to being thus separated from the rest of the army. He sent Lieutenant Colonel James Duncan of the artillery to investigate once more the only remaining road by which an advance could be made, a road that previous reconnaissances had reported to be impracticable. This was a route that, passing between the marshy southern shores of the two lakes and the steep mountain slopes that beetled above them, led to the village of San Augustín, the scene of the famous annual gambling-fiestas. Thence a highway curved northward round a great lava field, passed the hacienda of San Antonio, and went on over a bridge at Churubusco to the capital, which was distant from San Augustín only about ten miles.

Duncan reported that the road was practicable, though in some places there was barely room for a wagon to pass between the lake shores and the mountains. Scott, who had told

Trist that he would regard himself as a murderer if he should lose 900 men in taking the city when by another route he could have taken it with a loss of only 800, accepted the report with pleasure. On the morning of August 15 — "by a sudden inversion," as he described the movement in his autobiography — he sent Worth's division, with the dragoons ahead of it, marching southward and westward through the tortuous defile. It was "mud, mud, mud," all the way, as one artillery officer remembered it. It took most of three days to cover the twenty-seven miles. Mexican irregulars rose from the rocks and brush along the mountainside in a manner that reminded Lieutenant Semmes of the clansmen of Roderick Dhu and rolled down boulders and tree trunks, but their hearts were not in the fighting, and at a few shots from the American light-infantrymen they fled. On August 18 Worth stood at San Augustín, with the divisions of Quitman and Pillow close behind him, and El Peñon, the fortress that had balked the advance of a Spanish army not many years before, had been turned and made of no effect.

§2

The only trouble was that the enemy, since he held interior lines, had shorter distances to cover and so could meet promptly this new threat to his defenses. In order to mask his movement Scott had left Twiggs at Ayolta for one day after the other divisions had marched. But Valencia got wind of it and, when Twiggs moved out on the 16th, encountered him between Ayolta and Chalco with a strong force of cavalry and infantry. As usual in such circumstances, the American light batteries put the enemy to rout. But when Worth and the dragoons advanced from San Augustín on the road to Churubusco two days later, they met with such stout resistance at the hacienda of San Antonio that they retired.

Beautiful in a setting of silver poplars and Peruvian pepper trees, the place was so constructed as to earn from the Americans the name of "the White Castle." It was strongly garrisoned and well armed with cannon, and their first shot put an end to the troubles of the unfortunate Captain Thornton, whose clash with the irregulars on the Rio Grande had precipitated hostilities, and whom Taylor had brought before a court-martial after he was exchanged.

San Augustín was a charming town, shaded by orchards and interspersed with luxuriant gardens. Many of its houses were the summer places of wealthy residents of Mexico City, some of whom had sought a refuge in them from the expected attack on the capital. These gentlemen did all in their power to propitiate the invaders, short of introducing them to their womenfolk. But the Americans found little comfort there. Forage was lacking, hard bread rations were turning musty. The ground was wet, there was no tentage available, and rain threatened. The mood of the soldiers changed from elation over their successful march to discouragement and doubt as the check at San Antonio and reconnaissances of the routes farther west demonstrated that their laborious maneuver had been countered by a corresponding movement by the enemy. The strong position at San Antonio blocked what was practically a defile between a marshy overflow from Lake Xochimilco to the east of it and, to the west, fifteen square miles of lava bed, which was known as the Pedregal and looked like a raging sea that had been instantaneously turned to stone. A wild tangle of ravines and gullies, it appeared to present an impassable obstacle, especially to mounted troops and artillery.

Across its southwestern corner, however, Lee and Beauregard discovered a mule track that came out a little to the north of the village of Contreras on a highway running to the capital through the villages of San Ángel and Piedad. To make this track practicable for troops and guns, they reported, would not be too difficult; the distance from San Augustín to the highway was only five miles; and on the morning of the 19th Scott set Pillow's men to work on it with pick and shovel. Twiggs's division guarded and escorted them as they advanced, and Magruder's 6-pounders and 12-pounders, the rocket battery, and the mountain guns followed

until, on the ridge that overlooked the highway, they came
under a fire so heavy that road-building had to cease and the
guns must be manhandled forward in order to open fire.

Nine hundred yards away, across a valley through which
ran the highroad and a little stream, rose a rounded hill, its
slopes furrowed by entrenchments that bristled with bayonets and were punctuated with the muzzles of heavy guns.
At its foot, on the hither side of the stream, the small hamlet
of Padierna was occupied by enemy infantry, and the flanks
of the position were guarded by several regiments of lancers.
Since Lee and Beauregard had observed the locality the day
before, General Valencia had moved into it with 5,000 men
and twenty-two guns.

Pillow's orders contemplated no more than the building of
the road, but his self-sufficiency rose to the occasion. Undeterred by the memory of his blundering at Cerro Gordo, he
established his position on the hill of Zacatepec, whence he
could observe the whole field of action, sent Smith's brigade
to clear the Mexicans out of Padierna, preparatory to a
frontal attack, and ordered Riley's brigade to move to his
right front, across the edge of the Pedregal, to ford the
stream and approach the Indian village of San Gerónimo for
the purpose of threatening Valencia's line of retreat.

Smith's troops succeeded in taking Padierna. Riley's traversed a mile of lava, waded the stream, repulsed several
charges by three regiments of lancers under General Torrejón, and took cover in and around San Gerónimo to await the
success of the attack on Valencia's front. But that attack had
stalled. The light American guns, though officered by John B.
Magruder — the "Prince John" of Big Bethel and Malvern
Hill — by Jesse Lee Reno, who was to command a Federal
corps at Second Bull Run and be killed at South Mountain,
and by Lieutenant Thomas Jonathan Jackson, the "Stonewall" of First Manassas, were all but put out of action by
the more numerous and heavier Mexican artillery, among
which were several 68-pounders. Without adequate artillery
support the infantry could not attack up the slope with any

hope of success. For if they advanced in column, the enemy guns would plow them through and through; and if they deployed into line for the attack, their flanks would be exposed to the charges of the enemy lancers, from which they had no cavalry to protect them.

Back at San Agustín, Scott heard the unexpected noise of battle with anxiety and obtained from the roof of his headquarters a distant view of Valencia's position. He mounted his horse and, about three in the afternoon, joined Pillow at his command post. Even there the fire was so hot that he received a slight wound. The situation in which Pillow had involved his two divisions was more serious than Scott had feared. Santa Anna himself had marched swiftly to the support of Valencia and, with several thousand troops drawn from the capital, El Peñon, and San Antonio, had made an impressive appearance on the hills above and to the northeast of San Gerónimo. Even Polk's pet major general had been able to see that this development exposed Riley to annihilation. He had sent Cadwalader to reinforce him, and Smith, who was without orders now, marched his brigade in that direction also.

To prevent the possible crushing of these organizations between the two armies of Mexicans, Scott further reinforced them with Shields's brigade, which he had ordered to follow him from San Agustín. He urged Pillow to stand fast, promised to bring up the divisions of Worth and Quitman in the morning, and returned to his headquarters. He knew that he could rely upon the fighting spirit of his soldiers and on the courage and constancy of their officers. He well knew the Mexican dislike of night operations, and only about two hours of daylight now remained. Nevertheless, he passed an uneasy time until midnight, sending out seven of his staff officers in turn in vain efforts to get in touch with Smith and Riley. The intricate pathways of the Pedregal baffled them all.

If he had been aware of the situation that was rapidly developing between Santa Anna and Valencia, he might have rested more easily. The relations between the two had long been strained. Valencia shared fully in the jealousy and suspicion of Santa Anna's power and intentions that were widespread in Mexico. He was believed to cherish the highest ambitions for himself. His refusal to give up his heavy guns was not the only evidence of his unwillingness to co-operate with his Commander-in-Chief, and if he had been less powerful than he was politically, Santa Anna would have removed him from command before this.

He had greatly exceeded his orders in advancing to his present position. He had been charged with the defense of the southwestern sector, between Tacubaya and Coyoacán. The stalling of the American attack elated him beyond measure. He celebrated it as a victory, reported to Santa Anna that he had smashed the American army against the sharp edges of the Pedregal, made promotions of his officers as if he had been the President himself, and proceeded to get gloriously drunk.

Santa Anna, who had ordered him to retire earlier in the day and had decided that the nature of the terrain was unfavorable for an attack on San Gerónimo, had withdrawn about two miles northward under cover of darkness to the village of San Ángel. There he received information that the Americans, far from being destroyed, as Valencia reported them to be, were gathered by the thousand in the woods around San Gerónimo. Furiously angry, he sent Valencia orders to retreat, on receipt of which Valencia shouted that Santa Anna had betrayed him. Torrejón reported that Americans with lights were creeping up to the rear of the position, and panic swept through the camp that had lately been so jubilant.

But none of this was known to the Americans at San Gerónimo. The last they had heard from their foes had been the bands, the *vivas*, and the salutes of cannon that celebrated Valencia's fancied victory. One of those cold and violent rains that seem to be a feature of almost every night on the battlefield had begun in the midafternoon. With little food, shelterless, and without fires, they lay or crouched under the downpour. They were old enough soldiers to understand the peril of the position in which nightfall had found them; the fortunes of this war had not accustomed them to reverses; they supposed Santa Anna's troops to be still on the heights to the north of them; and to the best of their knowledge the coming day would bring a die-hard fight with between 12,000 and 15,000 of the enemy.

But among their leaders were men who, however lacking in academic training for their profession, were enterprising, confident, and experienced. Persifor Smith, who had seen plenty of the rough side of war in fighting the Seminoles, sent Captain Lee back to Scott with a plan for making a dawn attack on Valencia's camp from the rear in combination with a simultaneous frontal assault by the troops under Twiggs and Pierce. Where all others had been baffled by the black labyrinth of the Pedregal, Lee, whom Colonel Hitchcock called " 'the' engineer," made his way through to San Augustín and back again soon after midnight with the Commander-in-Chief's approval of the project and the requisite orders for it.

Meanwhile other engineer officers had found a ravine that seemed to lead in the right direction, and up this gully in the pouring darkness of three o'clock in the morning, blundering over rocks and slipping in clay that was like soft soap, Riley's brigade, supported by Cadwalader's and a part of Smith's, groped their way until the coming of daylight enabled them to prime the drenched pans of their muskets afresh and take up their positions for the attack. General Smith looked at his watch. It was about six o'clock.

Seventeen minutes later the battle was won. Valencia had neglected to fortify the rear of his camp. Only a couple of 6-pounders faced Riley's men, and they fired high. So did the guns that were swung hastily about to meet this attack. And up from Padierna rushed the 9th Infantry. The half-formed Mexicans, caught between two fires, broke; gunners who stayed by their pieces blazed away without aiming; flying lancers rode down the demoralized infantry; and a mob of camp women, laborers, and stampeded mules swelled the rout, which swept northward along the highway and scattered across the hills to the northeast.

Shields, who had been left at San Gerónimo lest Santa Anna fall upon the American rear, captured the fugitives by the hundred. Eight hundred of them, including four generals, were taken in all. Valencia and Torrejón galloped to safety along with most of the lancers, but J. M. Salas, one-time Vice President, who had issued the "no quarter" order, was among the prisoners. The booty included many horses, 700 mules, large quantities of ammunition, and twenty-two guns. The Mexican dead numbered 700. The American loss, both killed and wounded — "on the spot," as Scott reported it — was only sixty. Yet the numbers of the combatants were about equal, and, as Scott pointed out later, the Americans had pitted their 4,500 men against a potential enemy strength of 12,000.

It is small wonder that in his Report 32, dated August 28, he wrote of this Battle of Contreras: "August 20th opened with one of a series of unsurpassed achievements."

When he rode over from San Augustín about nine o'clock that morning, the men of the 4th Artillery had just recognized in a couple of captured brass 6-pounders the two guns that the Mexicans had taken from the 4th Artillery's battery at Buena Vista. He added his cheers to theirs, gave orders for the guns to be organized into a battery, and set off after the divisions of Pillow and Twiggs, which were by this time well up the road to San Ángel in pursuit of the fleeing enemy. Victory and glorious sunshine had warmed the spirits of the men and dried their sodden clothing, and they hailed the passage of the Commander-in-Chief along their columns with one continuous shout.

Before them, only about seven miles away in an air line and not much farther by road, lay Mexico City. Neither troops nor fortifications guarded this approach to it, and Scott was soon to be criticized by no less competent a judge than

Robert E. Lee and others in his army for not pushing straight on and seizing it. But his trains and his wounded were at San Augustín; he had ordered Worth to attack San Antonio from the south that morning; the Pedregal stretched between him and both those places; and, above all, somewhere to the eastward and to the northward of San Antonio, Santa Anna was still in the field with an army that Scott estimated at 27,000 and was in fact probably about 16,000 strong. To have taken the capital without first defeating such a force would have been a barren victory and perhaps a dangerous one. About a mile beyond San Ángel, therefore, he turned the column eastward on the side road that ran through Coyoacán to Churubusco, with the intention of coming down on the rear of San Antonio while Worth attacked it in front.

Worth, however, had not waited for this pincers movement to make itself felt. Sending one of his brigades to turn the right flank of the San Antonio position by a path that the engineers had worked out across the lava bed, he had advanced directly with the other to find that the enemy was already in retreat. Word of the defeat of Valencia, which rendered the San Antonio position untenable, had reached General Bravo, its commander; and his force, which consisted of 3,000 men, was retiring in haste up the road to Churubusco. Two of his guns and several wagons stuck in the mud. Emerging from the Pedregal, the American flanking brigade cut the disordered column in two, sent the leading half of it flying up the road, and dispersed the rest eastward across the swamps in the direction of Mexicalcingo. Worth with his reunited command pressed on, and Scott, who had by that time reached Coyoacán, received information that Worth was hotly engaged with strong Mexican forces in front of Churubusco.

Such serious opposition at that point was unexpected. Worth's first knowledge of the fortifications there came in a storm of grapeshot from a formidable bastioned tête-de-pont that covered the southern approach to the bridge across the Churubusco River at Churubusco village. About two hundred and fifty yards to the southwest of this work an old stone church, the massive stone Convent of San Mateo, and the thick walls of the convent garden formed a fortress, which had been strengthened with field works.

Convent, church, and garden as well as the bridgehead were crammed with troops and heavily armed with cannon. Sharpshooters filled the convent tower. The banks of the river, which was actually a broad drainage canal, were raised above the plain, and the northern bank from convent to bridgehead and on to the eastward was lined with infantry. Cavalry and reserves of infantry held the road to the capital as far as the hacienda of Los Portales, a distance of about a thousand yards. For Santa Anna, retiring from San Ángel that morning, had gathered here the whole of Mexico's remaining forces for what he intended to be a fight to the finish.

The ubiquitous and indefatigable Lee, with Kearny's troop as escort and the Rifles in support, made a swift reconnaissance and returned to Scott with a report of the enemy's position. Within the next ten minutes Pillow, with Cadwalader's Voltiguers and infantry, was crashing through the fields of tall corn to attack on Worth's left against the bridgehead; Twiggs was advancing against the convent; and Pierce, under Lee's guidance and followed by Shields's South Carolinians and New Yorkers, had been dispatched northward with his brigade to wade the canal and then, turning northeastward, to seize the highway at Los Portales and cut the enemy's line of retreat to the city, which was at that point only four miles away.

Pushing forward against the tête-de-pont and the convent, the Americans were met with a tremendous fire of musketry and cannon. The Mexicans fought as they had never fought before. Though built in haste, the tête-de-pont was strong, scientifically constructed, and surrounded by a ditch twenty feet wide, in which the water stood four feet deep. The high corn and numerous ditches impeded and confused the advance through the fields, and twice the veteran 6th Infantry, which attacked along the road, was beaten back. The light guns of the artillery could not face the fire of the enemy's more numerous pieces on the open highway, and they mired in the soft ground when the attempt was made to put them in action on either side of it. In front of the convent Twiggs's men were driven back again and again. The garrison made repeated sorties, and their guns killed and wounded twenty-four men and fourteen horses of a battery that attempted to shoot it out with them at four hundred yards and finally forced it to withdraw.

The battle had begun between noon and one o'clock, and it was past three before the attack showed any sign of succeeding. Then the Americans, working far to their right, turned the Mexican left by fording the canal and advanced toward the highway that led to the capital. To the troops in and about the tête-de-pont it looked like Contreras over again, for their numbers had already been diminished by withdrawals to face the threat against Los Portales. They were shaken, they wavered, and the Americans in front of them, though still subjected to a heavy fire, waded the ditch, stormed the rampart with the bayonet, and seized the work in a bloody melee.

The Mexican troops near by and such of the garrison as could do so began to stream away up the causeway or off to the right on the road to Mexicalcingo. But the garrison of the convent stood fast, although now the fire of the captured guns in the tête-de-pont was added to that already directed against them. For here two hundred and fifty of the deserters of the San Patricio Battalion were fighting with the American provost marshal's halter around their necks, and they would not permit their Mexican comrades to surrender. But ammunition began to fail, guns to fall silent. American infantrymen filtered in through breaches in the garden walls. Presently, to stop the useless carnage, an American officer raised a white flag, and the colors of the 3rd Infantry were flaunted from the convent balcony.

Meanwhile the troops under Pierce and Shields had traced

a wet and muddy course across the canal and over the spongy fields beyond it until, near Los Portales, they were confronted by the Mexican forces on the causeway. They were unfortunate in their leaders that day, although both Pierce and Shields had displayed excellent ability in the past and were to do so again in the near future. Pierce had been so severely hurt by the fall of his horse that he had been unable to advance on the previous afternoon. Thereupon a regular army colonel of the type that is afflicted with a congenital suspicion of the courage of all volunteers had called him "a damned coward," and this morning he rode at the head of his brigade in such agony that he fainted during the course of the action.

Shields made poor work of deploying his men. More than a third of them were killed or wounded, and for some time they were barely able to hold their own. But they ended by taking 380 prisoners and joining in the pursuit as the fugitives from the tête-de-pont poured up the road with Worth's and Twiggs's men hot on their heels and the dragoons galloping among them and sabering them as they fled.

Philip Kearny led two squadrons in this and, true to his training in the Chasseurs d'Afrique, failed to hear the "recall" when it was sounded. With only two squads he actually cut his way in at the city gate and lost his arm there. Second Lieutenant Richard Stoddard Ewell, who was to be one of Lee's ablest lieutenants fifteen years later, had two horses killed under him here. The other squadron leader, A. T. McReynolds, was seriously wounded but recovered and lived on to keep his brigade out of Ewell's clutches in the Valley of Virginia at the beginning of the Gettysburg campaign. First Lieutenant James Longstreet advanced against Churubusco as adjutant of the 8th Infantry, and Second Lieutenant Winfield Scott Hancock, who was to be wounded in fighting Longstreet at Gettysburg, charged with the 6th on this happier day.

§3

The cheering ran from the convent to the bridge and on up the road for two miles beyond Los Portales, as Scott, his handsome old face beaming with pride and gratitude, rode among his troops. It was, indeed, a magnificent victory. A third of Santa Anna's army had been killed or wounded or had gone missing since the dawn of that bloody Friday. The prisoners numbered 3,000, including eight generals, and two of these had been Presidents of the Mexican republic. Four thousand Mexicans had been killed or wounded. The capture of thirty-seven guns had more than doubled the strength of the American siege train and field batteries.

But all this had not been won cheaply. The American army had lost 139 killed, including sixteen officers among whom were the colonels of the South Carolinians and the New Yorkers. Sixty officers and 816 enlisted men were wounded. The casualties at Churubusco, wrote Thomas Mayne Reid, the English writer and adventurer, who fought there as a second lieutenant in the New York volunteers, were, for the numbers engaged, greater than those at Waterloo.

Seated in a tent pitched on the spot where the tent of Cortes had stood during the siege of the city in 1521, Lieutenant Semmes was not alone in feeling shame at his recent joy in the victory. The grim work of collecting almost a thousand American wounded and many more of the enemy was going on around him. The medical corps, desperately short-handed, was at its dreadful task of probing and amputation. Thunder rolled, lightning flashed, and again, as on the previous day, black night fell swiftly in a torrential downpour.

Many of the soldiers dropped where they stood and slept the sleep of exhaustion after thirty-six hours of almost continuous labor, marching, and fighting. Others found shelter where they could: Shields's at Los Portales; Worth's there and at Churubusco. Some of Pillow's men straggled back to San Antonio, and some of Twiggs's to Coyoacán and even to San Ángel.

Scott rode back to San Agustín, where he was at work on orders for the battering and assault of the city when, through rain and darkness, came Edward Thornton, secretary of the British legation, and a deputation of British merchants resident in the capital. They admitted that he might easily take the city amid the consternation that his victories had caused there, but they urged him not to do so lest the fall of the capital should so discredit the government as to "scatter the elements of peace."

It was among the considerations that had been present in Scott's mind when he ordered recall to be sounded to his troops that afternoon. His instructions from the President were "to conquer a peace," not a country. So it was toward Tacubaya, a pleasant suburban summer resort two and a half miles southwest of Mexico City, that he was marching with the dragoons and Worth's division the next morning (August 21) when he was meet by a fine carriage bearing an emissary from Santa Anna.

This was General Ignacio Mora y Villamil, Chief of the Mexican Army Engineers. He descended from his carriage. General Scott dismounted from his horse. A great tree stood near by, and in its shade the two held a brief conference while their staffs looked on from a respectful distance. The Mexican brought from Santa Anna an oral proposal for a truce to permit the burial of the dead. He was the bearer also of a letter from the Mexican Minister of Foreign Affairs to Secretary Buchanan, offering at long last to listen to such proposals as Mr. Trist might have to make. This letter was open for Trist's inspection, and with it was a note to him from British Minister Bankhead assuring him that the Mexican government was prepared to receive him as an envoy. Scott declined to grant the truce proposed. But he wrote to Santa Anna in return, proposing an armistice with a view to opening negotiations for peace.

Coming as it did from a victorious enemy, this proposal was a godsend to the all but discredited Santa Anna. He made haste not only to accept it but to utilize for home con-

sumption certain generous phrases that spilled into it from
Scott's hasty pen, such as "Too much blood has already been
shed in this unnatural war" and "I await with impatience
. . . an answer to this communication." Might they not be
made to sound as if the recent American victories had been
too dearly won? In Santa Anna's reply he called the war "a
scandal," alluded to "the lack of consideration of the rights
of the Mexican Republic" as the cause of it, and, in expressing his willingness that the American troops should find comfortable quarters, had the insolence to hope that they would
be found "outside the range of shot from the Mexican fortifications." The whole correspondence was published in the
Mexico City newspapers.

Quitman, Smith, and Pierce, all of them lawyers, put in a
night of stiff horse-trading with the Mexican commissioners,
and the armistice was signed next morning.

It provided for a cessation of hostilities for so long as the
Mexican government should be engaged in negotiations with
Mr. Trist, but it could be terminated by either party to it on
forty-eight hours' notice. The troops of both nations were
to remain at the places they then occupied. The Americans
were to allow provisions to enter the city for the use of the
inhabitants and were to be permitted to draw funds from the
city and supplies from both the city and the surrounding
country. But no preparations for the resumption of hostilities were to be made by either side.

Pillow and Worth were for insisting on an American occupancy of the castle of Chapultepec as a guarantee of the
fulfillment of these terms by the enemy. But Scott was determined to rely on Mexican good faith rather than offer an
affront to the Mexican people that might discredit the ex-
isting government and bring about its overthrow. For he
was assured by Mr. Thornton and a number of the resident
British merchants that if that government should fall, chaos
and anarchy would follow and he would be left with no responsible authority with which to negotiate a peace. The
armistice was published on the 24th, and Trist went to work

on the peace negotiations with ex-President Herrera and other commissioners of such excellent reputation that the sincerity of their government appeared to be indubitable.

The army devoted itself to much needed rest and recuperation. Quitman's division remained at San Augustín, which a medical officer with the marines described as "one grand hospital." With troops at Coyoacán and San Angel, Twiggs linked him to Pillow at Mixcoac, which was only two and a half miles from Worth's division and Scott's headquarters in the Archbishop's Palace at Tacubaya. The little towns were pleasant places in which to be billeted. The domes and towers of the church at San Ángel appealed to ear and eye with their many bells and their decoration of porcelain mosaic work. The many British residents of the capital who had summer places at Tacubaya were grateful for the non-interference with their mail throughout the war, opened their luxurious baths and fine billiard rooms to the American officers, and entertained them on *azoteas* that afforded magnificent views of plain and mountain and broad lakes flashing in sunsets that seemed to submerge the domes and spires of Mexico City in a white splendor. The legation courier carried the home letters of the American officers to Vera Cruz, and Mr. Kendall sent off his dispatches to the *Picayune*.

Fruit, green peas, and green corn were abundant. So were pulque, the "wine" of the country, and mescal, which tasted like Irish whisky. And there was money to buy these luxuries with. For Scott was able to cash his drafts in the city. Thence came specie and supplies, and more supplies by wagon train from the valley of Toluca. Americans held prisoner in the city were released. But there were grim interludes as justice caught up with the members of the San Patricio Battalion, of whom eighty had been captured. With his customary magnanimity, Scott had urged clemency on the courts-martial wherever possible. Fifteen of the culprits, who had deserted before the war, escaped with being branded on the face with the letter *D* and the wearing of an eight-pound, three-pronged iron collar at hard labor as long as the army re-

mained in Mexico, after which they were to have their heads
shaved and to be drummed out of the service. Fifty were
hanged in batches several days apart at San Ángel and Mixcoac. The others, it appeared, had never been in the American army or navy.

Rested and well fed, some of the troops began to insult and
rob the inhabitants, and the officers found leisure to criticize
the recent conduct of their leaders and each other: Pillow's
blundering in the Contreras battle; Shields's ineptitude at
Los Portales; Scott's two decisions against seizing the capital, when he might so easily have done so; the failure to make
careful reconnaissance — the only failure of its kind during the campaign — before the attack on Churubusco; and,
above all, the granting of the armistice.

The soldiers felt cheated by this: they had counted on the
fun of sacking the city. Opinion among the officers was divided. Four days after the publication of the armistice Captain Anderson cherished hope that the last great battle of the
war had been fought. But many others — and among them
Lieutenant Semmes, who had acted as secretary and inter-
preter for the American commissioners — soon became convinced that, as he put it, Scott had been "humbugged," and
that the peace negotiations were merely an artifice by which
Santa Anna was gaining time to reorganize and increase his
army and strengthen his fortifications. Many more entertained doubts that various occurrences seemed to confirm.

A mob attacked an American wagon train in the capital
with cries of " *Mueran los yanquis!*" and although it was
guarded by Mexican soldiers, prevented its loading and killed
an American teamster. Scott's agent had to resort to a private carriage and the cover of night to make his next deliv-
ery of money. Specie and food came through later under
Mexican guard, but the agent's storehouse was broken into
and plundered, and there were signs that only Scott's policy
of cash payments prevented the obedience of secret orders
forbidding the country people to sell supplies to the Americans.

Ominous military rumors kept coming in: that a foraging party escorted by a squadron of dragoons had been cut off — which was false; that the fortifications of the city were being strengthened — which was denied; that several thousand reinforcements had entered the city — actually about 400 of Valencia's scattered soldiers; and that Santa Anna had collected 18,000 men — twice the number of Scott's army — and had reviewed them on August 30. It was said that the principal Mexican generals had met in secret to oppose the making of peace: this came to Mr. Trist from Santa Anna himself through the British consul. And day and night, less than a mile away, loomed menacingly the strong castle of Chapultepec on its hilltop. The "*alerta*" of its sentinels answered the American "All's well" through the darkness, and the Mexican bugles responded to the roll of the American drums at dawn.

During the last week of August and the first few days of September the commissioners of the two countries met at brief intervals at the house of the British consul. But officers who studied the expression of Mr. Trist's features as a kind of thermometer at the close of the later sessions suspected that he was not making much progress, and it seemed like an ill omen when Scott broke up housekeeping in the Archbishop's Palace on September 3 and assigned it as quarters for a regiment.

The Mexican government, it appeared, was prepared to cede Texas and Upper California, for a consideration. But all Mexico was shocked by the idea of "selling" the loyal citizens of New Mexico to American masters, and Santa Anna, it seemed, had entered the negotiations under a misapprehension. Seizing on the report of a vague remark that Trist had made at Puebla, he had believed that the United States would consent to the neutralization of the disputed territory between the Rio Grande and the Nueces, or so he pretended.

Trist proposed to extend the armistice long enough to permit him to refer this point to his government. But the fact was that Santa Anna now realized that it would cost him his place to make peace on any terms he might hope to obtain. The country was against any cessions of territory whatever, and especially so since their sale would strengthen his position by placing many millions of ready money under his control. Paredes was reported to have returned from exile. Valencia, who was generally regarded as a martyr to Santa Anna's ambition, had already pronounced against him. And his other generals, though they one and all cannily refused to accept the supreme command of the army, which he craftily offered to them, only waited for an opportunity to drag him out of the saddle.

Early in the negotiations, moreover, he had come to the conclusion that Scott had proposed the armistice not from any humanitarian considerations but because his heavy losses at Contreras and Churubusco had convinced him that without reinforcements he could not go on with the war. Indeed, among the Mexicans generally the armistice was regarded as a masterful American stratagem. In the shadow of their great defeats it was comforting to believe that the enemy had been reduced to a state in which he wanted no more fighting.

Hence the difficulties encountered by the Americans in obtaining money and supplies. The fortifications of Chapultepec were quietly strengthened. Ammunition was smuggled in. Troops were concentrated. Appeals were issued for soldiers, for funds and materials. The clergy were set to preach a crusade, and the Virgin of Guadalupe was paraded through the streets in solemn splendor.

On September 6 the Mexican commissioners presented to Mr. Trist such a project for a peace as both they and Santa Anna knew that he would reject. There was no discussion, only a courteous parting with expressions of mutual esteem. Scott immediately declared the armistice to be at an end. The breaking of its terms by the enemy — infractions that the Mexican commissioners admitted — freed him, he maintained, from the requirement of giving the forty-eight hours' notice. Not to be outdone, the Mexicans marched out the very next day and formed for battle.

§4

Scott, for his part, was far from ready to resume hostili-ties. His army was spread out all the way from San Augustín to Tacubaya. So scrupulously had he abided by the provi-sions of the armistice that he had permitted no reconnais-sances to be made of the approaches to the city or of its forti-fications and had not decided whether to attack its southern or its western side. Close by, however, were two objectives of secondary importance that demanded attention and looked as if they might be easily captured. These were the Molino del Rey, an old foundry, in which, his spies informed him, church bells were being melted down and cast into cannon to replace Santa Anna's heavy losses in artillery in the recent battles, and, eight hundred yards to the northwest of it, the Casa Mata, which housed a large powder magazine.

Both buildings were constructed of massive stone. The Molino, which was a quarter of a mile in length, formed the western side of the great walled enclosure at the eastern end of which towered on its isolated hill the castle of Chapultepec. The Casa Mata was strengthened by a dry ditch and un-completed earthworks; the plain in front of both buildings was commanded by the castle's guns. But there were no forti-fications to link the two, and it was not believed at American headquarters that they were strongly garrisoned. Santa Anna appeared there on the 7th, but marched away that eve-ning to meet a threat that Scott had caused to be made against the southern gates of the city. Worth, to whom the attack was assigned, even entertained the notion of pressing on from the Molino to take the castle.

Scott reinforced Worth's division with Cadwalader's bri-gade, gave him adequate heavy artillery, and, making a cor-rect valuation of the 4,000 irregular Mexican cavalry that were to be seen in the neighborhood of Los Morales, a ha-cienda across a ravine on the enemy's right, added the 270 dragoons to guard his flank. Worth attacked at daylight on the 8th. The result was a bloody fiasco. The position was, indeed, finally taken, the powder magazine blown up. Six guns and 680 prisoners were captured; 2,000 of the enemy were killed or wounded, and about 2,000 more, discouraged by the defeat, deserted. But there proved to be no foundry in operation in the Molino — a thing that many American officers had already suspected: there had evidently been none there for a long time; and out of the troops under Worth's command, which entered the fight 3,447 strong, 116, including nine officers, were killed, and 665, of whom forty-nine were officers, were wounded.

For Worth loved the bayonet so well that he attempted to rush the position after only the briefest artillery preparation. That innocent-looking interval between the Molino and the Casa Mata which appeared to be the weakest spot in the line turned out to contain a deep ditch. In front of this the storming party huddled helpless, masking their own artillery fire, while a Mexican battery, hitherto concealed, and the musketry of troops massed among the thickets of maguey beyond it and on the sandbagged roof of the Molino cut them to pieces.

The Americans assigned to the assault of the Molino and the Casa Mata fared little better. The doors were stout, the walls too high for climbing. There were neither breaching pieces nor scaling ladders at hand, and roofs and barred windows flamed with enemy fire. Captain Anderson, whose wounded shoulder the surgeons kept under a poultice of bread and milk for many days, said the fire was heavier than he had thought possible. The leading elements fell back, and the Mexicans followed them, murdering the wounded they found in their way. Reinforcements restored the attack. The Molino was taken in fierce hand-to-hand fighting, but at the Casa Mata the assaults were repulsed until artillery fire forced the garrison to retreat. So gravely did Scott doubt the issue that he ordered up Smith's brigade and Riley's, which arrived just as the battle was won. The 5th Infantry came out, looking about the size of a company, with one of its captains in command. Fortunately the commander of the

Mexican cavalry decided that the ravine was too difficult to cross, though Sumner, who was to lead a grand division of the Federal army at Fredericksburg, led his dragoons across it and vainly dared the Mexicans to charge them.

"The foully murderous tragedy of Molino del Rey," Robert Anderson called it. Another officer wrote that human ingenuity could not have devised a better plan for the slaughter of our troops without result. Hitchcock wrote of it in his diary as "a sad mistake" and added: "There is general grief in the army for the loss of so many valuable men and because of the manner of it." Worse still was the blow to the army's confidence in itself and in its leaders. It was rumored that one division commander and one brigadier were in favor of entrenching and waiting for reinforcements. Simple arithmetic showed that the 10,300 troops with which Scott left Puebla had shrunk to 8,300, whereas the best information obtainable indicated that Santa Anna had now an army of from 18,000 to 20,000 men and seventy guns. Hitchcock thought that Scott might be compelled to attack the city and work his way in by inches, as Kleber had been compelled to do at Cairo in 1800. Scott turned irritable, as he always did when things were going badly.

The breach between him and Worth grew wider. Partisans of the latter — notably Semmes, who had served through the campaign as Worth's volunteer aide — were inclined to believe that through negligence Scott had misled Worth as to the difficulties before him in the attack on the Molino position. Hot words passed between the two generals, and when Scott summoned the division and brigade commanders to decide on the objectives of the next attack, Worth remained away.

The choice lay between an attack on the southern gates of Niño Perdido and San Antonio and the storming of the castle of Chapultepec as an essential first step in advancing against the city's western gates of Belén and San Cosme. Scott, who had reconnoitered the southern gates in person, opened the discussion by speaking in favor of the Chapultepec route: the artillery officers were confident of the ability of their guns to destroy the fortifications of the castle. But most of the generals were against it. Lee and, with one exception, the rest of the engineer officers, who had been scouting continually since the termination of the armistice, doubted the power of the artillery to reduce the castle and feared that if its failure to do so should make an assault necessary, such heavy losses might be suffered that it would be impossible to go on to the attack of the city itself.

The only engineer to favor the Chapultepec plan was young Lieutenant Beauregard. He pointed out that on account of the marshy nature of the ground and the numerous inundations the southern attack would have to be confined almost entirely to the causeways, which had been cut in many places and strongly fortified in others, and on which the advancing columns would be exposed to heavy enfilading fire without being able to receive adequate support from their own artillery. He held that, whichever side of the city might be attacked afterwards, Chapultepec ought to be taken as a pivot from which a movement could be made against any part of the city's perimeter. After he had spoken, Pierce changed his vote and sided with Scott, who was already supported by Twiggs and Riley.

"Gentlemen," Scott announced, "we shall attack by the western gates. The general officers will remain for orders. The meeting is dissolved." Later that night he ordered his siege guns into positions from which they could give the castle a thorough bombardment the following morning.

Since the termination of the armistice Quitman's division, with a convoy of hundreds of prisoners and their wives and *queridas*, whose bare legs and bronze busts made a squalid display through tattered skirts and ragged *rebozos*, had moved from San Augustín to Coyoacán. By a night march it joined Pillow's division at La Piedad, where they made a show of strength in threatening proximity to the southern gates of the city on the 12th. That night, under cover of darkness, Pillow's troops took position in the deserted Molino, and Quitman's men bivouacked close to Tacubaya. They were awakened by the screams of a soldier who had been sleeping on the roadside when a siege gun ran over his legs, and day broke to show them Chapultepec looming darkly against the dawn.

Throughout the previous day the great guns and mortars had been sending their 8-inch and 11-inch shells screaming over the five-hundred-year-old cypress grove that had been the delight of Montezuma and Cortes to burst against the castle walls. By nightfall some shot holes had been observed in these, but the bombardment had not forced the evacuation of the place, as Scott had hoped that it would, and the return fire of its batteries had continued to be too accurate for comfort.

When the generals assembled at Scott's headquarters that evening to receive their final orders for the attack on the morrow, they were not optimistic about its results. Pillow became discontented when a plan that he had evolved by the unaided light of nature was rejected; Worth remarked in an aside: "We shall be defeated"; and when the others had gone, Scott admitted to Hitchcock that he had his "misgivings."

The appearance of their objective was certainly formidable. Chapultepec, the Aztecs' Hill of the Grasshoppers, rose to a height of a hundred and fifty or two hundred feet above the plain. Cliffs and crags guarded its northern and eastern faces. On its southern side the one regular approach climbed so steeply from the fortified gate in the fifteen-foot wall that formed the outer enclosure that the road had to turn sharply on itself to reach the castle at the top, and a fortification guarded the bend. On the west the ascent from the Molino del Rey was more gradual. But troops advancing there must first cross fields and meadows under the fire of the castle's batteries, then penetrate the grove of ancient, moss-festooned cypresses, which grew in a morass, and finally scale a rough, boulder-strewn hillside that was sown with land mines and swept by fire from massive walls of masonry that rose from a deep fosse to enclose the terreplein on which stood the castle itself.

Intended originally to be a summer palace for the Spanish viceroys, this building had not been constructed to withstand bombardment, but its walls had been strengthened with timbers and sandbags. It housed the Military Academy of Mexico, and the cadets, a hundred youths who were spoiling for a fight with the Yankees, formed part of the garrison. To help them they had fewer than twelve guns and 240 poor troops, whom the bombardment had brought close to demoralization. But the gun crews were good; 600 infantry and artillery manned the outworks; and the courageous Bravo, who had held the village of San Antonio until he was maneuvered out of it, was in command. Santa Anna promised to send reinforcements as soon as they should be required, and he actually did place 4,000 troops on the causeways close to the eastern side of the castle hill for that purpose, although Twiggs kept up the demonstrations against the San Antonio gate.

At daylight on the 13th the guns and mortars reopened, pouring a storm of shot and shell upon the castle until half past seven, when for thirty minutes they searched the cypress grove with grapeshot and canister. Then a five-minute lull gave the signal for attack, and they turned their fire on the castle once more as the columns advanced.

Quitman, whose mission was to attack along the road from Tacubaya against the southern slope, was checked almost immediately, although he had been reinforced by Persifor Smith's brigade. Close packed between the marshy fields that bordered the road, his column was staggered by the direct fire of guns in a hornwork at the southeast corner of the castle's outer enclosure and enfiladed both by troops on the causeway leading to the Belén gate and by others who fired from scaffolds behind the castle's outer wall. He sent Smith's brigade to his right to feel its way across the wet ground toward the flank of the hornwork, Shields to the left against the castle enclosure, while on the causeway his guns fought it out with the enemy guns in front of them.

Of Pillow's division, Pierce's brigade poured out of the Molino, swept across the open ground, and, floundering through knee-deep mud, chased the Mexican sharpshooters out of the cypress grove. Four companies of the gray-coated Voltiguers followed Lieutenant Colonel Joseph E. Johnston swiftly eastward along the outside of the outer castle wall, stormed the redan at the gate and the strong point at the bend of the road above it, and joined the left of their line to Pierce's right for the last stiff climb to the fosse.

But there the attack was stalled, for the scaling ladders had been entrusted to inexperienced men who had failed to keep up with the swift advance. Unable to go on and determined not to retire, infantrymen and Voltiguers huddled among brush and boulders for fifteen terrible minutes, answering as best they could with rifle and musket the fire of cannon and musketry that was poured down upon them from wall, window, and roof. Fortunately the enemy's guns could not be sufficiently depressed to reach the nearest of them, and his infantry had to expose themselves above the parapet in order to aim at them. The narrow gravelike mounds among which they found themselves they recognized as land mines and either cut the canvas pipes that housed the powder trains or shot the Mexicans charged with firing them.

It seemed probable that enemy reinforcements from the plain might come round the shoulder of the hill at any moment. Pillow, nursing a bullet-bruised ankle, which he reported as a shattered leg, called on Worth to help him with his whole division, and Worth, who was advancing on the road north of the castle to support the attack, sent him a brigade. But there were already too many men in blue and gray crowded together with their bright regimental flags on that narrow front.

Santa Anna had in fact sent a battalion to reinforce the castle, but it had encountered American troops at the bend of the road and was not heard of thereafter. Round the shoul-

der of the hill, instead, came Shields's New Yorkers, the 2nd
Pennsylvanians, and the South Carolinians, who had in one
way or another penetrated the outer wall. The brigade from
Worth came up on the left. Lieutenant James Longstreet,
carrying his regiment's colors, fell wounded, but Lieutenant
George Pickett — he who was to put his whole heart into the
fighting at Gettysburg, as Longstreet did not — snatched
them up. And now, at last, the ladders arrived upon the
scene.

The first that were planted were hurled back with their
loads of climbing men upon them. But enough fresh ones went
up side by side to carry fifty men abreast. The bullet-torn
flag of the Voltiguers was planted on the parapet. The Mexicans broke and fled, vainly seeking safety, to fall under bullet or bayonet as the Americans in hot blood avenged the
murdered wounded at the Molino, until their officers stopped
them. General Bravo surrendered his diamond-hilted sword,
which was immediately returned to him. But some of the gallant cadets in their blue tasseled caps and smart gray uniforms fought to the death rather than yield. Little did their
vanquishers think that at New Market in Virginia seventeen
years later the boys of an American military school were to
die as bravely in battle against troops of the United States.

At half past nine the watchers who crowded every roof and
church tower in Mexico City saw the red, white, and green
tricolor come down with a jerk from the observatory on the
castle's summit and the Stars and Stripes of the United
States rise in its place. Scott saw this from the roof of the
house of Count Alcortez at Tacubaya. He mounted his horse
and galloped to the castle. With so much accomplished in
two hours, the whole war might be won by night.

§5

At Chapultepec Scott found the courtyard of the castle
swarming with excited soldiery, still reeking with blood and
powder smoke. The scent of victory, too, was in the air. As-

THE ASSAULT ON CHAPULTEPEC, SEPTEMBER 13, 1847

From a lithograph of a painting by Carl Nebel, as reproduced in The War between the United States and Mexico, by George Wilkins Kendall (1851)

*THE ENTRY OF THE AMERICAN ARMY INTO THE CITY OF MEXICO, SEPTEMBER
14, 1847*

From a lithograph of a painting by Carl Nebel, as reproduced in The Works of James K. Polk, United States

sailed on both flanks by Smith's brigade and troops fresh from the storming of the castle, the hornwork that had checked Quitman's advance had been captured, and the Mexican reserves behind and beyond it were in full retreat along both causeways leading to the city.

It had been Scott's intention to send Worth's division northward, along the Veronica causeway to its junction with the San Cosme causeway and thence against the San Cosme gate, which he knew to have been little prepared for resistance. Quitman meanwhile was to have distracted the enemy's attention and divided his forces by a feint directly eastward against the nearer but strongly fortified Belén gate. But Quitman and his men had had more than enough of playing second fiddle to the rest of the army. Scott's assurance that they had really held "the post of honor" in guarding the trains and the wounded at San Augustín, while their comrades were winning glory in battle, left them cold. No sooner was the castle taken than the words "Quitman's division to the city" passed from mouth to mouth. Quitman borrowed most of Pillow's troops and by the time Scott reached Chapultepec was well out upon the Belén causeway, the crimson sashes of the Rifles swinging in his van.

Scott sent him the first of several reminders that his advance was to be no more than a diversion — messages that neither Quitman nor any of his staff would ever admit that they received — then turned to the organization of Worth's movement against the San Cosme gate. He strengthened it with siege guns and Cadwalader's brigade. But this took time. Stonewall Jackson's guns cleared the way along the north side of Chapultepec, and Lee, who had not slept for forty-eight hours, guided the advance until he fainted from exhaustion, but stiff resistance by guns, foot, and horse had to be overcome on the Veronica causeway, and it was four o'clock when the column turned eastward on to the 1,100-yard stretch that led straight to its objective.

Quitman had only a couple of miles to go in all. About a mile out, a two-gun battery held him up for an hour. But the

Rifles, dodging from arch to arch of the aqueduct that ran down the middle of the roadway, finally rushed it. The gate itself, like all the other entrances to the city, was not a true gate but a *garita*, a mere customs barrier. A redoubt, however, guarded it on one side, and a ditch and parapet on the other. Moreover, the approach was enfiladed by troops and guns on the converging causeway from La Piedad, whose fire swept the arches of the aqueduct, and Santa Anna had lately been there, posting troops in the Paseo just north of the *garita* and others to the south and in reserve.

A storm of lead and iron checked the American advance until the artillerymen sweated a long 18-pounder and a 24-pounder howitzer into action on either side of the aqueduct. The nerves of the defenders had been shaken by one defeat that day: now shell and solid shot shattered them. Rifles and South Carolinians poured over trench and rampart. At twenty minutes past one o'clock the Palmetto flag and the green regimental colors of the Rifles were planted on the parapet, and between them stood Quitman, holding a lighted cigar in one hand and waving a red handkerchief tied to a rifle with the other.

But now ammunition had begun to fail, especially charges for the guns, and the flanking fire was so hot on the causeway that it was impossible to bring forward fresh supplies. Beauregard and every staff and artillery officer had been either killed or wounded. Among the wounded line officers was Fitz-John Porter, whose military career was to be brought so unjustly to an end after Second Bull Run. The enemy had retreated only to some strong stone buildings behind the *garita*, and across 300 yards of open ground to the north stood what was called the Citadel, a formidable structure well garrisoned and armed with cannon. The enemy counterattacked and although some of Worth's guns, unlimbering on a side road to the west, eased the pressure by shelling the Mexicans in the Paseo, Quitman could do no more than cling to the works he had taken and wish for the night.

And now Worth's men were having one long fight of it

along the San Cosme causeway. Both sides of the way were lined with buildings, and from their windows and the sand-bagged parapets of their roofs infantrymen sent a hail of bullets. Grape and canister swept the road from a redoubt that Santa Anna had caused to be hastily thrown up at the *garita*. It was like Monterrey over again as the Americans dug and blasted their way through party walls and rushed roof after roof. Some crept forward under the arches of an aqueduct that here, as on the Belén causeway, traversed the middle of the road. Raphael Semmes on one side of it, and Ulysses Grant on the other, manhandled mountain howitzers into church towers to cover the attack. A field gun galloped forward a hundred and fifty yards and, although almost every man and horse were wounded, went into action almost muzzle to muzzle with the enemy's guns.

Finally, about five o'clock, a flanking party gained a house commanding the interior of the redoubt and from its roof poured down a volley into it that killed or wounded almost every one of the defenders. They burst from the door as other Americans assaulted the opposite flank. The Mexicans fled in a panic so complete that they swept with them Santa Anna and the reinforcements he was hurrying from the Belén gate. It was too late in the day to advance farther into the city, Worth decided. He put his men in shelter in a church and other buildings near the *garita*, but he caused his siege guns to drop a few shells in the neighborhood of the National Palace as a sample of what might be expected if fighting were continued on the morrow. Quitman moved three siege guns into position under cover of the darkness and, when Scott sent him a suggestion that he withdraw his division until morning, replied that without a positive order he would not retire one inch, that his men had taken the city and, by God, they should have it.

Santa Anna still had 5,000 men with fifteen guns at the Citadel and probably 7,000 more not far away. Quitman and Worth were dangerously far apart for mutual support. But the Mexican troops were demoralized, the people disheart-

ened, the rich and influential more interested in the safety of
their possessions than in defending the capital of their country. At a brief council of war Santa Anna stated that honor
had been satisfied by the fighting of the day; that he wished
to spare the city the horrors of bombardment, assault, and
pillage; and that the army should be saved for carrying on
the war in the open field. At one o'clock in the morning (September 14th) the Mexican troops, minus some 2,000 stragglers, marched out on the road to Guadalupe Hidalgo, and
before daylight three members of the *ayuntamiento*, the city
council, were forwarded by Worth to American headquarters
at Tacubaya, where they offered terms of capitulation.

Scott received them sternly. He told them that the city
was already in his possession, had been so since the previous
evening; that his army would be bound only by such terms
as its honor, the dignity of the United States, and the spirit
of the age should imperiously impose; and that, even so, his
protection of the inhabitants would depend on the prompt
payment of $150,000, with which he intended to purchase
necessaries and comforts for his men.

He sent Worth an order to await his coming and, after a
hasty breakfast and a brief stop at Chapultepec, rode on by
way of the San Cosme causeway to join the First Division
in a triumphal entry into the captured capital. But again
he failed to take into consideration the impetuous and emu-
lous Quitman. At daylight Quitman had been aroused from
uneasy slumber by a flag of truce with the request that he
occupy the city for the preservation of law and order. The
officer left behind to surrender the Citadel promptly did so.
Quitman garrisoned it. Then, without waiting for orders
from Scott, he led his troops to the Grand Plaza.

Less than twenty-four hours earlier the populace had
crowded roofs and belfries to watch the battle at Chapultepec. Now, sullen and amazed, with many a white handkerchief and foreign flag displayed among them, they filled sidewalks, windows, and housetops to gaze upon their conquerers.
The latter presented a sorry sight. They were unshaven,

powder-stained, and bedraggled, in uniforms smeared with
mire and clay. Many a head bore a bloody bandage, many
an arm was carried in a filthy sling. The general himself rode
with one foot shoeless. He had lost the shoe the day before
when, on a reconnoitering venture with Lieutenant Beauregard, both of them had fallen into a canal. His men formed
line with no great smartness. They presented arms at the
word of command when, at exactly seven o'clock, a bullet-
torn flag of the United States rose on the staff above the
dome of the National Palace. But an hour was to pass before
there was any show of the pomp and circumstance to which
the Mexicans were so susceptible.

Then brazen music and the thunder of the kettle-drum
sounded from the direction of the Alameda, and up the street
came the mounted band of the dragoons, the squadrons riding with drawn swords behind it, and the general-in-chief
following them at the head of Worth's division of regulars.
Mounted on a tall bay charger, Scott was a magnificent figure in the white-plumed chapeau and gold epaulets of the
full-dress uniform he had donned for the occasion. The band
played *Hail Columbia, Washington's March, Yankee Doodle,* and finally *Hail to the Chief,* as, hat in hand, he rode
down the lines in brilliant sunshine that flashed from the bayonets of arms at the present. Even the conquered populace,
their hatred overcome by their love of splendor, cheered him
as he passed.

At a desk in the National Palace he wrote out the order
announcing victory. "We must not be too elated by our success," he said to his officers. But it had been astonishing. In
the five weeks since he had marched from Puebla he had
fought and won six battles. In the taking of the city he had
captured twenty colors and standards, seventy-five guns and
fifty-seven wall pieces, 20,000 small arms, and a great store
of ammunition, shot, and shell. The two days' fighting had
netted 863 prisoners, including four generals. The number
of enemy killed, wounded, and missing could only be guessed
at. For the whole campaign Scott estimated it to be 7,000.

The American loss for the last two days was ten officers and 128 enlisted men killed, sixty officers and 613 men wounded.

But there was now little leisure for rejoicing. Even the shooting was not entirely over. A mob of *léperos* was already ranging the city. Some of them were looting the National Palace when the Americans arrived there and had to be driven out by the bayonets of the marines. As the troops marched to their quarters, Colonel Garland fell wounded by a bullet evidently intended for Worth. A fusillade burst from neighboring housetops. Two thousand convicts, liberated by Santa Anna or someone else in authority, and a like number of disbanded soldiers joined the fray. It became necessary to sweep the streets with grape and canister, to blast with cannon fire houses that sheltered the rioters, and to place sharpshooters in the belfries to clear the roofs.

Only after a night and another day of terror was order re-established, and so stern were Scott's methods that the Mexicans said the Americans had killed more people in doing so than had died in the latest revolution, which had lasted for three weeks. Colonel Hitchcock was sickened by the sight of killings which were not always justifiable. But Scott could not afford to be less severe. He had now a force of only about 7,000 men with which to dominate a city of 180,000 people, and many thousands of the latter were ignorant, poverty-stricken half-barbarians who had everything to gain and only their miserable lives to lose in any disorder. Santa Anna, moreover, with the hope that the city had tardily risen against the invader, turned back for a day in his retreat, which was now directed toward Querétaro.

Forgetful in his haste, or moved by an almost touching confidence in the chivalry and discipline of the Americans, he had left his beautiful young wife in the city. The British consul obtained a passport for her. Scott offered her an escort of cavalry as well, but this she declined. He considered paying his respects to her in person, but decided that under the circumstances the visit "might by others be regarded as a vaunt."

Meanwhile her husband had resigned the Presidency and marched off to attack the little American garrison at Puebla. Its capture, he thought, might be the first step toward returning to the dictatorship of the country. His government simply disintegrated, and Scott found himself confronted by the task that he had done everything in his power to avoid: the making of peace with a country in which there was no one in authority with whom he could negotiate.

CHAPTER X

Old Horses Turned Out to Die

§1

M̲r̲. P̲o̲l̲k̲ was in no danger of suffering from that elation against which General Scott warned his officers as they stood victorious in the National Palace of Mexico. The capacity for it simply was not in the man. On September 14 the Southern mail brought him news of Contreras and Churubusco and the armistice that followed them; next day the New Orleans newspapers confirmed it, and a letter from Trist told of the beginning of negotiations. But he doubted Scott's wisdom in making the armistice so long, lest the Mexicans had agreed to it only to gain time for reorganizing their army, and he was so dissatisfied with Trist for not presenting the American terms as an ultimatum that when he heard of the proposal to neutralize the Nueces and Rio Grande territory he ordered Trist's recall. He would never, he said, consent to "the dismemberment of Texas," and he instructed Scott to levy on the property of wealthy Mexicans to bring it home to them that their country was beaten.

When, five weeks later, the telegraph office at Petersburg relayed the New Orleans courier's news that the enemy capital had been taken, that Santa Anna had resigned, and that the Mexicans had organized an interim government, with which, pending the assembly of their Congress, tentative negotiations had been opened, no word of pride or joy was entered in his diary. Of the many officers killed and wounded he wrote: "Some of them, indeed I may say all of them, [were] very valuable"; and of the official reports of the battles that had won what had become almost his personal war: "They were very voluminous, but in the course of the day I read them." Yet he had slaved for this victory, even to the point of investigating personally the loose system of keeping accounts in the Quartermaster Department, and had been planning to raise five additional regiments.

The fact was that he was tired out. He went to bed exhausted after Cabinet meetings, and a short carriage drive fatigued him. Mrs. Polk was still far from well. She had another chill, and her doctor called several times a day. He was saddened by the death of Silas Wright, lately Governor of New York, whom he mourned as a friend of many years' standing, though Wright had been a Whig and had promised to become the leader of all who were disposed to make a national issue of the abolition of slavery. He continued to be at the mercy of callers whom he described as bent on "the patriotic business of serving themselves by seeking office."

It was a pleasure to welcome General Stephen Kearny, who arrived in Washington from California, especially since the general made no allusion to the unfortunate case of Colonel Frémont. Frémont was in town, under arrest, pending court-martial on the charges Kearny had brought against him. Polk asked Marcy to see if that business could not be disposed of by a court of inquiry, but finally decided that Frémont should be tried like any other officer. Senator Benton called several times at the White House in a growing state of excitement over his son-in-law's case and ended by registering his anger at Polk's decision by refusing to head the Military Affairs Committee in the approaching session of Congress. And it did not help matters to have the Senator's son march into the President's office to demand a second-lieutenancy in the army. Polk treated him with kindly forbearance, "as he was young and on his father's account," pointing out that private soldiers who had been wounded in Mexico would be preferred over civilians who had remained at home. But the youth departed swearing and breathing forth threats of vengeance and the odor of too much whisky.

With the next general election only a year away, Secretary Buchanan had to be told that neither he nor any other aspirant for the Presidency would receive Polk's support until he had been nominated by the Democratic National Convention. For at a Cabinet meeting at which Polk reiterated his intention of demanding California and New Mexico as part of the indemnity that Mexico must pay for peace, Buchanan reversed his position and, though not explicitly, made it evident that he favored the annexation of the province of Tamaulipas and the country east of the Sierra Madre as well.

"Since he has considered himself as a candidate for the Presidency," Polk commented dryly, "it is probable that he looks at the subject with different considerations from those which he entertained before that time."

§2

One item in the news from Mexico — and one that the President should have received most thankfully — he seems to have taken for granted: namely, the information that there was still in that country, after its crushing defeat, a government with which his commissioner could negotiate. At Toluca on September 22 Manuel de la Peña y Peña, senior member of the Supreme Court, announced its formation, with himself as President. Early in October he removed it to Querétaro. Its first official act was to deprive Santa Anna of his command and to order him before a court of inquiry.

Santa Anna had been engaged in besieging Puebla. Colonel Childs, with a garrison of 2,193, of whom 1,800 were sick in hospitals, had been holding out there since September 13 against a combination of guerrilla and other ruffian bands, whose attacks troubled him less than the shortage of supplies they inflicted on him. Santa Anna brought 4,000 regular troops and ten guns against him. But the Mexican artillery was too light to be of much use against the American positions, and he had accomplished nothing when at the end of more than two weeks he went off to meet a force of 1,800 men that was marching up from Vera Cruz under the command of the Buena Vista veteran General Joseph Lane. Lane defeated him at Huamantla on October 9 and entered Puebla three days later. The siege was raised, and Santa Anna, turning over his command to General Reyes, wandered off into obscurity.

The Mexican Congress, which met at Querétaro on November 11, elected as President P. M. Anaya, who had been made substitute President when Santa Anna left the capital for Cerro Gordo. Anaya was a Moderado; Puros, Santantistas, and Monarchists were united in preferring a continuation of the war to peace under a Moderado government; but Anaya had reliable troops and, with the help of about two hundred American deserters who had entered his service, quickly put down an insurrection. He made Peña y Peña his Minister of Foreign Affairs, and informal negotiations for peace had actually begun when on November 16 orders recalling Trist and directing Scott to go on with the war arrived from Washington.

It was evident to both men that the administration did not understand the situation, but there seemed to be nothing to do but obey. Trist had his luggage packed and was only waiting for an escort to take him to Vera Cruz when Thornton, now temporarily in charge of the British legation, came to him at President Anaya's request and begged him to remain and continue the negotiations. Scott added his persuasions, and so did Mr. J. L. Freaner, the able correspondent of the *New Orleans Delta*. It was clear that the Washington government desired peace; Peña favored the proposed boundary of the Rio Grande to parallel 32° and thence westward to the ocean; and it was most probable that, should negotiations break down now, his government would not long survive. Anarchy would ensue and the United States would be confronted with the necessity of pacifying the whole of Mexico.

On the other hand Trist could be held traitorous if he, not only a mere private citizen but a discharged and discredited official, should presume to exercise the powers of which he had been deprived. If he should do so and the results of his action should not be sustained, ridicule and ignominy were the least of the penalties he would have to suffer. But Nicholas Trist, a Southerner by birth, tradition, and marriage, was to oppose Secession and cast his vote for Abraham Lincoln thirteen years later, and his moral courage did not fail him now. The decision, he wrote to his wife, was entirely his own. He withdrew the formal notice of his recall, which he had sent to Peña, then waited with such patience as he could command for the appointment of the Mexican commissioners. It was January 2 when they finally met with him secretly in Mexico City.

Scott, meanwhile, set himself to the delicate task of obeying the order to carry on the war without imperiling the frail prestige of Anaya's government. His liberal policy toward the conquered Mexicans now stood him in good stead. The capital, like Puebla, Jalapa, and Vera Cruz, had become "Americanized." There were American names over the doors of saloons and eating-places. The *American Star*, formerly of Puebla, appeared on the streets as the *American Star, Mexico* along with the *North American, Mexico*. American generals and members of their staffs, on their big American horses, mingled with the native cavaliers and the lumbering carriages of the rich and aristocratic on the Paseo.

American soldiers thronged the saloons, which were filled with Mexican girls, and stern moralists spoke of the "hells of Montezuma." Hackmen fled at the approach of a prospective American fare: they had been cheated out of their hire so often. But Scott had forbidden the billeting of officers and men in private houses without the consent of the occupants; the troops were quartered in the Mexican barracks and, following the Mexican custom, in the monasteries. And under Quitman, who was the first governor of the city, and Persifor Smith, who succeeded him, active and vigilant patrols kept the troops in such good order that foreign observers wrote home about it and even the Mexicans were of the opinion that no other soldiers would have behaved any better in the circumstances.

Moreover, there was a strong desire for peace throughout

the country. Three members of the Puro Party told Colonel Hitchcock that they wished that the American forces would remain until the Mexican army was annihilated, so that a proper civil government might be established. They wanted no payment of money by the United States to the government of Mexico. It would, they said, only corrupt those in power. Others proposed to Scott repeatedly that he declare himself dictator of Mexico as a preliminary to the annexation of the whole country by the United States, and even offered to finance his doing so.

It was fortunate that such feelings prevailed. For by the beginning of December Scott had fewer than 6,000 men fit for duty, with some regiments reporting only 150 effectives. Along every road traversed by the Americans a warfare of merciless atrocities and equally merciless reprisals sputtered and flared between gangs of brigands and self-styled patriots and unresting American patrols. Eastward of Jalapa on the road to Vera Cruz the guerrilla bands became so bold and numerous that strong columns such as Lane's and, later, one commanded by General William Orlando Butler had to fight hard to make their way inland. The garrison of at least one strong point grew so nervous that, although it was under the command of young Major John R. Kenly, a veteran of Monterrey, who was to be a major general of United States volunteers in the War of Secession, it opened fire with its cannon when Minister Bankhead, who was going home on sick leave, appeared on a distant hilltop with his escort of dragoons.

When, by the middle of December, reinforcements had given Scott between 13,000 and 14,000 men, the new organizations were riddled by mumps and measles, erysipelas was frequent among them, and Daniel Webster's son Edward was only one of many who died of camp fever. Scott reported bitterly on the deplorable lack of clothing. The storehouses at Vera Cruz had been emptied, and requisitions that had been made twelve months before were still unfilled.

Fresh from West Point, Lieutenant Ambrose E. Burnside, who was to take such a beating at Fredericksburg in 1862,

and Lieutenant John Gibbon, a wheel horse of the Army of
the Potomac from 1862 to 1865, came up to join their regiments. But the character and behavior of the new arrivals in
general caused Captain Anderson to believe that the army
would soon be no place for a gentleman. The decline in morale and discipline common to all victorious troops in conquered countries showed itself among officers and men alike.
The frequent funerals of officers who finally died of their
wounds were depressing. A few soldiers who were convicted
of murder were hanged, and there was the grim necessity of
shooting certain Mexican officers who had broken their parole. Desertions became so frequent as to call forth from the
General-in-Chief a reminder of the punishment that had
overtaken the members of the San Patricio Battalion. Three
officers — one of them, to Colonel Hitchcock's horror, a West
Pointer — were convicted of robbing a bank. And General
Pillow was brought before a court on the charge of attempting to make a personal trophy of one of the small howitzers
captured at Chapultepec.

Lacking a disposable force of 4,500 men, which he considered not more than adequate for a march on San Luis
Potosí, Scott proceeded to obey the President's order to make
the Mexicans pay for the war as best he could. He occupied
the cities of Pachuca, Lerma, and Toluca and levied heavy
assessments on them as well as on other places in the two states
of Mexico and Vera Cruz, which were in the possession of his
troops. By these means and from customs duties, and government monopolies he actually collected $3,000,000 of the
$23,000,000 that a careful study of the Mexican treasury
reports led him to hope for, and at the same time avoided
interfering with municipal revenues, which might have disorganized the life of the inhabitants. The *ayuntamiento* of
Mexico City acknowledged the wisdom and justice of his rule
by giving him a magnificent picnic at the ruins of an ancient
convent some miles out of town.

With an escort of two troops of dragoons to guard against
guerrillas, and a regiment of infantry on the road halfway

between the convent and the city, Scott could give himself up to the enjoyment of food and wines such as few men were better fitted by taste and inclination to appreciate. The music of a fine Mexican band alternated with that of guitars and flutes. "The gentlemen," Colonel Hitchcock observed, "became pretty well warmed." The alcalde and several members of the council made speeches, some of which expressed the wish that the Americans would not leave the country until they had destroyed the influence of the army and the Church. Only one thing marred the pleasure of the occasion. Of the generals who might have been expected to participate in it, Pillow and Worth were absent. They were in Mexico City, under arrest.

It is a sorry story, motivated by cheap ambition, envy, jealousy, wounded vanity, fantastic egoism, and contemptible intrigue. In early October Pillow's reports of the battles of Contreras and Chapultepec had contained such extravagant pretensions to credit for those victories that Scott had felt it necessary to ask him to alter them. It was gently done, but not wisely. "Your report," he wrote, ". . . seems, without intending it I am sure, to make you control the operation of the whole army, including my own views and acts"; and again: ". . . a seeming effort, no doubt unintentional, to leave General S. entirely out of the operations." Common justice to others and respect for historical truth demanded that credit should be distributed among the officers who had earned it. But this might have been accomplished without the manifestation of apparent anxiety about his own reputation.

Pillow's reply was smoothly evasive. He made some alterations in the reports but refused to give Persifor Smith and Riley their due for Contreras. Scott forwarded the reports to Washington and would have let the matter rest. But up in the States strange letters from the army began to appear in the newspapers and were soon reprinted in the *American Star, Mexico* and the American Tampico paper. The *New*

Orleans Delta published one, signed "Leonidas," which was copied in the *Picayune*. Another was in the *Pittsburgh Post*. And the *Washington Union* of October 23 carried two, one of which appeared over the signature "Veritas."

In them one read that Pillow's plan of battle at Contreras resembled that of Napoleon at Ulm, and that he slew a Mexican officer in single combat with sword and revolver that day. "Veritas" praised the "judgment, skill, strategy and science" that had placed Pillow "in the estimation of the army, in the first rank of American generals." The *Post's* letter represented Worth's and Duncan's recommendation of the Chalco route of advance as having been the means of extricating the army from a dangerous situation in which it had been involved by Scott's blundering.

Recognizing the letters for what they were, the army read them with derision and disgust. Universal ridicule would have disposed of them. But Scott's sense of humor was never great. The tone of Pillow's reports and Worth's behavior toward him ever since the Puebla episode convinced him that the letters had been contrived by them or their supporters, and he was stung by their ingratitude, for he had treated them both with marked kindness and consideration. He smarted, moreover, with injured vanity, and, strong in the knowledge that the regulations forbade officers to write for publication private letters commenting on active operations, he proceeded to unlimber his heaviest quill pen. With such phrases as "partizans and pet familiars," "pruriency of fame, not earned," "despicable self puffings," and "malignant exclusions of others" he stated in a general order dated November 12 that it required "not a little charity to believe that the principal heroes of the scandalous letters alluded to, did not write them, or specifically procure them to be written."

Worth promptly demanded to be told whether the order was aimed at him, since, he wrote, the whole army seemed to think so. And when Scott would reply only that the order was directed at "the authors, aiders and abettors of those

letters" and that, if he knew who they were, he would court-
martial them, Worth appealed to the Secretary of War, describing himself as the victim of "arbitrary and illegal
conduct" and "malicious injustice" and accusing Scott of
"conduct unbecoming an officer and a gentleman." Scott
placed him in arrest. Colonel Duncan now brazenly acknowledged the authorship of the *Post* letter in an open letter to
the *North American, Mexico*. Scott placed him in arrest also
and wrote to Washington asking the appointment of courts-
martial to try both officers.

Pillow, who had managed to slip the "Leonidas" letter
into Mr. Freaner's dispatch bag without that gentleman's
knowledge, hastened to find a scapegoat in a paymaster who
confessed that he had written it. Pillow had by this time succeeded in laying the guilt of the theft of the howitzer on a
couple of young lieutenants. He had returned the piece, but
the court had expressed a grave doubt of his having intended
to do so and had found him morally guilty. Scott approved
the verdict, and Pillow, like Worth, appealed to the Secretary of War in such improper terms that he, too, was
arrested.

It took forty days to send a message to Washington and
receive a reply in the most favorable circumstances, and
these appear seldom to have attended the transit of official
dispatches. On January 13 the latest official communication
Scott had received from Washington bore the date of October 26. Private mail, though slow and irregular, did a little
better. Both Freaner and Kendall had organized swift courier services for their newspapers, but at least one of their
messengers was found hanged by the neck with "*Correo de los
yanquis*" on a paper pinned to his clothing.

So throughout the rest of November, December, and January, Pillow, Worth, and Duncan kicked their heels in a kind
of limbo, confined to the limits of the city but not, thanks to
Scott's magnanimity, to their quarters, as they might have
been. General Lane, and Captain Hays at the head of a company of Rangers, employed the time by becoming a terror to

guerrillas and banditti. Trist, in growing apprehension —
which was shared by Scott — lest each day should bring positive orders to end all negotiation, wrought feverishly for
peace.

It was slow and irritating work. The Mexican commissioners shilly-shallied and quibbled. Anaya's term as President expired. Peña, who became provisional president once
more, pending the assembly of the Congress, was scared by
an attempted insurrection at San Luis Potosí, and his government balked stubbornly when told that on account of the
prolongation of the war only fifteen millions would be paid,
instead of thirty, for the territory that was to be ceded. On
January 29, his patience exhausted, Trist formally declared
the negotiations at an end, and Scott sent Peña a hint
through the British legation that if the treaty was signed, he
would protect the Querétaro government from insurrection,
but that otherwise he would march against it and disperse
it to the hills. Four days later, in deepest secrecy, at the suburb of Guadalupe Hidalgo, where the proximity of Mexico's
holiest Virgin might seem to lend the act something of her
sanctity, the treaty was signed. Freaner of the *Delta* stuffed
it into his saddlebags and was off at a gallop for Vera Cruz
and Washington.

Scott wrote to the Secretary of War that day, asking to
be allowed to go home if the treaty was accepted. But one
week later the arrival of private letters and clippings from
the newspapers put an end to hopes of that kind. From these
he learned, as he wrote to Marcy, "that the President has
determined to place me before a court, for daring to enforce
necessary discipline in this army against certain of its high
officers!" He learned with pleasure, he went on, that he was
to be superseded by Major General Butler. But he closed,
with characteristic waspishness: "My poor services with this
most gallant army are at length to be requited as I have long
been led to expect they would be."

§3

Freaner rode with all haste, past Puebla, Perote, and Jalapa, to Vera Cruz, leaving behind him, one after the other, escorts furnished by the Mounted Rifles, the spy company, and other mounted organizations. Since he was a government messenger now and not a mere correspondent, the U.S.S. *Iris* steamed off with him from Vera Cruz. To make sure that for once the newspapers should not outstrip the official dispatches, the steamer *New Orleans*, ready and waiting for the *Picayune's* messenger, who was close behind him, was held in harbor for two days after his departure.

But that swift ship reached New Orleans about the time that Freaner landed at Mobile. Gaining on him in the long gallop across Alabama, the *Picayune's* man caught up with him at Charleston and telegraphed the great news to the New York newspapers from Petersburg. But it was the end of the week. They could not get it on the streets until the following Monday, and on Saturday evening. February 19, only eighteen days after the signing of the treaty, Freaner handed it to Secretary Buchanan.

It was not entirely unexpected. Early in January a private letter from Vera Cruz had informed Secretary Marcy, on the authority of the courier of the British legation, that Trist was negotiating for peace in spite of his recall; Mrs. Trist had showed Buchanan a postscript of one of her husband's letters, in which he had asked her to inform the Secretary of State of what he intended to do; and on January 14 Buchanan had received a dispatch from Trist, announcing that he had actually reopened negotiations.

In Polk's opinion the dispatch was "arrogant, impudent, and very insulting to his government, and even personally offensive to the President," and had probably been written "at General Scott's instance and dictation." Trist appeared to Polk to have become Scott's "perfect tool" and "to have entered into all Scott's hatred of the Administration." It is probable, though it cannot be proved, that a private letter from Pillow was responsible for this idea. At all events, the President had been up in arms in defense of his favorite since the arrival of the charges against him and Worth and Duncan. He saw Pillow as another "persecuted" Democratic officer and a victim of Scott's anger at not being made "the exclusive hero of the war." After a good deal of discussion in the Cabinet he had decided that Scott should be superseded by Major General William Orlando Butler, who was not only a veteran of Monterrey and the Battle of New Orleans but a sound Democrat as well, that the accused officers should be released from arrest, and that a court of inquiry would be better than a court-martial for dealing with the charges against them.

Thus easily could a president whose sense of gratitude had been deadened by party feeling and personal prejudice dispose of a general who might well have been the presidential candidate of the rival party. It would be strange if Scott did not emerge with reputation sadly deflated from an investigation in which he must appear as both prosecutor and accused.

As for Trist, the indignant President sputtered in his diary: "If there was any legal provision for his punishment he ought to be severely handled." If he was still at headquarters, General Butler was instructed to "order him off and inform the Mexican government that he had no authority to treat." The arrival of the treaty raised a more serious question. Should the President reject it or, irregularly negotiated though it was, submit it to the Senate for ratification? Although February 20 was a Sunday, the Cabinet met that evening to advise him on the subject. It met again at noon next day and learned that he had decided to submit the treaty.

The boundaries laid down in it, he explained, were, in the main, in accord with the instructions he had given Trist the previous April. Although he would have demanded more territory now, he doubted that Mexico would yield more without further fighting, and it seemed to him unlikely that Congress, of which one branch charged him with making the war for conquest, would vote more men and money if he should reject this treaty, which was made on his own terms.

Only Buchanan spoke against the decision, and Polk observed shrewdly in his diary: "No candidate for the presidency ought ever to remain in the Cabinet. He is an unsafe adviser." For he was convinced that his Secretary of State really wished the treaty to go to the Senate, but wished also to avoid displeasing the growing number of people in the country who favored annexing the whole of Mexico.

The Senate fell upon the treaty with anger mingled with derision. With different motives the annexationists, the no-territory men, and those who clamored for all Mexico attacked it. Some thought, as Lieutenant W. T. Sherman did, that it was exactly the sort of treaty Mexico would have imposed had she been the victor. Since it had been negotiated by an agent whom the President had discredited, many considered it mere waste paper, an instrument that it would be absurd and undignified to treat seriously.

But while the storm of oratory was raging in the Senate, the cry of "Look to Mr. Adams!" interrupted debate in the House. He had slumped suddenly over the arm of his chair. They carried him to the Speaker's room and thence home. At seventy-five he had written for his own eye alone that he was "surrounded by remorseless enemies and false and scary and treacherous friends." Now, in his eighty-first year, he muttered: "This is the last of earth; I am content," and spoke no more. All next day, which was the birthday of Washington, he lay unconscious. He died the day following.

Both houses of Congress adjourned. The government offices were hung with black, and there was crepe over the front door of the White House. The body lay in state in the Capitol, where thousands flocked to do it honor. For a review of this man's life was like a pageant of the history of the country. Son of its second President, he had been Washington's Minister to the Netherlands and his father's Minister to Prussia. Though a United States Senator from Massachusetts, he had supported Jefferson's Embargo Bill. Madison

had sent him to Russia. He had been a negotiator of the
Treaty of Ghent, Minister to Great Britain, Secretary of
State when Florida was acquired and the Monroe Doctrine
promulgated, the sixth President of the United States, and,
since 1831, a Representative of Massachusetts in Congress.

The President, the Vice President, and the Cabinet, the
judges of the Supreme Court, the members of the Senate and
the House, the diplomatic corps, and officers of the army and
navy in uniform attended the funeral service in the hall of
the House of Representatives on the following Sunday. A
long procession, composed of the military, the Odd Fellows,
the fire companies, and a throng of people in carriages, on
horseback, and on foot escorted the remains to the Congressional Cemetery where they were deposited in a vault to await
removal to Massachusetts. "It was a splendid pageant," Polk
thought, and he transacted no business "of any importance"
in his office that day.

The Senate returned to the consideration of the treaty in
a more sober mood. A good many of its members had arrived
at the opinion that the treaty was better, at least, than its
probable alternative, a continuation of the war. But its progress toward ratification gave the President several days of
painful anxiety. He heard that Buchanan and Secretary
Walker were intriguing against it and that the Committee on
Foreign Affairs had resolved to recommend its rejection.
Webster had said that California and New Mexico were "not
worth a dollar." Benton was opposing the treaty, apparently to get even for Polk's part in Frémont's case. The
court-martial had sentenced Frémont to dismissal from the
service. The President had approved the sentence, but remitted the penalty, and Frémont had resigned from the army
in disgust. But on March 8 the Senate had asked the President for additional information, and two days later the
treaty was ratified by a vote of thirty-eight to fourteen.

There was no such delay, however, in the settlement of
Polk's account with the officious Trist. With Polk it went for
nothing that his zealous agent had risked disgrace and pros-

ecution for treason to negotiate a treaty that not only brought him all the territory he really desired for half the price he had been willing to pay, but also gave him the peace that was essential if his party was not to be defeated at the approaching election. The man had disobeyed his orders and, in his estimation, had "proved himself to be an impudent and unqualified scoundrel." A paragraph was added to the dispatch to General Butler, directing him "to require [Trist] to leave the headquarters of the army as soon as a safe escort could be furnished to conduct him to Vera Cruz." A subsequent refusal to pay Trist for either his services or his expenses after his recall placed the pinnacle on an edifice of presidential ingratitude and smallness of mind that it would be hard to match in all American history.

§4

At Mexico City enlightened native opinion was edified by the spectacle of the victorious general of an admiring army laying down his command at the mere written order of his government, which was two thousand miles away. The generals the Mexicans were accustomed to had not acted like that. But at the British legation it was said openly that the order removing Scott from command would be condemned in Europe "as the result of a low and vulgar intrigue by inferior men." Hitchcock heard "unmitigated condemnation" of it in the army. Robert Lee wrote: "the discontent in the army at this state of things is great." In giving his opinion of the treatment of Trist he wrote: "I presume it is perfectly fair, after having made use of his labors, and taken from him all that he had earned, that he should be kicked off as General Scott has been . . . turned out as an old horse to die."

The court of inquiry assembled in the National Palace on March 14. "And such a court!" Scott wrote contemptuously many years afterwards. It was composed of Brevet Brigadier General Nathan Towson, paymaster general of the army, Brigadier General Caleb Cushman of Massachusetts, an offi-

cer of the war volunteers, and Colonel E. G. B. Butler of the
3rd Dragoons, all of whom were Scott's juniors in rank and
age and inferior to him in experience.

Worth promptly asked leave to withdraw his charges
against Scott: the President, he said, had already done him
full justice. Scott declined to press his charges against Pillow. He had asked for the trial of three of his officers by
court-martial, he explained, and the result was this court of
inquiry, before which "the innocent and the guilty" were
thrown together "to scramble for justice as they might."
Some of the necessary witnesses, he added, had already gone
home, which would make an adjournment to the United
States obligatory; peace was imminent, and the moment it
was declared, Pillow, by the explicit wording of his commission, would revert to civilian status and be no longer
within the jurisdiction of a military court.

But this did not suit Pillow. He now felt pretty sure that
his friend in the White House would not permit him to be
convicted, and he did not wish to return to civil life with the
blot of untried charges against his name. General Towson
proposed to write to Washington for additional instructions
in these circumstances. But rather than endure such a delay,
Scott preferred to let the inquiry proceed, and on March 21
the dreary and squalid business of taking the testimony of
scores of witnesses began.

Pillow's scapegoat acknowledged the authorship of the
"Leonidas" letter on oath, though it was proved that he had
often denied it. Freaner told how he had refused to forward
the letter when he received it from Pillow's headquarters.
Lee, Hitchcock, Longstreet, and others exposed the extrava-
gance of the claims that Pillow had written into his reports
of the battles. The President had read the garbled newspaper
story of the plan discussed at Puebla, by which a million dollars was to be paid in advance of the conclusion of a peace,
and although Shields had explained to him that no "proposi-
tion to bribe Santa Anna" was considered, the matter was
dragged into this investigation. Scott refused to answer

questions about it. Certain foreign diplomatic representatives were involved in that affair, he said, and he felt himself to be in honor bound to communicate it to nobody except the President "and *perhaps* the Secretary of War."

Scott continued to live very comfortably at Mexico City. When young officers whom he knew came up from outlying posts on leave, he invited them to late suppers of cold fowl and champagne and joked with them about his being superseded. In March, Santa Anna, who was now reunited with his lovely young wife, passed through Jalapa on his way to exile. The American officers stationed there entertained the couple at luncheon and furnished them with a strong and by no means superfluous mounted escort to protect them from certain vengeful Texans. At the capital a formal race meeting was organized in April. The *"demonios yanquis"* entered a horse that looked like a sure winner but, since it was not accustomed to the altitude, collapsed in mid-career. And late that same month Ambrose H. Sevier, chairman of the Senate Committee on Foreign Relations, and Attorney General Clifford, who was to be the new Minister to Mexico, arrived as commissioners to explain to the Mexican government certain amendments that the United States Senate had made in the treaty, to obtain acceptance of them, and to exchange ratifications.

It was some weeks, however, before the Mexican Congress, which was assembled only with great difficulty, ratified the treaty, and the American commissioners could proceed to Querétaro for the concluding formalities. Even so they went with a strong mounted escort, for the opponents of the peace were threatening and vociferous. The commissioners were received by the government with every courtesy; a resplendent colonel of Mexican cavalry entertained American and Mexican officers together at a breakfast that began with wineglasses filled with cognac; but streets and plazas rang with yells of " *Viva la guerra!*" and "*¡Abajo la paz!*" The headquarters of the commissioners was guarded by American riflemen, and strong bodies of Mexican cavalry patrolled the city until, on the last day of May, the ratifications were exchanged.

By that time Scott had reached home. On April 21 the court of inquiry had adjourned to the United States to take the testimony of various witnesses who had preceded it. Scott departed next day, leaving the contents of his wine closet to be distributed among his favorite officers, and deprecating the spontaneous demonstration of loyalty and regret in which, despite his expressed wish to the contrary, officers and men united to bid him farewell.

Six months earlier Taylor had returned as a conquering hero. Thirteen vessels had escorted his ship up the Mississippi to New Orleans. A hundred guns saluted his landing, and he was led beneath a triumphal arch of evergreens in the Place d'Armes to hear the *Te Deum* chanted in the Cathedral of St. Louis. Mounted on Old Whitey, he headed a long procession through the Vieux Carré to the St. Charles Hotel. A banquet and a visit to the city's various theatres closed the day but not the demonstrations in his honor. His progress up the river was one long ovation from both banks and from passing steamboats; flags flew by dozens and cannon thundered. Little Donaldsonville gave him a banquet. Baton Rouge, which was his home, if the old campaigner could be said to have one anywhere, welcomed him as an old friend and neighbor. There he settled down, and his wife began her nightly prayers that all the talk of making him president would come to nothing.

If Scott had landed at New Orleans, he, too, might have made a triumphal journey home. Congress had voted him its thanks and requested the President to have a magnificent gold medal struck for him. The Louisiana legislature had voted him a splendid sword. Kentucky and New Jersey had passed laudatory resolutions. At Conner's orders the naval ships manned the yards, and the guns of the flagship *Cumberland* saluted his departure from Vera Cruz. But he chose to return in obscurity, sailing for New York on board the slow brig *Petersburg,* which was loaded with guns, mortars, and ordnance stores, and from the Narrows, on May 20, he was rowed to Elizabethtown, where his wife and daughters awaited him in the old house to which he had brought his bride more than thirty years before.

He was near the end of his sixty-second year, very weary, suffering severely from what he called "the Mexican disease," and smarting from the injustice and humiliation that the administration had heaped upon him. But New York was not to be balked of doing honor to the hero of Vera Cruz, Churubusco, and Chapultepec. Five days after his return a committee of notables escorted him to the metropolis. The guns at the Battery boomed to welcome him, a former President rode in his procession, and the acting mayor presented him with a silver medal. "Hail to the Chief!" wrote Philip Hone, who knew and loved him in spite of his irritating foibles. ". . . General Scott's reception has been splendid . . . 'the hasty plate of soup' was forgotten in the shouts of 'battles won' and conquests secured."

Scott was ill in bed for a week afterwards, but he reported promptly at Frederick, Maryland, when the court of inquiry resumed its sessions there on June 6. The testimony of Quitman, Twiggs, Pierce, and many other witnesses was added to the mass of evidence accumulated in Mexico, and from that mountain the court proceeded on July 1 to deliver a mouse. It found that Pillow had indeed appropriated to himself more than a just share of the credit for the victory of Contreras, but since Scott's own reports indicated that Pillow's conduct had been excellent in all operations, it was of the opinion that no further proceedings were called for by the interests of the public service. The President approved this decision without delay and, to make his attitude thoroughly understood, invited "the gallant and highly meritorious" general and his wife to dinner at the White House a few days later.

Scott established his headquarters at New York, taking to himself the command of the Eastern Department. At his sug-

gestion the command of the Western Department was given
to Taylor.

§5

"Little Jimmy Polk of Duck River," the small man who
had one great vision and one great ideal, had made the vision
a reality. Envious Whigs, like Philip Hone, might sneer at
the treaty with Mexico as "negotiated by an unauthorized
agent with an unacknowledged government" and "submitted
by an accidental President to a dissatisfied Senate." But
critics who called it robbery could be reminded that, although
the war had cost the United States a hundred million dollars
and many thousands of lives, fifteen millions were being paid
for territory for which Slidell had been empowered to offer
only $3,325,000 more. Those who wished for additional ter-
ritory could be asked whether they had been prepared to pro-
long the war in order to get it. They had not been prepared
to do so.

Through the seaports on the Gulf and up the rivers of the
South and West the armies were coming home. At Vera Cruz,
Persifor Smith, efficient as always, had shipped off 25,000
troops by July 12, and on the last day of that month the last
detachment of American soldiers in Mexico left San Juan de
Ulloa. The regulars went back to chasing Indians or to the
somnolent garrisons of seacoast forts, their officers to taming
Western rivers or building harbor defenses against the perennial alarms of aggression by "England."

At New Orleans, Colonel Hitchcock was busy for weeks,
discharging volunteers, who returned in riotous high spirits.
Precisian that he was, he considered them "unworthy of the
name of soldiers . . . their officers, for the most part, little
better than the men." But they carried home with them the
reputation of a splendid military accomplishment: the Duke
of Wellington was reported to have said that Scott's march
to Mexico City was the most brilliant episode in modern war.
They had wiped out in sweat and blood the old imputation of
the War of 1812 that American citizen soldiery would not

fight. The people at home knew only of the battles they had fought, the losses they had endured, and the victories they had won, and amid the tumultuous joy of their return and the sorrow for those who would return no more there was little inclination to criticize the fruits of their labors.

The Whigs were quick to trim their sails to this new slant of public sentiment. No longer was there talk of impeaching the President for having exceeded his constitutional powers by beginning "an illegal, unrighteous, and damnable war." That lanky giant, Abraham Lincoln, sole Whig from Illinois, had once taken time off from telling stories around the stove in the House post office to ask in a speech on the floor of the House whether the first American blood had not been shed actually on Mexican soil. But he was now busy organizing the Young Indian Club for Taylor for president. When the *Washington Union* called the war "one of the most brilliant wars that ever adorned the annals of any nation," the *National Intelligencer* implied its concurrence by printing the statement in its own editorial column. And the Whig Party, assembled in National Convention in Philadelphia in June, chose as their candidate for president Old Rough and Ready, the man who had pointed his cannon at Matamoros and brought on hostilities by causing the mouth of the Rio Grande to be blockaded. As a platform they presented only a letter from him to Captain J. S. Allison.

But now that the United States extended to the Pacific and the danger of a foreign state or a European protectorate on its western frontier was ended forever, Polk saw his great ideal, the integrity of the Federal Union, brought into jeopardy. For with the last nine months of his administation came the rise of the Free Soil Party and the doctrine of Squatter Sovereignty, which were to end by tearing the Union in twain.

When the Democratic National Convention met in Baltimore in May, the rival delegations from New York — the Barnburners and the Hunkers — walked out of it, though both of them had been seated. Senator Lewis Cass, who was described as a Northern man with Southern sympathies, was nominated for president, and it was declared that no countenance should be given to any effort to interfere with slavery. But on June 24 Polk heard with great uneasiness that the Barnburners had held a convention at Utica at which they had bolted from the regular Democratic ticket and nominated Martin Van Buren "distinctly on the ground of the Wilmot Proviso." "A most dangerous attempt to organize geographical parties upon the slave question," Polk called it, "more threatening to the Union than anything . . . since the Hartford Convention in 1814."

He had long been apprehensive of some such occurrence, writing in his diary in the previous November that the activities of John Van Buren, Preston King, and other antislavery politicians were "inexcusable." In April the attempt of certain abolitionists to smuggle a number of slaves out of the District of Columbia on board the schooner *Pearl* had caused such a furor in Washington that the building occupied by the *National Era,* an abolition newspaper, was in danger of destruction by a mob. When Congress got down to business again after the national conventions and set about providing governments for the newly acquired territories, it was immediately evident that the essence of that question was the status of slavery, and the President began to exert all the influence he could wield for a settlement by the prolongation of the Missouri Compromise line to the Pacific.

Calhoun and his followers denied the right of Congress to legislate on the matter. It could be settled, they maintained, only by the constitution that the citizens of a territory adopted when it became a state. On the principle that the best defense is an offensive, they attacked the antislavery provision in a bill for the permanent territorial government of Oregon. Things looked brighter when a committee, of which Calhoun had consented to become a member, worked out a compromise bill for not only Oregon but California and New Mexico as well, and the Senate passed it. But in the House, which, Polk observed, the members had "converted

. . . into a political arena," it was laid on the table by a majority that was made up of all the Northern Whigs, about half the Northern Democrats, and eight Southern Whigs. Here was another omen of the formation of political parties on geographical lines and, to the clear-sighted Polk, a fearsome one. And in confirmation of it there came news from Buffalo that a strangely assorted congeries of Whigs, abolitionists, and Barnburners had nominated Martin Van Buren for president, with Charles Francis Adams, John Quincy Adams's son and an avowed abolitionist, as his running mate. They had formed what they called the Free Soil Party and proclaimed that its policy was to "limit, localize and discourage" slavery.

Mr. Whittier, who had published an article the previous winter in which he likened the bombardment of Vera Cruz to the September Massacres of the French Revolution, hailed the event in "Pæan 1848":

> *The slumbers of the North are o'er,*
> *The Giant stands erect at last;*

and after welcoming "the repentant ones" to the "toil worn ranks," adjured his comrades:

> *Sound for the onset! Blast on Blast!*
> *Till Slavery's minions cower and quail;*
> *One charge of fire shall drive them fast*
> *Like chaff before our Northern gale.*

Amid the humid heat of a Washington August and the hurry and impatience of the last days of the session in a presidential year a bill providing for the territorial government of Oregon alone was passed by both Senate and House with, as Polk wrote, "the restriction of slavery in it." Calhoun called upon him to give it his veto on constitutional grounds. But Polk told him that, in deference to what their predecessors had done, individual opinions ought to give way on questions affecting the very existence of the Union, and that he considered this to be one of them. He signed the bill; Congress adjourned; and, "much fatigued," the President took "the morning train of cars" to seek rest at Bedford Springs in the Pennsylvania mountains. It was the first time he had been more than three miles from the White House since his tour of New England thirteen months before.

He was back at his desk ten days later, however. Most of the Cabinet were still on vacation, and he enjoyed using his intimate knowledge of the details of every department, took steps to prevent a rumored filibustering expedition into the northern provinces of Mexico by certain Southwestern adventurers, and removed a district attorney from office in New York because he had "united himself with Federalists and abolitionists."

November 2, his fifty-third birthday, caused him to moralize on "the vanity and emptiness of worldly honors" and "the wisdom of preparing for a future state." A week later he received the news that Cass and the Democrats had been defeated in the election. It was a blow. It was a disaster to the country in the opinion of Polk, who believed, like a greater President who was to come after him, that the Democratic Party included all the trustworthy men of intelligence in the United States. He considered Taylor to be without opinions or judgment of his own on any public subject, foreign or domestic, compelled to rely on "the designing men" of his party, and made to reverse, so far as it should be in his power to do so, the whole policy of his predecessor's administration. Mrs. Polk's departure for New York, accompanied by her husband's private secretary, her nieces, a maid, and a manservant, to buy furniture for their new home in Nashville, seems to have cheered the tired and disappointed man with its implied promise of retirement and rest.

Early in December, Secretary Marcy brought him samples of the gold that had been discovered in California at the beginning of the year. In the early years of his administration the consul at Bremen had showed him samples of gun-cotton, which had been lately invented in Germany. Polk might have felt some doubt as to which packet was the more explosive. California was said to be in a state of anarchy. At the end of September the *New York Herald* had published a letter to the people of California from Senator Benton, advising them to set up a government of their own to serve until Congress should provide one for them, and Polk feared that if this were done, California and Oregon, influenced by the Whigs' desire to get rid of the new territories, would unite to form a republic independent of the United States.

In dealing with the subject in his message to Congress he determined, first, to recommend non-interference with the slavery question by Congress, which he considered to be the true course; second, the extension of the Missouri Compromise line to the Pacific; third, to leave the matter to the decision of the courts. But December was not over before a resolution to abolish the slave trade in the District of Columbia exacerbated the resentment of the Southern members, Whigs and Democrats alike. In January they began to hold meetings, at which Calhoun asked for their signatures to an address to the Southern states. But the Whigs declined to sign it, saying that they believed the cause of slavery would be safe with Taylor, who was himself the owner of three hundred slaves.

Polk refused to become involved in the movement. To the importunities of Calhoun he replied with expressions of his "strong attachment to the union of the States" and "the great importance of preserving it." To a member of the House who wished to leave the responsibility of settling the question to Taylor's administration he said that the Democrats "had a country to save as well as a party to obey, and that it was the solemn duty of the present Congress to settle the question."

Alexander Hamilton Stephens of Georgia and Stephen A. Douglas of Illinois worked hard to help him. But the Southern members, led by Calhoun, issued an address to the Southern people in which they dwelt on the growing antagonism between North and South, the attacks on slavery by Northern congressmen, and the failure of the North to obey the fugitive-slave laws and to respect the Missouri Compromise. They charged the North with trying to defraud the South of a just share of the Mexican cession, and called on the South for united action against these injuries.

This was near the end of January. Time was running out, and not too soon for James Knox Polk. He had made a just estimate of his physical strength when, during the previous spring, he had refused repeated demands that he reverse his original decision and become his party's candidate for re-election. He had recorded with a certain zest the reception at the White House on New Year's Day, the fine music of the Marine Band, and his skill in shaking hands with several thousand people without suffering a sore arm. But after the fashionable levee on February 7, in which he once more passed through the crowded rooms with Mrs. Madison on his arm, he went to bed "much fatigued." A week later he wrote with evident satisfaction: "I will soon cease to be a servant and become a sovereign." He dealt "very summarily" with a throng of office-seekers who hoped that Taylor would not be "proscriptive," and he took time to sit for his daguerreotype to Mathew B. Brady, who was to become the photographer of the war whose seeds the President was now striving so hard to kill.

Late in February the President-elect arrived in Washington from his home at Baton Rouge. He came by way of the Mississippi and the Ohio, and his journey was one long triumph, interrupted only when his steamboat stuck in the ice below Wheeling. The usual salutes of artillery, bands, fireworks, and speeches from the balcony of Willard's Hotel celebrated his entry into the capital. Accompanied by Jefferson Davis, now Senator from Mississippi, by the indispensable Bliss, who had lately married Miss Betty Taylor, and by Colonel Garnett, General Taylor called on the President and remained, chatting pleasantly, for about half an hour.

The President and Mrs. Polk held their last levee on February 28. He seems to have been much gratified by the large attendance. Army and navy officers came in a body in full uniform; the foreign diplomats and their families were there in court dress; the line of carriages, he was told, extended for several hundred yards. Such was the crowd, however, that he was glad of the protection of the marble center table at his back, and again he was "exceedingly fatigued."

The next night there was a dinner at the White House for General Taylor and Mr. Fillmore, the Vice-President-elect. It was a party of various affiliations: the members of the Cabinet and their wives, Seaton, Ritchie of the *Union*, Senator Davis, and Senator Cass, the Democratic candidate lately defeated. But it was perfectly successful. The dinner was "finely gotten up in Julian's [the French cook's] best style," and no allusion was made to any political subject.

Two days later, about sunset on Saturday, March 3, the President, having disposed of all the business on his table, left the White House, with his family and servants, for the apartments engaged for them at Willard's Hotel. But from there he went at once to the Vice President's room in the Capitol to receive such bills as might be presented to him for his signature in the last hours of the session. A wild night followed. A provision for the temporary government of California and New Mexico was tacked on to the civil and diplomatic appropriation bill, there seemed to be danger that the Wilmot Proviso might be attached to it in the House, and it was by no means certain that the Senate would not give way and yield to the Proviso. If this should happen, Polk determined to veto the bill, although such action would necessitate the convoking of an extra session of Congress.

Late at night the House amended the bill so that the laws of Mexico should remain in force in the new territories until Congress should change them. Since the Mexican law abolishing slavery would thus remain operative, there was great excitement among the Southern members. "It was," Polk felt, "a moment of high responsibility, perhaps the highest in my official term." Some members of the Cabinet favored the signing of the bill so amended. But again he determined on a veto and let his determination be known.

At midnight many asserted that the President's term of office, and those of the House and of one third of the Senators as well, expired at that hour. Others insisted that, since the President had taken the oath between noon and one o'clock on March 4, 1845, his term had still twelve hours to run.

For hours the wrangling continued. Between three and four in the morning Polk retired to his hotel, where his steadfast wife awaited him. He was, and certainly with good cause, "exceedingly fatigued and exhausted." But he had something to eat and, still fully dressed, went immediately to his parlor, when, about six o'clock, the civil and diplomatic bill was brought to him for his signature. It did not contain the obnoxious amendments that would have caused him to veto it, and the session was ended. So far, so good. If the question of slavery in the new territories had been left like an open sore in the body politic, he had, at least, prevented it from being scabbed over to breed infection within.

It was half past six in the morning when the matter was disposed of; he had had no sleep since the previous night, but at the accustomed hour the President, accompanied by his wife and nieces, attended divine worship at the First Presbyterian Church as usual.

§6

Next morning Polk rode with Taylor to the inauguration in an open carriage, though the weather was dreadful, heard the new President read his address in a low voice and "very badly as to his pronunciation and manner," and shook him by the hand at the end of it, saying: "I hope, sir, the country may be prosperous under your administration." One gathers that it was a feeble hope. To him Taylor appeared to be "no doubt a well meaning old man" but "uneducated, exceedingly ignorant of public affairs" and "of very ordinary capacity." His views on California and Oregon alarmed the ex-President: in the carriage on the way to the Capitol, Taylor said that they were too distant to become members of the Union.

At ten that night, while the beauteous Mme Bodisco queened it in a diamond tiara and a court dress of crimson velvet at the most brilliant of three inaugural balls, and young Mrs. Bliss was taking her first steps toward becoming "our Betty" in Washington society to the strains of Gungl's orchestra, Mr. and Mrs. Polk took the steamboat on the first stage of their long journey home by the southern route. Hundreds, including a whole military company from Baltimore, had called on them at their hotel that afternoon. There was a poem, "Farewell to Mrs. Polk," in the *Union:*

> *Lady, farewell! amid the gloom of grief,*
> *How many a heart will utter that sad sound.*

It was a wet night, but Buchanan, the Marcys, and the Masons came to the dock to see them off.

If Polk was depressed by the impression that Taylor had made upon him, his homeward progress was such as to cheer him. Enthusiastic crowds waited for his train at every station. There were ovations and receptions at Petersburg, Wilmington, Charleston, Savannah, Montgomery, and Mobile. At Richmond the Assembly of Virginia received him formally in the Hall of the House of Delegates. Tar barrels blazed at Weldon. Forts saluted with their cannon as his ship steamed past them. Macon had a six-horse carriage for him. At New Orleans not even the presence of cholera in the city could prevent its people from giving him a splendid welcome.

But there was no rest for the exhausted man. He caught a severe cold and was too ill to leave the steamboat for the festivities planned for him at Jackson and Vicksburg. He allowed his strict sense of courtesy to overcome his prudence at Memphis and had to call a doctor at Paducah. A day in bed at Smithland, where the Cumberland joins the Ohio, gave him the strength to reach Nashville on April 2, to drive through the cheering crowds on Broad and Cherry streets, and to reply to the official address of welcome. But he felt "scarcely able to do so" and found himself "exceedingly feeble and exhausted" when he retired to his quarters at the Verandah Hotel.

Some part of his strength returned. Soon he and his wife moved into the large substantial house they had chosen for their retirement. Through the pickets of the tall iron fence he could be seen for the next few weeks, as erect as ever, superintending the improvements in the garden. But at the end of May he felt too ill to go to church, and on June 19 he died, worn out by his incessant devotion to his duties. He had written in his diary near the end of the previous year: "No President who performs his duty faithfully and conscientiously can have any leisure." And he had had none.

History has dealt harshly with him. Written chiefly by his political opponents and their descendants, it has presented him as little more than a small-minded mediocrity and denied him due credit for either the vision that gave his country its continental extent or the steadfastness with which, party man though he was, he placed the integrity of the Union above every other consideration.

In Washington that summer, those who attended the concerts of the Marine Band on Saturday afternoons might see knock-kneed Old Whitey, his "warfare o'er," looking more like a family buggy horse than a battle charger as he roamed about the White House grounds in well-earned ease. An old gentleman in black, with his hat on the back of his head, mingled affably with the heterogeneous crowd. He might have been taken for an alderman by anybody who did not know that he was the President of the United States, the hero of Monterrey and Buena Vista.

In November, Henry Clay reappeared. He had lately recovered from an attack of cholera and injuries received in a stagecoach accident, and he was seventy-two years old. But his carriage was erect. His collar was as high, and his hat as jauntily cocked, as they had ever been. In Congress neither party was strong enough to dominate, and nothing was done to settle the question of slavery in the new territories until the beginning of the next year, when the perennially young old man — "the immortal Harry," they called him — turned his attention to it.

"The preservation of the Union," he said, was "the leading and paramount object of his public life." It was he who had devised the Missouri Compromise. He proceeded to devise another. In its original form it dealt with so many issues that President Taylor dubbed it in derision the Omnibus Bill. But Daniel Webster spoke for it with all the power of his matchless oratory on March 7. Upon the succession of Fillmore to the Presidency at Taylor's sudden death in July, it received the support of the administration, and as the Compromise of 1850 the five measures that composed it became the law of the United States.

By these measures California was admitted to the Union with an antislavery clause in its Constitution. The old New Mexico was divided into two territories — the one of the same name including the present state of Arizona; the other, which was called Utah, including the present state of Nevada — and both were left to make their own decision about slavery when they became states. A more drastic fugitive-slave law was enacted, but the slave trade, though not slavery itself, was abolished in the District of Columbia. The territory claimed by Texas west of the Rio Grande was given to New Mexico, but Texas was paid $10,000,000 for it.

So was the Union preserved for ten years more. But an era was approaching its end. The men who had kept the states united for so many decades by a spirit of give and take, live and let live, were dying off — both Clay and Webster in 1852. The spirit that animated them was dying also, and a new spirit, a spirit of fierce intolerance and blind fanaticism, was spreading, fostered by such men as Stanton and Salmon Chase in the North, and in the South by Jefferson Davis.

It was only four years until the Kansas-Nebraska bill was

answered by the creation of the Massachusetts Emigrant Society, and Kansas began to "bleed." Another year, and a United States District Court in Wisconsin declared the fugitive-slave law unconstitutional. One more, and Preston Brooks of South Carolina had beaten Charles Sumner into insensibility at his desk in the United States Senate. In 1857 came the Dred Scott decision, like a premonitory signal for the guns around Fort Sumter, and the end of the decade saw the blood-bespattered soul of John Brown start "marching on." In the North and in the South the sprouting dragon's teeth that Polk had striven so hard to plow under had sprung to their full height by thousands. The Irrepressible Conflict, for which he had all unwittingly staged a rehearsal, could be repressed no longer.

BIBLIOGRAPHY

ADAMS, E. D.: *British Interests and Activities in Texas, 1838–1846*. Baltimore, 1910.

ADAMS, JOHN QUINCY: *Diary of John Quincy Adams*. Allan Nevins, ed. New York, 1928.

ANDERSON, ROBERT: *An Artillery Officer in Mexico*. New York & London, 1911.

Appleton's Encyclopedia of American Biography. New York, 1887.

Appleton's Railroad & Steamboat Companion. New York, 1847.

BACOURT, THE CHEVALIER DE (ADOLPH FOURIER): *Souvenirs of a Diplomat*. New York, 1885.

BASSO, HAMILTON: *Beauregard, the Great Creole*. New York, 1933.

Battles and Leaders of the Civil War. New York, 1887–8.

BAYARD, SAMUEL JOHN: *Sketch of the Life of Com. Robert F. Stockton*. New York, 1856.

BEMIS, SAMUEL FLAGG: *The Latin American Policy of the United States*. New York, 1943.

BENTON, THOMAS HART: *Thirty Years' View*. New York, 1854–6.

BRACKETT, ALBERT G.: *History of the United States Cavalry*. New York, 1865.

BRYAN, W. B.: *History of the National Capital*. New York, 1916.

California Historical Quarterly. San Francisco, June, 1923.

Chronicles of Oklahoma. Vol. III. Oklahoma City, 1925.

CLAIBORNE, JOHN F. H.: *Life and Correspondence of Anthony Quitman*. New York, 1860.

CLAY, MRS. CLOPTON: *A Belle of the Fifties*. New York, 1905.

COLMAN, EDNA M.: *Seventy-five Years of White House Gossip*. New York, 1925.

COPELAND, FAYETTE: *Kendall of the Picayune*. Norman, 1943.

CULLUM, G. W.: *Biographical Register of Officers and Graduates of West Point*. New York, 1868, 1879.

DAVIS, VARINA HOWELL: *Jefferson Davis, A Memoir*. New York, 1890.

DELLENBAUGH, FREDERICK S.: *Frémont and '49.* New York, 1914.

DEPEYSTER, JOHN WATTS: *Personal and Military History of Philip Kearny, Major General of United States Volunteers.* New York, 1870.

DEVOTO, BERNARD AUGUSTINE: *The Year of Decision, 1846.* Boston, 1943.

Dictionary of American Biography. New York, 1935.

Dictionary of National Biography. New York, 1896.

ELLET, MRS. E. F.: *The Court Circles of the Republic.* Hartford, 1869.

ELLICOT, JOHN: *John Ancrum Winslow.* New York & London, 1902.

ELLIOTT, CHARLES WINSLOW: *Winfield Scott, the Soldier and the Man.* New York, 1937.

Encyclopædia Britannica, 11th edition.

FREEMAN, D. S.: *R. E. Lee, a Biography.* New York, 1934, 1935.

FRÉMONT, JESSIE BENTON: *Souvenirs of My Time.* Boston, 1887.

FORCE, WILLIAM Q.: *Force's Picture of Washington.* Washington, 1848.

FURBER, GEORGE C.: *The Twelve Months Volunteer.* Cincinnati, 1857.

GIDDINGS, LUTHER: *Sketches of the Campaign in Northern Mexico.* New York, 1853.

GOBRIGHT, LAWRENCE AUGUSTUS: *Recollections of Men and Things at Washington.* Philadelphia, 1869.

GODWIN, PARKE: *Life of William Cullen Bryant.* New York, 1883.

GOODWIN, MAUD WILDER: *Dolly Madison.* New York, 1896.

GOUVERNEUR, MARIAN: *As I Remember.* New York, 1911.

GRANT, U. S.: *Personal Memoirs.* New York, 1885.

HAMILTON, HOLMAN: *Zachary Taylor.* Indianapolis, 1941.

HENDERSON, G. F. R.: *Stonewall Jackson.* London & New York, 1898.

HENRY, CAPTAIN W. S.: *Campaign Sketches of the War with Mexico.* New York, 1847.

HITCHCOCK, ETHAN ALLEN: *Fifty Years in Camp and Field.* W. A. Croffut, ed. New York & London, 1909.

HOLLOWAY, LAURA C.: *The Ladies of the White House.* Philadelphia, 1880.

HONE, PHILIP: *Diary of Philip Hone.* B. Tuckerman, ed. New York, 1889.

———: *Diary of Philip Hone.* Allan Nevins, ed. New York, 1936.

HOUSTON, ANDREW JACKSON: *Texas Independence.* Houston, 1938.

Illustrated London News. 1846, 1847.

INMAN, COLONEL HENRY: *The Old Santa Fe Trail.* New York, 1899.

JAMES, MARQUIS: *Sam Houston.* Indianapolis, 1929.

JEFFERSON, JOSEPH: *Autobiography.* New York, 1889.

Journals of the Late Brevet Major Philip Norbourne Barbour and his wife, Martha Isabelle Hopkins Barbour. R. van B. T. Doubleday, ed. New York & London, 1936.

KEARNY, THOMAS: *General Philip Kearny, Battle Soldier in Five Wars.* New York, 1937.

KENDALL, GEORGE WILKINS: *The War between the United States and Mexico.* New York & Philadelphia, 1851.

KENLY, JOHN R.: *Memoirs of a Maryland Volunteer in the War with Mexico.* Philadelphia, 1873.

KINGLAKE, ALEXANDER WILLIAM: *The Invasion of the Crimea.* Edinburgh & London, 1863–87.

LEWIS, CHARLES LEE: *Admiral Franklin Buchanan.* Baltimore, 1929.

LODGE, HENRY CABOT: *Daniel Webster.* Boston, 1883.

LOGAN, MRS. JOHN A.: *Thirty Years in Washington.* Hartford, 1901.

MACKALL, S. S.: *Early Days of Washington.* Washington, 1899.

McCLELLAN, GENERAL GEORGE B.: *Mexican Diary.* W. S. Myers, ed. Princeton, 1917.

McCORMAC, EUGENE IRVING: *James K. Polk, a Political Biography.* Berkeley, 1922.

McMASTER, J. B.: *History of the People of the United States.* New York & London, 1910.

M'SHERRY, RICHARD, M.D., U.S.N.: *El Puchero.* Philadelphia, 1850.

MAURY, GENERAL DABNEY HERNDON: *Recollections of a Virginian.* New York, 1894.

MAURY, SARAH MITTON: *An English Woman in America*. London, 1848.

MAYER, BRANTZ: *Mexico as It Was and as It Is*. Philadelphia, 1847.

MEADE, GEORGE: *Life and Letters of General George Gordon Meade*. New York, 1913.

MEADE, ROBERT DOUTHAT: *Judah P. Benjamin*. Oxford, 1943.

METCALF, CLYDE H.: *History of the United States Marine Corps*. New York, 1939.

MINNEGERODE, MEADE: *The Fabulous Forties*. Garden City, N. Y., 1924.

MORDELL, ALBERT: *Quaker Militant, John Greenleaf Whittier*. Boston, 1933.

National Intelligencer. 1846–8.

NELSON, ANSON and FANNY: *Memorials of Sarah Childress Polk*. New York, 1892.

NEVINS, ALLAN: *Frémont, the West's Greatest Adventurer*. New York & London, 1928.

NICHOLS, ROY FRANKLIN: *Franklin Pierce, Young Hickory of the Granite Hills*. Philadelphia, 1931.

Niles' National Register. 1846–8.

NYE, RUSSEL B.: *George Bancroft, Brahmin Rebel*. New York, 1944.

O'CONNELL, J. HARLIN: "*U.S.S. Princeton.*" *Princeton University Chronicle*, June 1940.

ODELL, GEORGE C. D.: *Annals of the New York Stage*. New York, 1928.

Ogden's Uniforms, United States Army. Copyright, 1885.

OSWANDEL, J. JACOB: *Notes of the Mexican War*. Philadelphia, 1885.

PARKMAN, FRANCIS: *The Oregon Trail*. Boston, 1906.

POLK, JAMES KNOX: *The Diary of a President*. Allan Nevins, ed. New York, 1929.

——: *Diary*. Milo Milton Quaif, ed. Chicago, 1910.

POORE, BEN PERLEY: *Perley's Reminiscences*. Philadelphia, 1886.

Private Correspondence of Henry Clay. Calvin Colton, ed. Boston, 1856.

RAMSEY, ALBERT C.: *The Other Side of the Mexican War*. New York, 1850.

Records of the New York Stage. New York, 1866, 1867.

RHODES, JAMES FORD: *History of the United States.* New York, 1893–1906.

RIVES, GEORGE LOCKHART: *The United States and Mexico, 1821–1848.* New York, 1913.

ROGERS, JOSEPH M.: *Thomas H. Benton.* Philadelphia, 1905.

ROOSEVELT, THEODORE: *Thomas Hart Benton.* New York, 1914.

ROWLAND, DUNBAR: *Jefferson Davis, Constitutionalist.* Jackson, Miss., 1923.

SANDBURG, CARL: *Lincoln, the Prairie Years.* New York, 1926.

SCHLESINGER, ARTHUR M., JR.: *The Age of Jackson.* Boston, 1945.

SCOTT, WINFIELD: *Memoirs of Lieut. Gen'l Scott, L.L.D.* New York, 1864.

SEARS, LOUIS MARTIN: *John Slidell.* Durham, N. C., 1925.

SEATON, JOSEPHINE: *William Winston Seaton of the National Intelligencer.* Boston, 1871.

SEITZ, DON C.: *Braxton Bragg.* Columbia, S. C., 1924.

SEMMES, RAPHAEL: *Service Afloat and Ashore in the Mexican War.* Cincinnati, 1851.

SINGLETON, ESTHER: *The Story of the White House.* New York, 1907.

SMITH, JUSTIN HARVEY: *The War with Mexico.* New York, 1919.

SPAULDING, OLIVER LYMAN: *The United States Army in War and Peace.* New York, 1937.

SPEARS, J. R.: *A History of the United States Navy.* New York, 1908.

SPROUT, H. and M.: *The Rise of American Naval Power.* Princeton, 1939.

STEELE, MATTHEW FORNEY: *American Campaigns.* Washington, 1909.

THOMPSON, WADDY: *Recollections of Mexico.* New York & London, 1847.

THRALL, HOMER S.: *Pictorial History of Texas.* St. Louis, 1879.

TINDALL, WILLIAM: *Standard History of the City of Washington.* Knoxville, 1914.

TREVELYAN, GEORGE MACAULAY: *Garibaldi's Defense of the Roman Republic.* London & New York, 1910.

VAN ALSTYNE, RICHARD W.: *American Diplomacy in Action.*
   Stamford University, 1944.
VESTAL, STANLEY: *Kit Carson, A Biography.* New York, 1928.
WALLACE, LEW: *An Autobiography.* New York, 1906.
WATTERSON, GEORGE: *A New Guide to Washington.* Washing-
   ton, 1842.
WHARTON, CLARENCE R.: *The Republic of Texas.* Cleveland,
   1922.
WHITTIER, JOHN GREENLEAF: *Complete Poetical Works.* Bos-
   ton, 1873.
WILLIAMS, ALFRED M.: *Sam Houston and the War of Independ-
   ence in Texas.* Boston & New York, 1893.
WILLIS, NATHANIEL PARKER: *Poetical Works.* New York, 1850.
WISE, HENRY ALEXANDER: *Seven Decades of the Union.* Phila-
   delphia, 1872.
WISE, LIEUTENANT HENRY AUGUSTUS, U.S.N.: *Los Gringos.*
   New York, 1849.

INDEX